INTERNATIONAL PRAISE FOR FOOLS RUSH IN

'Bill Carter is one of those guys who seek answers to questions most of us are afraid to ask. His heart and eye have always seemed set on describing and revealing the world just as he sees it, and his heart and eye are so clear that it almost breaks your heart.'
— BONO

"In this gripping chronicle of his time in war ravaged Sarajevo, Bill Carter bears witness to both the evil we can do each other and the remarkable resiliency of the human spirit."
— EMMYLOU HARRIS

"Bill Carter's book Fools Rush In gives those of us who have suffered great loss, hope and inspiration A ferocious read."
— CALEXICO

"This book is such a sock to the stomach. We never planned on meeting the people of the world who write important books, or make movies that effectively change the course of the world, but that's exactly what we did when we met Bill Carter. "Fools Rush In" reminded us that even though some folks can dig themselves deeper than they probably should, they also only do what's mostly necessary and true when they're dug down deepest. If only such dreadful circumstances weren't sometimes required for these traits to shine through."
— GRANDADDY

"The ilk of Cronkite is gone from these tubes for good. We are left with someone else's daily idea of what we should see and hear ... and it's never good. Never enough information and never enough time to tell the story. Just bite after bite. In the literal mean time, this man Carter managed to yank the window wide open enough to get a view of what we do to ourselves when we don't know why. And even more pertinent, why we can't stop. The book is a must." —HOWE GELB

"No one can keep the wars straight anymore as they hopscotch from continent to continent. The slaughter in Bosnia has slipped beneath the rising tide washing over our minds. But Bill Carter takes us to his killing ground in Sarajevo and for a while we are there, just as we are in the current killing ground and the next one, also. This fine book is the best guide you are going to find to the rest of your life. And, yes love is always the answer."
—CHARLES BOWDEN, AUTHOR OF DOWN BY THE RIVER

'Bill Carter is more than a digital age Huck Finn. He is not merely writing here, he is singing, as if his life depended upon it. And you get the very real sense that it does. This drama is an honest, wry, immensely humane look at coming of age at the edge of a bomb crater. Carter tells this story with a sense of grandeur.' —DOUG STANTON, AUTHOR OF IN HARM'S WAY

"Carter's book reads like a novel, evoking a lost city inhabited by angels, bandits, punks and adrenaline fiends. In the end, Carter reaches far beyond personal experience to find the story of a wounded city, and a war that pitted neighbor against neighbor in a nightmare of mindless hated."
—NEWSWEEK INTERNATIONAL

A brutally frank education about the nature of survival."
—JANE MAGAZINE

"This lively book is like Good Morning Vietnam crossed with a Conrad novel." —THE TIMES

"Fiercely intelligent . . . It is a deeply felt emotional reaction to the horror and the humanity that Bill Carter would witness . . . Told with the passion of one who came to identify himself with the tragedy of Bosnia, not as an observer."
—GUARDIAN

Fools Rush In

...where angels fear to tread

Fools Rush In

BILL CARTER

WENNER BOOKS NEW YORK

Numb : Words & music written by U2 © Copyright Blue Mountain Music Limited for the
UK/3BU/Mother Music Limited for the Republic of Ireland/Polygram Music International B.V.
for the rest of the world. Used by Permission of Music Sales Limited. All Rights Reserved.
International Copyright Secured.

This edition is published by arrangement with Transworld Publishers,
a division of The Random House Group, Ltd.

Library of Congress Cataloging-in-Publication Data

Carter, Bill
    Fools rush in : a true story of war and redemption / Bill Carter.
        p. cm.
    ISBN 1-932958-50-9
    1. Sarajevo (Bosnia and Hercegovina)—History—Siege, 1992–1996—Personal narratives,
American. 2. Carter, Bill. 3. Americans—Bosnia and Hercegovina—Sarajevo. I. Title.

    DR1313.32.S27C37 2005
    949.703—dc22   200402752

ISBN: 1-932958-50-9

Wenner Books are available for special promotions and premiums. For details contact Michael
Rentas, Manager, Inventory and Premium Sales, Hyperion, 77 West 66ᵗʰ Street, 11ᵗʰ floor, New
York, New York 10023, or call 212-456-0133.

FIRST EDITION

10 9 8 7 6 5 4 3 2 1

For my parents,
Susan and John Lalaguna

Author's Note

Although everyone in the story is a real person, I have changed a few names in the writing of the book. And although a true story, the book is not intended to be a historical account, one that seeks to answer any burning academic questions surrounding this period in time. That said, I have sought to make it a testimony to what really happened, and how it was for me.

Furthermore, this is a story pieced together from my memory. I have included dialogue, all of which I believe to be fair and accurate. As for the facts, the editors have checked and rechecked to the best of their ability, and any remaining errors are entirely my own.

HUNGARY

CROATIA

ROMANIA

Vukovar

Novi Sad

Belgrade

public

Tuzla

Serb Republic

Zenica

Srebrenica

Kiseljak

Sarajevo

THE

Višegrad

Goražde

STATE UNION

Metković

OF SERBIA

Serb Republic

AND

MONTENEGRO

KOSOVO

Dubrovnik

ALBANIA

MACEDONIA

0   MILES   100

0   KILOMETRES   150

Map by Neil Gower

Living, there is no happiness in that.
Living: carrying one's painful self through the world.
But being, being is happiness.
Being: becoming a fountain,
a fountain on which the universe falls like warm rain.

Milan Kundera, *Immortality*

PROLOGUE

My fondest memory of when I was young is the smell of dirt.
Every day I would wake before sunrise to water the trees, one
of my chores on the ranch. I remember hating the cold of the
early morning, but cherishing the smell of the earth as the black
of night turned to daylight blue. Sometimes, if there were cumulus clouds, it looked like a fleet of ships was sailing across
the world, their hard-edged shadows spread out before me. At
that hour the air was wet, crisp and filled with the rich aroma
of the night's organic deaths. The worms, bugs, leaves, roots,
rotting apples, plums, almonds, watermelons all decaying into
one big clump of soil. Those mornings I would stand under the
rising sun and feel the undeniable existence of all the living
creatures around me, as if the earth itself was the chest of a
mighty giant that breathed slowly and deeply, not bothered
much if I stepped on its skin.

But if the experiences of childhood are, as they say, where
we form lifelong impressions, then I must go back further, to
my first memory. The first thing I remember is the ringing. I
was young, too young to know what the ringing was, but
I knew it was too loud. I climbed the breakfast stool. It was as
tall as a young tree. I climbed that tree to the top, where the
ringing was. I remember from up there the world seemed a little
dangerous, but light. It was good to be free of all that gravity on
the floor. I picked up the phone because it sounded like the ringing was coming from inside that black contraption. My father's
voice was on the other end. I thought this was odd, actually
fascinating. There was also another voice, another man, and

probably a father too. My first word into the never-never land of the world's airwaves? The word that by now will be flying past Pluto and on its way to Vega: "Hello?"

I remember feeling scared but happy when I fell from the top of the stool. I had a sensation as if I was floating somewhere. Like I was underwater, free from the weight of my own being. My father had kicked out the stool, sending me flying to the floor. Father was a large man. Six feet two. He sometimes laughed in public and always ran his hand through his hair, which he parted in such a way that it went from one ear clear over his skull to the other ear. He never drank, never smoked and never showed any anger to strangers. He kept his anger for the ones he loved so much that he seemed to hate them. The fact is he was never all that mad until he started in on us. That morning his steel-toed boot was a perfect fit under the small of my back and that's how I took my next big trip. He kicked me clear across the room into a wall, where I slid down onto a couch. Crumpled, I cried, but not too loud. He leaned over me. "The phone is not for you."

Looking back as I type, it is almost comical that those words were most likely the best advice he ever gave me.

Then there was movement . . . Memories of car rides through a world of open fields and white birds with skinny legs. Hawks and eagles rested on the tops of telephone poles. The mountains weren't far, but far enough to be a hazy charcoal sketch on the horizon. There wasn't anyone around except us: my mother, my brother, my father, and me. We had moved to a piece of property that had a name. The Thomas Creek Ranch, named for the creek that flowed nearby into the big river down the road called the Sacramento. The farm had orchards and big open fields of dirt. There were watermelons, blackberries, plums, apples, pomegranates, apricots, and walnuts. The oak trees were as big as barns and the barns as big as—well, bigger than anything I'd ever seen, including the bridge down by the river.

Apart from the orchards, which never made us any money, we raised worms, what fishermen called night crawlers. I believe these were the first words in English to capture my imagination. Night crawler: a thing that crawls around at night. It felt dangerous and secret.

First we built containers for them. There must have been more than a hundred six-by-three-foot boxes, all made from plywood with no lid. Each one was lined with plastic, to hold in the moisture and soil. Then we rigged lights to keep them warm. After that it was just a matter of letting worms do what they do best, make more worms. In truth the boxes looked like coffins for very large people. I used to spend hours digging my hands into the wet soil and bringing up handfuls of pink worms. Sometimes, as an experiment, I would tear one in half just to see if the other half would live. It always did, for a while.

The first truck would arrive near the beginning of the month, dropping off a shipment of round white styrofoam containers. And then on most Friday afternoons another truck would come and take the containers away, each one packed tightly with dirt and a dozen or so worms.

For a while we made money selling the worms to wholesalers who then sold them to fishermen. Then one day the water system broke and the worms all died. It was no one's fault. The wiring had gone haywire. Still, Dad found me in the bushes and brought me into the barn. As he calmly lectured me about the cost of all the dead worms he poked me with the pitchfork. It was the same way he had taught me not to step out of the batter's box in baseball—with a pitchfork to my back as my brother pitched.

Then there was Christmas. Then another. No one ever visited but it didn't seem strange at the time. Cookies and carrots for Santa Claus and one present each. It was always cheerful and hopeful, like there would be more days like this. I always asked for the same thing, a subscription to the *National Geographic* magazine.

Each month, when the magazine arrived, it was filled with enough information to drive me crazy with desire to travel. One issue had women with naked breasts. Another had a lion eating the stomach of a gazelle. There were pictures of people on top of mountains, crossing the Sahara and everything else I couldn't see out my window. Then one day an issue came with a map of the world. I stuck the world, measuring three feet by five, on the wall next to my bed with a few strips of tape.

At night, on the top bunk, I would secretly stretch out across the world. If I extended fully I could put my toes in the jungles of Sumatra, my navel at the tip of Argentina and my head in the Indian Ocean. Most nights I would place an ear against the map, my hot flushed cheek touching the imaginary cool deep waters of the Pacific Ocean. I think I was listening for the sound of breaking waves. Instead most nights sounded the same. Just on the other side of the world, I could hear the cry of a woman. She was crying out for help. Her husband was slowly beating her to death.

So it began. My urge to be anywhere but where I was. I would drape the world around me like a cape against the rain. Sometimes I would be in rough seas with a hearty crew in a faraway place. Once we landed, safely navigating the danger-ous coral reef, the local king would greet us with exotic food. We would drink from coconuts and dance naked in the glow of a roaring fire. I'd learn to fish with a spear and swim for miles underwater without needing a breath. They promised I could return any time, any time at all. They would wish me luck and pray to God for me.

And what about God? Where was He? Or She? Or It? Be-ginning at a young age I had a tendency to look for God in the oddest of places. It all started when the preacher said God was everywhere, he was even there when you were sleeping. Espe-cially when you were sleeping. This kept me awake for years.

I would eyeball the inside of decaying fruit and peer down gopher holes. I would search birds' nests, spiders' webs and ant colonies. Sometimes I'd follow my brother when he sleep-walked onto the lawn. That seemed otherworldly.

Then the preacher, who had fat fingers and breath that smelled like mildew, said, "Every step you take, God is walking that path with you." Every step? This made walking slightly daunting. Once after school I went into the field to find a piece of wet ground. Walking slowly, with my eyes closed, I took a few steps and stopped. I opened my eyes and spun round to watch the footprints rise up from the mud and slowly disappear. Maybe that was the Holy Ghost following me. I didn't know.

But this is all just background. For the day in question was a typical warm autumn day. I heard someone at school call it an Indian summer. Actually they said "Injun summer." The sun was spraying yellow on everything in sight. When we heard the sound of tires on the gravel road I followed my brother as we ran into our designated hiding spots in the blackberry bushes.

Mom, a schoolteacher, was home earlier than usual. She put her hand up to shield her eyes from that bright sun. She yelled out our names. My older brother, Cliff, shrugged his shoulders. He didn't seem convinced. Mom was not the enemy, but she slept with the enemy. My brother was good at seeing traps. If he smelled trouble he would run to the back of the property where he had tunnels and hiding places. Usually he took me with him, but sometimes, if there was no time, I would get caught in the open wishing I had a hiding place.

That afternoon, once inside the house, Mom told us to sit down.

"We're leaving," she said.

"Leaving?" I asked.

"When?" my brother asked.

"Now."

"Where are we going?"

"Away."

"Are we coming back?"

"What about Dad?" I asked, beginning to cry. I was eleven and I suspect I was more afraid of the unknown that lay ahead than of the actual leaving.

"He's not coming," she said, leaning her head back and taking a breath.

"Will we ever see him again?"

"Yes, but later. We have to go."

There was a noise. It sounded like Dad's car on the gravel drive. I was terrified. That was my only fear about leaving: if he caught us the punishment would be severe.

I jumped up and started toward the bedroom, Cliff toward the door.

"It's just the neighbors," my mother said. "Hurry."

We were gone within twenty minutes. Driving the blue Skylark, Mom turned east at Santa Clara road and headed for the river. We passed the Fox Gravel Company. I always wondered how they could sell stuff anyone could get for free from the river. We passed a few farms. At one, playing baseball in the yard, there were kids I knew from school. It seemed odd, but not sad, that I had seen them at school that afternoon but would never see them again.

The back roads intersected like the rivers on my world map. One fed into the next and then another, as if they were the blue veins of the earth. Feeling a brand new sensation, maybe boldness, I sat up and put my head out the window. Then I put my arm outside, letting it go up and down as it pleased, riding the wind in wild movements. Down below, the yellow lines on the asphalt zoomed by like ticks on a clock. In the fast lane cars passed us with kids playing games with their parents, back and forth from the back seat to the front, as if the world were one large lollipop waiting to be licked.

Who knows? Maybe God lived out here on the road.

"Can we go to the ocean?" I asked, now imagining the car to be a mighty ocean steamer cutting through the Straits of Malacca.

"Sure, honey, sure," she said. "Nothing will ever happen to either of you again. I promise." She checked and rechecked the rear-view mirror every few seconds.

"Never," she said, clenching her teeth and nodding her head left to right. She cried quietly to herself, which made her lip quiver.

"Mom?"

"Nothing. Everything's fine now."

We headed south, keeping the river to the west. Outside, the fields glowed in the late afternoon sun. The thin blond wheat bent in the breeze without a care, like an entire population of people quietly acting as one continuous motion. I stuck my face in the wind. The air smelled like ripe peaches and wet earth. On the side of the road I saw a dried-up rattlesnake skin. It was just hanging there on a barbed-wire fence.

Mom pressed her shoe down a little harder on the gas pedal. Pretty soon she even stopped looking in the mirror.

Boy oh boy, you should have heard it. I'll never forget it. The sound of those wheels humming down Highway 99.

Part One

1

Just after two o'clock, I rose up from under a plastic garbage bag in a freezing rain. The night was silent except for the pitter-patter of the rain, which rolled in from the edge of the sea in thick heavy clouds. Darkness pulled in from the edges of the night, leaving only the pale sepia glow from a single lamp-post across the street in front of a school. The street was shiny, with water trickling down the gutter to the beach. I closed my hands around my mouth and breathed out a steady stream of mist. The locals had said something about a *burra*, a freezing wind that blows off the mountains and into the Adriatic Sea. I re-membered reading about war, how it changes a person, makes them go crazy or in some cases straight sane. And it was the thought of this mental gamble that made me feel much calmer.

Then the road began to rumble and squeal at the same time. It sounded like a bus had slammed head on into a pig farm. I jumped behind the concrete railing running alongside the road and lay flat on the ground. I wasn't afraid of anything in partic-ular. It just seemed like a good idea.

It's funny what we notice when our senses are in high gear. Moments before I'd barely registered that the rain had turned to snow. But now, startled and alert, I smelled air like wet black rye bread, and across the street a white dust blanketed the school. It looked peaceful and yet a little empty, stuck in the yard as if waiting for the demolition ball. Then like a herd of killer elephants on speed, five Warrior tanks whizzed by head-ing south. Union Jacks were painted on their sides. Headlights splashed across the white cinderblock walls of the houses.

They lit up like sheets of stretched canvas, empty, pale, and silent.

My body calmed down again, my nerves straightened out. The muscles relaxed and the senses diminished. Now the school across the street just looked like an ugly building with a sloppy white paint job.

So there I was, some time around mid-March 1993, in Split, Croatia, standing on a two-lane road, with the Adriatic Sea to my back. To the east, less than a hundred kilometers away, was Bosnia, where a violent war had been raging for almost fifteen months. That was where I was going.

A few times, thinking about actually going into Bosnia, I had started down the road toward the pension, back to a warm bed, back to safety. But each time I had this overwhelming sensation—call it providence, call it fate or destiny or just call it faith—that my life would change if only I waited a little longer.

And so I did.

Besides, the Englishman had been clear. He told me, if I was serious about going to the war, to wait on the side of the road for his convoy. When I asked how I would recognize his trucks, his reply was quick and without irony.

"Look for the circus," he said.

So that's where I was—so full of hope that all I needed was a tap on the shoulder and I would happily have jumped into a boiling volcano. Anything to keep some movement under my feet.

2

I had met Graeme Bint, the Englishman, two days earlier while sitting at the back of a United Nations security briefing. These daily meetings were extended as a courtesy to those non-governmental organizations (NGOs) that were running humanitarian convoys into Bosnia. I was trying not to be noticed; after all, I didn't belong there. As for Graeme, the first thing a person noticed about him was his hair. It was orange and stood straight up, like he had just removed his finger from a light socket. He wore a bomber jacket and dirty Doc Martens with worn-out soles. And as far as I could tell he was always smiling. At one point during the briefing he leaned over to me and said something like "Everyone in this room is completely nutters." Playing along, I smiled back and nodded my head. It was around then that he said to meet him in the Split Hotel lobby at sunset if I was serious about going to Bosnia.

I arrived early.

The Split Hotel was a large concrete high-rise originally built for tourists coming to enjoy the Mediterranean climate of the Dalmatian coast. Since the Bosnian war, the hotel had become a stopover for foreigners going to or coming from Bosnia, or "upcountry" as they referred to it. Locals, wearing white dinner jackets, served the journalists, who lounged in the lobby in their chinos and tan photographer's vests. It all had a slightly soiled and colonial feel to it. The journalists' laughter set my teeth on edge, as they chatted giddily to one another over cappuccinos or wine. As far as I could make out, everyone liked to act as if the war was near, but in truth the closest it had ever got to here was the swimming pool. There was no water, only a big black hole at the bottom: an errant grenade from some drunken soldier had reduced this resort pool to an oversized bathtub with a huge black drain.

Don't get me wrong, I had nothing against the journalists. That is, nothing except everything I could imagine they had and I didn't. They had armored cars, expense accounts, free food and beer, and a license to go anywhere they pleased. They were the world's eyes and ears, the scribes of history. That alone used to set me thinking I might one day want to be a war correspondent, but that was before I spent time listening to them.

That afternoon I strolled around the lobby with a beer in my hand and caught snippets of conversation. "And then, while the woman was standing over her dead daughter, Marco—what a cold bastard—moved her to the left, toward the window. I mean he had to kind of tug at her elbow with one hand and her shoulder with the other. No shit. This woman is in shock, shells are falling and he whispers to me, 'The light is better over by the window.' Fucking balls, man."

So had ended my dreams of being the next Ed Murrow.

From the lobby, not far from the journalists, I had a clear view to the store, where I suddenly noticed Graeme. He was busy stealing chocolate bars, porno magazines, peanuts and beer. I found it astonishing he could steal things so deftly while another customer, innocently, kept the clerk busy with some question. That took talent. On his way out of the lobby he reached out with his right hand, as if to shake mine, but when I reached out in kind, instead, with the speed of the artful dodger, he handed me a can of beer.

"Ta." He laughed and disappeared out the front door.

After spending two weeks trying to get into Bosnia, either by offering my services to aid organizations or attempting to tag along with journalists, it suddenly occurred to me that sitting around this lobby waiting for a ride was a dead end. I followed the Englishman out the door.

I caught up with him near the sea wall.

"What do you think of those gits?" he asked.

"Who?"

"Those geezer reporters."

"Seem pretty jaded, you know?"

"Those fuckwits wouldn't know the truth if it was shoved up their arses," he shouted. He cracked a beer and took a bite of a Mars bar as we strolled along the beach.

"I've seen them drive right by people with no fucking arms. Screaming and bleeding out their fucking eyeballs and those cuntheads take a snapshot and move on."

"Pretty cold stuff," I said.

"Are you being supercilious?"

"Being what?"

"A fucking smart arse!"

"No." His anger threw me.

"So you aren't a journalist?" Now he was laughing, which threw me even more.

"I'm not."

"Don't need any more of those wankers. That said, without them the whole fucking country would be gone by now. I hate this catch-22 bollocks."

He handed me a porn magazine. "Fancy that one there, mate," he said, pointing to a dark-haired beauty pouring a gallon of milk on her enormous breasts. "Wouldn't mind getting your nuts off with that one now, would you?"

Graeme was my age, twenty-seven, and walked with a confident gait that lilted slightly to the left. He had a loud and contagious laugh, which announced clearly that he didn't care what anyone thought. He seemed earnest, thoughtful, self-educated and slightly soiled from lack of hygiene. He wore large beaded necklaces and had earrings in each ear. Although he said he came from a working-class background in Reading, when he spoke he tended to mix in words that sounded like he had spent half the night crash-reading the dictionary and the other half in a Charles Dickens novel. At times it was like a steelworker reciting *Oliver Twist*. "Bloody hell, life is a conundrum, but the array of possibilities are . . . oh fuck off and pass the bloody vodka." This was always followed by a mannerism: either a small noise from his mouth indicating *oops!* or perhaps a quick shuffle in his step and a giggle to punctuate the moment. In other words his humor was based on undermining whatever he or someone else had just said.

I couldn't figure out if he was a hippie or a punk. He wasn't a liberal in any American sense, which meant he didn't have that tedious cynicism that Californian coffee-shop philosophers spout so effortlessly while doing nothing about the situation they so clearly detest. Unlike them he didn't hate everything, just the lazy and uncommitted. He worked hard, but only for the principles in which he believed; and those, I would find out soon enough, he was willing to die for. His thievery was selective: never against the poor or righteous. He stole only from those he deemed morally on the wrong side of the fence, albeit the fence he had built.

I asked him about the organization he was part of.

"It's a traveling circus."

"You mean it's disorganized?" I asked.

"No. It's a bloody circus. Dress up like clowns, that sort of thing. Know what I mean?"

"Bitchin."

"Bitchin?"

"Excellent."

"Actually it's a bunch of mates from London looking to do something better than be cunts our whole lives. So we deliver food but with a little bit of laughter."

"Sounds perfect."

"Choice," he said.

"Choice?" I asked. "What's that mean?"

"Means the dog's bollocks."

"The dog's bollocks?"

"The dog's balls."

"Oh." I was confused.

"Or you could just say Bob's your uncle."

"Choice?" I said.

I was catching on.

We walked and he talked. His group referred to themselves as The Serious Road Trip or TSRT, and for the past two years they had traveled to Romania and Russia, delivering food to orphanages. Now they were in Bosnia dressed as clowns. To finance their journeys they had garage sales, food drives, and a few donations trickled down from some reclusive old hippies in northern England. For the most part they ate from the cargo they were carrying and slept in the back of their trucks. Currently they had five trucks, each loaded with five tons of food, ready for delivery to Sarajevo. They just needed money for fuel.

"We siphoned one UN vehicle yesterday but it was only thirty liters. We need two hundred for the trucks."

I told him I was staying with my friend Jason Aplon, who had a job with a large US aid group that regulated the movement of all NGOs to and from Bosnia.

"Jason. I know him. Good guy. Serious one, isn't he."

"That's him. So got any room for an extra set of hands in Sarajevo?"

"Got any money?"

"No." I felt my life savings: $200 under my big toe in my left boot.

"Can you drive a five-ton truck?"

"Never tried."

"Are you good with tools?"

"If my life depended on it? I would have to say no."

"Well, you aren't much bloody use, are you?" He laughed.

"I'll do whatever. And I can take a decent photo and I write."

He stopped suddenly. "You just said you aren't a wanker journalist. So are you or aren't you?"

"No. It's more of a documentary kind of thing. Same with the camera."

"That could be good for raising some more money," he said to himself, walking faster and mumbling as if taking mental notes. "Can you juggle?"

"Not really."

"Can you play music? Guitar or harmonica?"

"I . . . no."

"Why are you here?" he asked with a new level of suspicion.

"Seems like the place to be."

"Fair enough," he said. "Wait by the side of the road down by Jason's pension. We should be there around midnight."

The sun was dropping like a lead ball and the air was getting colder. I caught a bus going south out of town toward the pension. I had to pack. If all went right I would be in Sarajevo in a few days, by the end of the week at the latest. That's when it dawned on me. I was going to the very center of the most violent war in Europe since World War Two and I didn't even know who was fighting whom.

3

I did have a loose mental sketch of the war. I had seen a map at the United Nations security briefing a few days earlier. A Scottish army captain jabbed the map with his pointer stick to indicate the movements of troops. Like all soldiers everywhere in the world, he seemed quite pleased with his uniform and even more pleased with his pointer. The topography map had lines close together, indicating a steep mountainous country. There were several peaks and deep gorges with rivers. It resembled the topo maps of the hikes I'd done in the Sierra Mountains or the Rockies.

The blue pins were the Serbs, who it seemed had the upper hand on everyone. They had the tanks, indicated by small blue markers with pieces of blue paper glued to the tops. I wondered what kind of job it was to glue those pieces of paper.

The red markers said either HV or HVO. Both indicated Croatian troops. If it was HV they were soldiers from Croatia. If it was HVO they were technically Bosnian Croats: Croatians living in the area of Bosnia known as Herzegovina, which was heavily Croatian-populated. The green markers were the Bosnian army, and by all accounts they were a civilian army scrapping for their lives. The Serbs were fighting the Bosnians and the Croats, but in some places, such as Herzegovina, the Croats and Bosnians were beginning to fight each other as well as the Serbs. The Bosnian army was the only one with a mix of all three ethnic groups: Serbs, Croats, and what people were referring to as the Muslims, even though "Muslim" usually refers to someone's religion, not their ethnicity.

The Bosnians, meaning mostly the Muslims, the green pins, were clearly the underdogs. They lived in towns with names like Zepa, Goražde, Srebrenica, Tuzla, Zenica, and Sarajevo. They were the ones in need of help.

Waiting on the road, I thought of what I'd been through in the past two weeks in Split as I tried to get a ride to Bosnia. Every aid organization with a field office there had said I was unqualified. They'd said they only hired professionals trained for extremely stressful situations. They'd told me how they administered psychological tests to assess a person's ability to deal with grief and mass murder. I told them I was qualified and they smiled as if I might be a bit dangerous.

Besides, they told me, I had to apply through Geneva or New York, where the testing was done. And since I didn't have enough money for a return trip to the States that was out of the question. Everyone wanted references and résumés. They preferred people with degrees in engineering or accounting from schools like Harvard or Princeton. I knew a guy in Bangkok who could forge me a degree from MIT for $20 or an MBA from Harvard for $30, but what was the use?

I thought, it's a war. Doesn't anyone need an extra body to do something? Anything? I got one taker, a burned-out humanitarian pro looking to retire soon. He said go see the guy down in Metković, a town three hours south along the Dalmatian coast. I knew it from studying the map. It was a border town that served as a gateway to a mountain road leading to central Bosnia. He said the work would involve taking inventory.

I caught a ride to Metković, to a warehouse that had been commandeered by the IRC, the International Rescue Committee, a large American aid organization founded by Albert Einstein after World War Two. The guy I was supposed to talk to was a recent college graduate. He began the conversation by telling me how good this job would look on his résumé when he returned to the States. He was slightly overweight, punchy, but armed with a wry sense of humor with a twinge of bitterness. Who could blame him? For the next month he had to burn 100 tons of army uniforms that the United States had sent as aid to the Bosnians for the cold winter.

"OK, let's see if you can guess what happens when a civilian population puts on army fatigues?" he asked. He whipped around, his eyes taking in all of us in the room, a clipboard in his hand. "Wait. Before you answer, remember it doesn't matter how cold they are. Does . . . not . . . fucking . . . matter." He pronounced each word clearly. "What happens if you put civilians in fatigues? Give up? I'll tell you. They get shot.

Sniped, executed, and buried in some parking-lot-sized mud pit."

He yelled this at the top of his lungs, but still no one in the building reacted. I didn't know if it was because they were used to it or because they didn't speak English. "*Shot.* Yeah, *shot . . .*" Forklifts moved more pallets of fatigues toward a pile of clothes fifteen feet high and as wide as a country-club swimming pool, at the foot of a large incinerator, which was not yet burning.

"So we burn them," he said, clearly defeated.

"Burn them?"

"For the Pentagon."

Confused, I shifted the weight on my feet.

"Why, you ask? A very good question," he yelled. "When next year's budget comes around the army tells Congress they don't have enough clothes for its fighting troops. Congress can't say no to buying clothes for our boys and girls fighting for the red, white and blue. Can they? So it gives them the money for clothes. And some Congressman from Mississippi gets a fat hundred million in pork-barrel cash. All because he made a few phone calls and got this shipment of clothes to some Balkan war and had a press conference to call it humanitarian aid."

By the way he was yelling I guessed he had been having this conversation with himself for months, at home, in the shower, at the bar, in his sleep.

He told me he made $4,000 a month doing this job, subcontracted by the USA. If he stayed a bit longer it would be bumped up with perks to $8,000 a month.

I told him I had to get going. It was a three-hour drive back to the pension.

"You are going to the action, aren't you?" He handed me a sleeping bag and a down-filled army jacket. Then he passed me an army-issue flak jacket and said, "It's good for a small piece of shrapnel, but a sniper? Forget it."

I told him I was trying to get on a food run to Sarajevo, but after that I didn't know what I was going to do.

"You are one lucky motherfucker," he told me.

Strangely, at the time, I believed him.

4

Back then I never thought too far ahead, maybe a day or two at most. I was twenty-seven and had two college degrees, one in Economics and the other in Political Science. I graduated with honors and with many words of encouragement from my professors, which as far as I could tell made me qualified to sit in a bathtub and read the classifieds the same as any other graduate.

So, instead of seeking the doomed life of mortgages, credit-card debt and sitcom television, I had spent my post-college life thus far roaming the earth, west to east and then north to south. I had journeyed by land or sea from Alaska to the Amazon, and from floating casinos in Macao to the high glacial valleys of the Himalayas. The net result of those miles, other than a few bouts of dysentery and a fish-tank of memories, was a notion I have come to think may be important: planning is the fatal blow to any journey. Tourists plan. And, even worse, they plan in groups. Lunch here, shopping there, snapshots in front of the statue, and then back on the bus. It's rare a tourist ever remembers anything about where they have been, except for the oddest of details. How much a beer was, how lovely the maid was, or what a strange language those people spoke. But a traveler just goes, with no plan and with as little baggage as possible, and at some point the journey itself becomes the destination.

I was flat broke. I didn't have a proper job and had no property. I did have a duffel bag and a heavily stamped passport. The contents of the bag had always changed from continent to continent, region to region. In Indonesia I had a few sarongs, books to read, toilet paper, and knick-knacks from Bali. In Nepal I bought some warm clothes and an extra pair of hiking socks. In Egypt I traded the warm clothes for cotton shirts and baggy desert pants. In Colombia I gave it all away and walked across the border with a tent.

At the pension in Split I packed my duffel bag with a leather jacket, some bread and cheese, a few rolls of toilet paper and a bottle of whiskey. I had five books, some mixed music tapes and a camera with twenty rolls of black and white film.

Just before midnight I crept downstairs and lit a candle. I made a cup of tea with a splash of whiskey and ate some left-over bread sitting on the counter. I watched the clock tick away as I huddled against the cold. I sat like that and, as always, reminded myself why I had come here.

Over and over again I watched the movie in my head, the whys and what ifs. Sometimes I replayed the long version, sometimes the short version, but the ending was always the same.

Every time she died and every time I lived.

I couldn't be sure what I was doing here, but I knew this: I wasn't here to hide or forget. I was here to seek something.

I think I was here to find a new ending.

5

It was a few hours before dawn when I heard the throbbing rhythm of a bass drum. At first I thought it was the pulse in my ear; the last surge of blood going to my head to wake me from the cold.

Coming up the road were four sets of large round lights swerving from side to side, weaving back and forth behind the lead vehicle. The music grew louder. It sounded like English trance or trip hop. Again I ran for the barricade, thinking it was a convoy of drunken Croatian soldiers on their way home from the bar.

The first truck to pass had a large painting on the canvas of the Roadrunner running through the desert. I stood up. The next truck had a colorful image of Wile E. Coyote running through the same desert with his hand stretched out, as if he was reaching after the Roadrunner. The next showed a tribe of Smurfs wearing blue helmets scratching their heads in a pine forest. Then came a truck bearing a giant image of Bart Simpson with squiggly streaks of anger coming off the top of his head. The final truck had a painting of the Tasmanian Devil doing a spread eagle on the side of the canvas.

In the window of all the vehicles were stickers that read

More Balls Than Most. Other stickers had the words *BTKA—Born to Kick Arse*.

I ran into the road just as a Land Rover painted in Rasta colors drove past. It had a large smiley face stretched across the grill and the hubcaps were painted in red, yellow, black, and green. It screeched to a halt fifty yards down the road.

Graeme, the Englishman with orange hair, stuck his head out the back door. "Well, come on then. What are you waiting for? A bloody invitation from the Queen herself?"

The silence of the night was broken and, along with it, all my doubts. Yes, I told myself, you are the ones. And with each step I could feel it, that tug telling me that my life was in the process of changing. I wasn't all the way inside when the truck lurched into first gear. I fell backward, hitting my face against the rear window.

"Easy now, Spam," said Graeme.

I wiped the outline of my nose and cheek from the glass and at the last moment I caught a glance out of it. There on the side of the road near the barricade was my flak jacket. It was just standing there on its own, green and erect, like a tortoise shell for sale in a Chinese market.

"Tea?" asked Graeme.

Near the door sat a portable propane stove with a small flame heating up a kettle.

"Tea?"

"What, you expecting eggs and bacon?"

"No." I laughed, still trying to take in the sight of the stove. "Tea would be great."

"Cheers."

"Cool trucks," I said, trying to ease my way into this band of merry pranksters.

"Works every time," he said.

"What works?"

"Bloody Serbs think we are a joke," said the driver. He gave his name as Tony Gafney, from Galway. "Pleased to meet you . . . not," he said. This made the shotgun passenger, who was crouched over in the dark, laugh hysterically.

"That's Christophe. A git," said Graeme.

"A git?"

"Frog. French."

"So the trucks?" I said.

"They think we are a joke and don't much bother us and we slip in twenty or thirty tons of food right under their stupid bastard noses," said Tony. "But the Croats, they'll slit our throats and take the Rover before we're done choking on our blood."

"Did you bring anything to drink, mate?" asked Graeme.

I produced the bottle of whiskey.

"Right," said Graeme. "See, I told you he wouldn't be a total waster."

As we got closer to the Bosnian border I remembered something that had been mentioned in the security briefing the day before. They said convoys traveling in Herzegovina should be especially careful: they had found three Italians in a riverbed in the Croatian-controlled sector of Bosnia. The story going around was that Croat irregular soldiers, most likely drunk, had stopped them at a bogus checkpoint, taken them out of their car, and shot them one by one at the edge of a bridge. And then there were the Turkish drivers hauling fuel and food to central Bosnia. The trucks were missing and the drivers were still at large.

"Did you hear about the Italians?" I asked.

"Yeah, poor buggers," said Graeme.

"Don't worry," said Tony, "we'll just give them you and tell them you are a spy."

"Thanks," I said.

"So what do you do in California?" asked Graeme, as he poured powdered milk into his tea. We hit a bump and he spilled a little on his shirt. "Oh, for fuck's sake, this isn't an amusement park, is it?"

"It isn't?" said the Frenchman.

"Right, sorry then, you were saying?" said Graeme. "You can't find good help these days."

"Sod off," said Tony.

"So what do you do in California?" asked Graeme.

"Work a little, this and that," I said.

"Yeah, right, mate, nice one," he said. "You aren't some rich geezer here for a look-see, are you?"

"No."

We drove on. The night was black. The only things visible were the ghost-like branches of trees caught in the headlights. Soon we gained altitude and turned east toward the mountains, away from the sea.

"How about we make the Spam the logistics officer?" asked Graeme. With precision he was forging papers with my name on them. He said they had to be done before we got to the border. I asked what would happen if they weren't done by then.

"They will rob us and maybe throw us in jail and we won't ever be allowed to cross the border again." He hesitated, making me wonder if he was lying or just didn't care.

"It will be impossible that he is ze logistics officer," said Christophe. "I am already ze logistics officer."

"Right you are, git. How about entertainment officer?" asked Graeme.

"What does a bloody Yank know about having fun?" exclaimed Tony.

"You gotta point there," said Graeme. This time his laugh lasted twenty seconds and then stopped just as suddenly as it had begun.

"Mate, you sure you haven't got any money?"

"A few bucks in my pocket, that's it. Why?" I asked.

"Need to get a case of vodka in Kiseljak. Mind you, the cheap Russian shit. Ah, no worries, we'll just nick it."

I gave a wiggle of my foot, squeezing the two hundred dollars between the flaps of my toes.

The voice on the CB radio was unmistakably Australian. It yelled, "Smurfs," and, as if prompted by a secret signal, everyone in the car began humming the theme song to the Smurf cartoon. Just then a convoy of United Nations trucks with bold white letters that read *UNPROFOR*, United Nations Protection Forces, rumbled past in the opposite direction.

"Useless blue hats couldn't find their way out of the bloody forest if they had to," said Tony.

At the border the Croatian guards didn't flinch at the forged paperwork dangling round my neck. They stole a few boxes of food and waved us across.

We passed an old woman riding a cart full of hay being

pulled by a horse. A young boy seated on the back of her cart waved and I watched them disappear as the woman lightly whipped the horse's ass.

And just like that, we were in Bosnia.

At daybreak the morning sun rose on the horizon like a low blue flame. Dangerous, but quietly mysterious as it hung against the silhouette of steep mountain peaks. There wasn't a cloud in sight, and straight ahead the two-lane road sliced through a landscape of rock and forest.

The driving was rarely interrupted, usually only for an occasional piss stop. And the radio was never silent, as the drivers from the other trucks cracked jokes or made observations on almost everything outside. About the local people walking the roads, how they were "dodgy". Or the UN troops standing guard behind a razor-sharp fence, "useless sods". I sat in the back trying to picture what war would look like, but it was useless. All that came to mind were clichés from television or the movies.

Toward sunset Graeme took a break from his GameBoy and cracked his neck with his hands, as if he'd done that exact move on someone else in a way that caused pain.

"You play?" he asked.

"No, thanks."

"So you've never been to a war?"

"No," I said, "close a few times, but no."

I felt humbled and thankful to be in the hands of veteran road warriors. Graeme giggled a bit, like a fourteen-year-old boy who had just peeked up a schoolgirl's skirt.

"That's OK, neither have we." He laughed.

So there it was. I had finally found a group of misfits—jokers, conmen and possibly drunks—all dead set to do anything other than let the red tape of life hold them back. Already I found something heart-warming about the fact that no one in the vehicle seemed to care why I was here. Except for a few courtesy questions, I hadn't asked them and they hadn't asked me. It was as if we were all going to allow our secrets to remain our own. Our motivation for being here wasn't the point. Being here was.

6

Just after dark the temperature dropped further as we began our ascent of the mountain pass east of Tarcin. The snow on either side of the muddy track was hip deep and perfectly still in the amber glow of the full moon. On the road the mud was shin deep. At one point we spent an hour stuck in the mud before getting pulled out by a UN tow truck.

The entire day's driving had been a chaotic series of pristine yet surreal images: deep river gorges with turquoise rivers flowing toward the sea, and bombed-out bridges replaced by temporary UN floating bridges. Up top, the alpine peaks were as jagged as the French Alps and the forests thick and dark with pines. Down below, on the side of a road leading to the forest, was a man standing on top of a UN tank waving, while behind him another soldier was taking a piss. At every checkpoint there were machine guns, tanks, and hand grenades. Just beyond the guards were bunches of children asking for chocolate. Like a band of pied pipers we drove through towns and the children ran after the trucks of cartoon characters, perhaps desperate for the color as much as for food. Sometimes we stopped and threw out juggling balls. One time Graeme got on top of the Land Rover and drank something out of a bottle. He set a stick on fire and blew on it. The flash of flame must have been five feet long. The kids went crazy with laughter.

Everywhere we went, the calculus of ethnic cleansing was visible. One village would be burned but then the next was full of homes with smoke coming out the chimneys, chopped wood in the driveway, and two cars parked out front. The most disturbing were the villages that had both the destruction and the calm. When a burned house stood in ruins next to an untouched house.

"A hundred quid says his neighbor did him in," said Graeme as we passed through, keeping quiet in the hope no one would notice us.

To bed down for the night we drove to Fojnica, a village at the end of a box canyon nestled under a foot of snow. There were children running down the street throwing snowballs in each other's faces. The war, wherever it was, hadn't come to this small hamlet. Yet.

"How close are we to the front lines?" I asked.

"Fifteen to twenty kilometers to Serb checkpoints," said Graeme.

We stashed two fifty-gallon drums of diesel for the ride home with the parents of Achman, a kid we befriended when he offered his parents' boarding house as a place for us to stay. Instead we opted to sleep in the trucks to protect the cargo.

We parked across the street from a large rectangular hotel that had a constant stream of people going in and out the front door. I wandered inside. It was a piece of concrete socialist architecture once used by cross-country skiers and weekend lovers. Now the hotel had been turned into an amputee recovery ward. There was a low hubbub about the place, as if the walls had asthma. Dozens of people milled around the lobby, holding the ends of their newly missing limbs. And when I asked them questions they talked as if nothing had happened. They treated me like I'd just got off a double-decker tour bus on my way to Budapest for a holiday.

"Have you seen the monastery on the hill?" the man missing his left arm asked. "It is very beautiful this time of year."

"Not yet," I said.

"You must try and stay awhile. It is a beautiful town."

I didn't understand what he was talking about. I pulled my wool cap down on my ears and walked out the door.

We slept two people to the back of each truck. On the black market our goods were worth a small fortune and we figured our physical presence was the best defense we could offer. I climbed in after Graeme and arranged a stack of sanitary towels and baby diapers to form a soft mattress under my sleeping bag. As I slipped into my warm bag I said a quick thank you to the man in Metkavitch burning US army-issued gear. It seemed like I had visited him some time last year even though it was only two days before.

A low booming noise was barely audible, like it was coming from many miles away.

"Artillery?" I asked, noticing it for the first time.

"Sounds like it," said Graeme in a worried voice.

"How far away do you think that is?" My ears had pricked up at the first noise of war.

"A couple of feet. That's my finger tapping on the tarp, you stupid geezer." He laughed so loud I thought he'd wake the amputees across the street. Then I wondered if they ever woke up scratching their goddamn missing limbs.

"Jumpy, eh, Spam?" He was slurping down a container of yogurt he had pulled out from under his leg.

"How do you guys live in London and not work?" I asked.

"Ah mate, every one of these punters is on the dole, living with mates in flats, that kind of thing. There ain't no brain surgeons here, if you know what I mean."

"Tough to keep it all going?"

"Give it all you got and it always comes back. That's the ticket."

"I hear that."

Graeme was like that, a Zen warrior, a believer in the full power of karma. I already trusted him and wanted to tell him everything, but not yet. I wanted to say the truth: that I drew in my next breath because I was convinced life was, above all else, about love. It was this or it was nothing.

Trying to sleep I was beginning to drift, to think of things not related to being here at all. Fishing in the Sacramento river; hiking Zion Canyon; teaching English to Taiwanese executives on a golf course in southern Taiwan. Outside, there were voices speaking in some language from another galaxy.

"So you were lying before, right?" I asked.

"Bloody hell. Which lie was that?" asked Graeme.

"You've been here before."

"Yeah," he said and chuckled. "Knew you'd fall for that one too. You Yanks are quite a gullible lot, aren't ya?"

"Oh, I don't know about that," I said, surprised how defensive I felt at the comment, even though I guessed that, for better or for worse, he was probably correct.

"I was here last year for a couple of weeks. Messed me up a bit though." He held up a yogurt. "Want one?"

"So what brought you back?"

He threw me the yogurt. I noticed it was from a German company.

"No place like it in the world, mate. Besides, doing this, delivering food to people who really need it, there just isn't any feeling like it."

"How long do you think it will take to deliver the load?"

"No saying. Roads could close. Fighting could get nasty. Maybe three days, maybe three weeks." He lay back down. "So you've been around the world, eh?" he asked.

"Backpacked a lot of it."

"Ever been to Africa?"

"Egypt."

"I would love to set up a camp in one of them wildlife reserves. Just wild animals and open land forever."

"So you keep calling me Spam. What does it mean?" I asked.

"Spastic Plastic American Motherfucker."

I didn't respond and in the quiet I swear I could hear the snow falling. My mind continued racing over things from my other life, the one I had left behind a few hours ago when I crossed that border.

Spam. There was no denying it. I came from a Spam culture. Everywhere in America it was just another day. Tomorrow people in Dallas, Chicago and New York would meet for coffee and talk about the stock market. America, the land of milk and honey, where in times of crisis citizens are often asked by their leaders to do their part for the country by "going shopping". And this night, like every night, millions would gather around the black box, remote in hand, for their daily dose of novocaine. Oblivion, one night at a time. Wouldn't it make sense if the politicians, instead of asking us to shop our way out of duress, were to encourage us to take a hike to the top of the nearest mountain or go fishing or make more love? Or never take them at their word? I'd vote for that candidate.

Dizzy from thought, I lay back and closed my eyes. The Navajo believe we have several lives. They say life is the arena in which the human spirit gets to interact, and by doing so we achieve the thing we find hardest—we change; whereas when we are dead we are permanently who we are when we cease living. So the idea is to go a step further than you did the last time you were here in the hope that your dead soul will be more content not to be here. A comforting thought, that our job of being human is simply to go about the nasty process of change, but I still didn't want to think about it.

I had other things on my mind.

Like who in God's name was going to use these sanitary towels and soil these diapers that I was sleeping on tonight?

And where was she, the girl I loved? Where was she hiding and how would I find her again? After all, that was why I was here—to find her. How long would she be gone? I kept asking myself over and over: if I tried with all my might, with all my love, would she reappear?

It was cold all around me but warm in my bag. For almost two years I had been sleeping only when either drink or exhaustion had worn me down. On most nights I caught an hour here, two hours there, but never more. Sometimes I went to bed with a woman, but that was only when they felt they were fixing me up like some broken angel. With the war not far away and the storm brewing outside, the thin wall of tarp suddenly seemed like a protective sheet against the past. A blanket of frozen time where the past was firmly out of reach and the future was on hold. Pleasantly suspended, I found myself drifting into a deep sleep for the first time I could remember. I had a giddy sensation that could best be described as contentment. I had finally found a place that promised some balance. It felt like those precious moments of free floating when I first hold my breath under water. And then I dreamed.

I had only one dream back then. It was always the same. I dreamed of Corrina.

7

I sometimes don't remember my dreams, but I usually remember waking up. That temporary feeling that comes only from awaking out of a deep sleep. When everything seems possible. But then there is the sound of a car, a distant conversation, or the voice of a stranger, and the dreams get sucked back into the dark hidden corners of the medulla and we are once again faced with what is often referred to as "real time".

The crew were noodling around in the snow, clearly waiting for someone to lead them, like sheep in a field puffing out clouds of breath. It must have been quite a sight for the amputees across the street, as they stood behind the lobby window staring into a world blanketed in white except for the five trucks painted in bold yellows, greens, and blues that sat in their car park. What did they make of an eight-foot Wile E. Coyote with a mad smile on his face? Maybe it looked crazy or farcical, but it must have been better than seeing a tank.

There was a trace of electricity in the air. It came from us. We were pumped. Today was the day. Today we would drive into the belly of the beast. Today we would change our lives. Everyone talked in hurried breaths and said things they didn't mean.

"I love this place. It's the most beautiful place I've ever been," said one driver.

"Bloody hell. I will definitely come back here after the war."

"Absolutely."

Everyone was bouncing around like we'd done speedballs for breakfast. My brain again slipped into a montage of my own travels. So many road trips, so many countries, but always alone. Now I was being thrown together with twelve freaks, and suddenly they were the closest thing I had to family. For a moment there, I could even say I loved them all like cousins.

We drove into Kiseljak, the official black-market town of central Bosnia, which was essentially run by Croatian HVO. It was the last stop before the Serb checkpoints. There was something shifty and mean about it. Towns in Arizona, where I live now, might have been like this in 1888. Boomtowns built on promises of money and whoring. This was no place to be caught drunk walking the streets.

As focused as bank robbers we pulled up at a store on the main drag. UN tanks patrolled the streets while HVO soldiers with Kalashnikovs slung across their chests walked the sidewalks.

"Stay cool, dude, and just keep asking about the price of cooking oil," said Graeme as we entered the store. My job was clear. I was to keep the shop owner busy.

The owner turned out to be an older woman, gray-haired and hard of hearing. She had tattoos on her arms and one on her forehead, just above the eyebrows. It was a faded shade of green and in the shape of a U. I almost panicked when a couple of HVO soldiers poked their heads in, machine guns first. She shooed them away. Graeme and a few of the others got busy stealing the vodka, potato chips, candy bars, and foot-long rolls of salami.

"How much is cooking oil?" I asked in English. She answered in incomprehensible Serbo-Croat, the language of all the ex-Yugoslavian nations. But depending on where one was standing, it was important to call it Bosnian, Serbian, Croatian, or Serbo-Croat. In truth, apart from minor distinctions resulting from regional dialects, it can be argued that the difference between them is more political than linguistic.

By the way she was rolling her eyes and moving her hands, I guessed the store lady was talking about how hard things were compared to the old days before everything went bad. I paid her ten German marks for a handful of oranges and some cooking oil. She smiled a toothless grin and I walked out behind the others.

We drove less than half a mile to a UN compound. There, Tony went inside to let the UN command know we were driving through no-man's-land, to Sarajevo. The idea was that they would rescue us if we disappeared or were shot in the two-kilometer death zone that separated the Serbs from the city.

Never idle, Graeme grabbed a hose and walked toward a nearby UN truck, parked by the fence. I couldn't stop thinking of our stealing from the old lady. It seemed a wrong had been committed.

Graeme hurried back just as Tony left the building.

"Wankers had a lock on the tank," said Graeme, disappointed he couldn't siphon any petrol. We quickly loaded up and were off, heading for the Serb checkpoints.

"Here we go, ladies. Keep sharp and no bullshit," said Tony over the CB. "If the driver is shot push him out of the way and keep on driving. Do not stop for anything. Not even for SMURFS."

"I don't know about stealing from that old lady," I said from the back seat.

"What's that?" shouted Graeme over the music.

"The old lady. I mean, what if she's just trying to make it too?"

"Did you see the tattoos?" Graeme cranked up the music.

"Yeah. The one on her forehead."

He was bobbing his head left to right and beating the dashboard with his hands. As far as I could tell, he was lost in a rave inside his head. A sign off the side of the road read *Warning— Mines*.

"Stands for Ustasha," he yelled.

"Ustasha?"

"Croatian Nazis. Hitler's pals. A million people croaked in Croatian Nazi camps. She's lucky we didn't burn her to the ground."

The music was loud and the bass vibrated through my spine. I had to admit it was beginning to have an effect on me.

Yes. I definitely felt like dancing.

8

At S4, the Serb checkpoint, Graeme and a few of the others brought out juggling balls and began entertaining the Serbian guards. The soldiers laughed and pointed and showed their rotten-toothed smiles.

"Aren't these the bad guys?" I nervously asked Graeme. All I knew was that ever since the Bosnian Serbs first surrounded Sarajevo, effectively laying a siege on its citizens, this road was the only way in and out of the city. These guards were quite literally the gatekeepers.

"Listen," he said, "they are fucking dangerous, but we gotta deal with them. And they tend not to shoot at our trucks because we don't act like the UN."

Meanwhile old men in blue overcoats and faded blue caps used forklifts to take seven tons of our supplies.

"It is only fair," said the guard with what looked like chicken grease still on his thick beard. "They get all the aid and we get so little."

"Who gets all the aid?" I asked.

"Those dirty Muslims. They are killing all the Serbs in the city."

I asked him if he would shoot at us if he saw us in Sarajevo.

"Of course." He laughed as if horrified at my stupidity.

I walked into their warehouse and found it lined wall to wall with boxes labeled *UNHCR*, the United Nations Humanitarian Center for Refugees.

It would become one of the well-known secrets of this war, and was most likely the reason the Serbs allowed humanitarian aid to flow into their own private siege. By agreement with the UN, the Serbs were allowed to take up to 40 percent of every load entering the city. Of course one could hardly argue with the logic. After all, the Serbs had all the bargaining power. To get food to the starving Sarajevans the UN had to make a deal, but the irony was that by making the deal the UN became involved in providing goods that would later sell on the black market. And it can be argued that throughout history it has been the black markets of war that have given those in power a reason to continue fighting.

Further down the road we stopped at one more checkpoint. There we ran into a bunch of twenty-year-old Serb soldiers who begged us for heroin, smacking their hands onto their forearms like a junkie prepping his veins. We told them we didn't have any. They insisted we must at least have cocaine.

Graeme gave them some breath mints and said, "Of bung-holes and arses you do smell on this day of waddle, taddle." He laughed and they laughed right along, not knowing he had just insulted them.

"But then perhaps you would care to lick your own arse and have me stick a bayonet in your eye, in the sky, want some pie, I hope you all bloody well die?"

They seemed perplexed by Graeme's smiling face.

"I say we give them some bleach and tell them it's coke," said Graeme. "They'll snort it straight off and go fucking knockers."

I told him it could be risky.

"You're probably right."

We drove at top speed through no-man's-land, the last desperate two-kilometer stretch before entering the besieged city. Every angle looked the same. Every home lay in rubble. A burned-out tank sat at the side of the road. Shots rang out somewhere. It was like traveling through a Nevada atomic-bomb test site. Nothing lived here. It was an ideal place for the dead to mingle in the shadows.

Yet before I could digest what I was seeing we turned a corner and just like that we were in Sarajevo, home of the 1984 Winter Olympics. My first impression was of its geography. The city spreads out in a valley, its eastern end tucked up against the steep slopes of a mountain with a ski resort at the peak. On all sides the city pushes against the rim of mountains, except at the western end, where it opens up into a valley that runs several miles before ending in another set of mountains. As we drove down the main street, the funny thing was there were all kinds of people out and about like there wasn't a war going on here at all. Many buildings were mangled and crumbling as a result of the bombing, but where were the trenches, the flying missiles, the screaming babies covered in napalm? It was sunny and people were walking slow and easy, as if they were on their way home from church. One man on a bicycle, with flowers in his basket, stopped and stared at us as we honked. Yelling kids ran after us for a short sprint before giving up. What were they saying?

As we approached downtown almost every building we passed was missing something: doors, windows, walls, roofs. Many trees were limbless, and sometimes just stumps remained. Cars stripped of their steel exteriors were stacked on top of one another and container units lined the streets on the west side, all ripped with bullet holes. More cars burned to the shell sat in front of flat buildings. The whole place was a bombed-out center of something, but the center of what I wasn't yet sure. It wasn't anything I'd ever seen on television. But the oddest thing was that in the middle of all this destruction there were people just walking along, most with what looked like toy carts and baby strollers.

"Poor bastards," said Graeme. "Use whatever they can to carry water to their homes." He indicated the strollers and carts.

Graeme's head hung out the window the whole drive into the city. We passed by two women with long black hair wearing black skirts.

"Home, sweet home." He waved and they waved back. "Oh la la, Sarajevo," he said. "Mate, the women here are bang on."

We drove straight for the UNIS towers, the tallest buildings in the city. Located on Marijin Dvor street, the office building was actually two forty-story towers that rose out of the guts of the city center, burned and abandoned. You could see right through the damn thing. It looked ready for a construction company to finish the job of putting in the windows and doors.

We pulled up at the entrance to an underground car park at the back of the towers. One guard emerged, an older man with a machine gun across his chest. Graeme jumped out and handed him some cigarettes. Within moments he and the guard were laughing, as if reminiscing about that fishing trip they took together off the coast of Sicily with their wives a few years back.

While we unloaded the food a herd of fifty children attacked the trucks. They tried to steal a battery from one truck and did steal several boxes of food from another. Eventually three guards with AK-47s dressed in polyester slacks and black, polished shoes ran them off.

Tony yelled out, "All right, someone stays with the food

all the time. And no one goes outside unless we're making deliveries."

There were a few crackles of gunfire but nothing to worry about. Apart from the destruction everywhere and the pack of starving children, there was no indication that a battle was raging.

We put the food in the parking garage in a steel-wired cage that had a lock on it the size of a baseball glove—"otherwise," Graeme said, "the guards themselves will sack it before sunset."

Our building was 300 meters from the nearest front line, which was across the Miljacka river at the Jewish cemetery. I grabbed my sleeping bag and followed Graeme upstairs to the eighth floor. "This is where we stayed last time. A little cold but it'll do," he said.

From the looks of it, our floor was once the office suite of an advertising business. In one room were scattered posters of people frolicking on beaches in Thailand. In another were pictures of trekkers on the trail in Machu Picchu. Now the empty office smelled of urine and excrement, or cauliflower and rotting pumpkin; the only relief was the breeze coming through the missing windows, which was also a grim reminder of our exposure to Serbian snipers—all the windows on the side facing the river had been shot out long ago.

We picked the safest room, away from the river side, and quickly stacked filing cabinets to the ceiling to block off the window. Someone found an old Yugoslavian flag—solid red with a large communist star—jammed in a desk upstairs and draped it over the cabinets to hide any signs of light. A few flights up we located a table and some plastic chairs. We even found a blue vinyl sofa. We brought in the portable stove and some supplies and called it our living room. Off to one side were two doors that led to smaller rooms where the windows still had glass. We spread out our sleeping bags and called those the bedrooms.

We didn't have any glasses so we drank our cheap Russian vodka straight from the bottle. To cut the nastiness and make it last longer we mixed it with powdered lemonade. I was pretty certain if we drank enough of this concoction our livers would disintegrate long before we got shot.

Somewhere there was an explosion that shook the ground a little bit. Another explosion. This one vibrated through my feet into my groin. That felt like war. Stunned, we all looked at each other for what seemed the longest time.

Finally, breaking the silence, Graeme spoke. "Right then. Who's going to sort out the toilet?"

9

Everyone in the Trip had a skill or contribution to make, even if they didn't quite know what it was yet. That was the Trip's whole philosophy. Do it, baby, think about it later. Roger, a polite Englishman who stood five feet five and had a thick north London accent, was a driver but also a designated truck mechanic. "Bits and bobs," he said when I asked him to describe what he did before he came here. He had worked primarily as a roadie for rock bands.

Allen and a different Roger, both designated truck drivers, were Australian. Their skill was unique in that they were able to laugh at each other's jokes for several hours straight. I made the mistake of telling them I'd been to Australia once, which only encouraged them to believe I loved their country as much as they did. I told them I got stuck in Sydney with no money and worked in an Indian restaurant until I could buy a ticket to Indonesia. Their response was, "Ah, but you had the time of your life, am I right?"

They spent most of their day telling anyone who would listen about the wonders of Australia. "Mate," Allen would say with a big drunken grin across his pale freckled face, "the chickies at Bondi Beach. What do you make of that, mate?"

Peter, also a driver, was the other Australian. He was a good driver but his talent was drinking. He had long red hair, a square jaw and bushy eyebrows, which made it difficult to see his eyes. The locals called him "ape." He rarely talked in the day but at night, after the vodka kicked in, he would walk around the room like a caged lion ready to pounce. One minute he would quietly tell you he was so proud of being able to help another human being, and in the next he would go into a tirade. "You're nothing but a cunt trying to cut me down. A parasite and fucking whore. You smelly cunt," he said, speaking in my direction once. And his driving? Well, he seemed to have a steady hand in stressful situations, but then there was the time he drove one of the trucks off a cliff, down by our pension in Split. All I really knew about Peter's past life was that he couldn't go back to England with the Road Trip because his passport had a black X in it.

Colin, a burly but soft-spoken Kiwi, was interested in medicine and planned on becoming a doctor or nurse working in troubled countries. He wore brightly colored bandanas that highlighted his dark features and full beard. On call as our "medical aid' in case of minor injuries, he kept himself busy by working with English Roger on the trucks.

The other Kiwi was Dougie. He was like Steve McQueen's character, the Cooler King, in *The Great Escape*. He never lost his cool, had a dry sense of humor and was good with his hands. He was the gopher of the group. He could make just about anything mechanical work and rarely got rattled. By the end of the first week he had jerry-rigged a wire into the Bosnian army press office below, which gave us electricity a few hours a day.

Josh, the only other American on the crew, could drive a truck, but his real talent was dishing out advice. He wore a black leather coat that came down to his knees. He had closely cropped red hair and talked about how he loved the far-right rantings of Rush Limbaugh. This made me cautious. Before this trip to Bosnia he had been living on the dole in London, in self-exile from America. One of the others said it had something to do with a run-in with the police in Petaluma. I was inclined to believe he was slightly dangerous or, more likely, pretending to be. Like the time he tried to convince us he should carry a handgun in his cab while driving through Bosnia. Apart from standing still on Snipers' Alley, there was probably no better way to make sure of being shot. Over time I realized there were only two ways to handle him. Either like a nurse trying to coax a mental patient into taking his downers, or with a loud forceful voice like a prison guard getting the bitches in order.

Then there was Meni, a British subject but whose ethnic background was Iraqi Jewish. He had a big lazy smile and an equally big heart, but spoke so slowly it was hard not to imagine something was a little loose upstairs. He laughed at most of the Australian jokes but sometimes he would become inexplicably angry and insist, "It is not funny."

His father had been imprisoned in Iraq for almost twenty years before landing in London, where he translated the first Hebrew–Iraqi dictionary. Meni wore overalls and could usually be found somewhere under a truck, smiling, working on a cracked oil pan or fried alternator.

Tony, the Irishman from Galway, had left his high-paying job as an accountant in Brussels to come here. He and a few friends had started the Road Trip a few years earlier. "I figure I can't do shite sitting behind a desk that I could ever tell me grandkids about." He was the boss, but when making a decision he usually consulted Graeme or sometimes me. And then quite often, as if simply to defy us, he would do the opposite of what we had suggested.

Graeme was the Ken Kesey of The Serious Road Trip. The only thing to add is that when he acted as diplomat to resolve the infighting among the drivers he usually ended up yelling something like "If you want to carry on being wankers when we are fucking surrounded by people rolling in their own shit, then go ahead. Be cuntheads for all I care."

As for the Frenchman, Christophe, he seemed either very nervous or very scared. Like me, he couldn't drive a truck, but because his Bosnian was passable he acted mostly as a liaison between Tony and Graeme and the locals.

"He was with me when I first came here," said Graeme. "He's scared out of his git mind to be here again."

"So why is he here?"

"Why do you think?"

"I don't know," I said.

"Why do most men do stupid things?"

I knew what he meant but I pretended not to and shrugged my shoulders.

"He has a girlfriend here. Or did. She escaped not so long ago." He poured another round of vodka and lemonade. "She was a dancer and wanted to get to a dance contest in Belfast."

"How did she escape?"

"Ran across the airport. The first time she tried, French UN soldiers stopped her. Hit her across the face with a rifle butt. Imagine that. Trying to escape her own city and turned back by the fucking UN, the same geezers here to protect her."

"What did she do?"

"She talked to her friends in the army and they gave her a hand grenade. The next time, when the UN soldiers told her she couldn't leave, she held up the grenade, finger on the pin, and said, 'Either I'm leaving or you are never leaving.' "

"And?" I asked.

"What's a twenty-year-old Frenchman scared shitless going to do?"

"Let her go?"

"Fucking right they let her go."

10

Escape.

As far as I could tell, there were three ways out of the city during the siege of Sarajevo.

Well, there were four ways if you counted dying.

None of the options was easy and most demanded either money or a great deal of courage. Or both. First there was the mad dash across the airport runway. This small stretch of land was the only hole in the Serbian noose around the city. One catch was the Serbian snipers, who limited any escape attempt to after dark. The other catch was that this small strip of land was officially under UN control, and troops were well known to turn back Bosnians fleeing in the middle of the night. The UN reasoning was always the same: they did not want to let Sarajevans escape because that would be contributing to the ethnic cleansing policy of the Serbs who were surrounding the city. So instead, like some Orwellian nightmare, the citizens were told to go back to Sarajevo, where they could then patiently wait their turn to be ethnically cleansed by snipers and grenades within the city limits.

The second choice was to obtain the coveted blue card, the gold standard for identification papers in the war. The blue card allowed anyone carrying it access to UN-protected transportation within Bosnia. With that card you could get on a UN armored transport vehicle and just ride out of the city. Or get on a UN military cargo jet for free and in less than an hour be drinking cold beers and eating lamb in Split. As for getting a blue card, it was usually tied to a person's direct connections with a foreigner. If a local befriended someone working in the UN or with the means to manufacture a blue card, then the usual arrangement was an exchange of work for freedom. In general this was an avenue of escape limited to those employed by the international aid groups as drivers, translators, or assistants. It was also a traded commodity, available to a few wealthy citizens. And of course there must have been cases where blue cards were issued as the result of a romantic relationship with a well-connected foreigner.

The third choice for leaving the city also had its share of complications. It was the Dobrinja–Butmir tunnel, a hole nearly one and a half meters wide and one and a half meters high that ran for about 800 meters directly under the Sarajevo airport.

A person needed a permit issued by Bosnian officials to use the tunnel. Controlled by the Bosnian army and off limits to foreigners, it was used primarily to move food and supplies in and out of the city. It was also the main conduit for getting

Bosnian army troops out to fight in surrounding villages. And, at times, the route served to move politicians to and from central Bosnia to attend sessions of Parliament.

Of course the tunnel was also a traded commodity and various warlords and mafia types "rented' it to import everything from carrots to cigarettes to fuel to drugs and contraband. So it moved goods and troops, but as an escape route it was available only to those few who had the means or the connections. And if someone did manage to secure a permit to use the tunnel for escape, when they left it they were still over a hundred kilometers from the border of Croatia, most of it on a road that ran through a thickly forested war zone with constantly shifting front lines.

And in keeping with Sarajevo's black humor, anyone who made it through the tunnel was quickly reminded how far they had yet to go. At the exit a sign read *Paris 3765 km.*

11

Since I didn't have any mechanical skills to contribute I decided to volunteer to see to the bathroom. I took a crowbar to the bathroom door in the hallway, near the burned-out elevator shaft. Inside there wasn't a breath of fresh air, only the smell of rotting human crap. I tore off a piece of cloth and tied it around my mouth and cleaned up the mess, little round pile by little round pile. All I could think of was this: where had 250,000 people been going to the bathroom for fifteen months? I wondered what their homes looked like. Did they shit in the gutters?

The thought, as soon as I formed it, became a physical need. I had to go. I ran up two stories to the tenth floor and found a hidden spot behind a broken desk. There were piles of feces everywhere. Dry piles of human excrement. It hit me then—we are a simple creature, we humans. Hiding our dumps in large white porcelain shrines can't disguise it. We eat, piss, and shit. If we are lucky, we have sex. If we are very lucky, we love.

But no matter what, we always eat, piss, and shit. Once you see the underpinning of life, you can't pretend you didn't. Once you see piles of crap in the hallway, and spread on the mirrors and on the ceilings, there is no turning back.

I needed paper to clean myself. I reached up and grabbed whatever was on the desk. It was an advertising blotter. A farmer and his son were looking into a field of golden wheat. The slogan read *Coca-Cola. It's got the whole world in its hands.*

That first night in the towers we played euchre, drank vodka, and went over the rules.

"Two in a truck. Never stop unless at a police checkpoint," said Tony as we sat around the long rectangular table. His hair was messy and his voice stern.

"Remember we don't have the UN blue cards so nobody will be coming to save our arses. We deliver and get back to the garage fast."

Everyone nodded their heads. The vodka had a way of making everything feel important.

"Graeme?" asked Tony.

"What?"

"You wanna add something?"

"Say something to this lot?"

"You've been here before. Any advice?"

"Right. All I can say is if you let it, this place will put a spinner on your head. Stay loose and don't do anything *stupid*. Most of you are useless cunts so this will be the most important thing you ever do in your life. Don't screw it up," said Graeme.

"How we supposed to get the ladies up here, mate?" This from one of the Aussies.

"For starters you might want to brush your fucking teeth."

Later, when everyone was asleep, I went into the front room, facing the river. I stepped on some glass and stopped. No one was following me. All I heard were drunken snores. I stood at one of the broken windows that looked into the hills with the snipers. There were a few lights flickering in the otherwise dark night. It wasn't far to freedom, just over the hills into the black of the forest. I knew she was out there somewhere, calling my name.

"Skidder," whispered Graeme.

"Oh hey," I whispered back.

"Duck down."

I ducked. He ducked and joined me as we peeked over the windowsill.

"That mate of yours with the army clothes in Metković. Maybe we could get ourselves a couple of truckloads and drive it to London. It'd be worth heaps there," he said.

Graeme always had a scheme brewing. On the way in he had been talking about setting up a program where kids would be taken from the war zone and put in circus schools in France. I asked him how he would finance it. He told me to stop being so damn negative.

"You been to the Himalayas?" he asked.

"Yes."

"Sorted."

We stared in silence at the flickering lights up on the hills, where the snipers and artillery gunners were quietly passing time.

"We're giving to the Krishnas tomorrow. You up for that?"

"Absolutely."

"OK, dude. I'm knackered." He headed back toward the office.

"Do you mean Hare Krishnas?" I asked.

"Spot on."

I pushed the thought of Hare Krishnas out of my mind and shut my eyes. I felt a familiar sensation come over me. It was like landing in any new city as a traveler—foreign, but somehow comforting, as if by being totally lost I had regained a sense of calm. I listened carefully, with all my might. A few gunshots. A barking dog. Then the rippling of a cold draft curled through the matrix of my earhole. Then silence. There. Like a siren call from the hills I could hear her calling my name. Or was it? Probably not. Yeah, probably not.

12

Before catching a ride into Bosnia I was quite happy making a few bucks in odd jobs and hitting the road every chance I got. Six days after I graduated from college I took $500 and a one-way ticket to Asia. After a quick stop in Japan I settled in Taiwan and taught English for a year. Apart from picking up a little Chinese and dengue fever, I also saved enough money to travel around the world. Then one day, after two years away from America, I got homesick for a home I didn't have. I caught a red-eye flight from Paris back to California.

I was twenty-four at the time and probably a bit cocky, feeling worldly and cosmopolitan after lounging in cafés in Cairo, Kathmandu, Istanbul, and Prague. You know the type: for every story a friend from my home town told I had a world story to up the stakes. Damn annoying habit, but hey, I thought, at least I wasn't wearing a cheap suit, drinking cocktails, and building a white fence for a wife I didn't like in the first place.

Anyhow, upon my return I immediately wanted to leave again, but to do that I needed money. Every dollar I made was calculated in terms of how far it would get me in the Third World. With this in mind, after a few weeks of culture shock in California, I decided on a job in Alaska working in the salmon-fishing industry. To be exact, in a cannery.

The job sounded perfect. They paid for my travel to Alaska and even kicked in the room and board. It paid $6.25 an hour, which wasn't much, but they promised heavy hours during the peak of the season. I figured I'd pocket enough for a trip to South America.

On my first day the foreman, a high-school math teacher from some place in Oregon with a well-manicured beard, put his hand on my shoulder and leaned into me with his full weight. He was tall and well built, like he snuck off and did push-ups during the breaks. He pointed to the ovens, which were hissing and hollering, belching steam out their snouts.

"Want to work the ovens?" he yelled in my face.

"OK."

"Ever been to London?"

"No."

"Me neither. Ever eat canned salmon?"

"No."

"Good. Why would you? Right?"

"Right."

"Stick with the fresh stuff." He pointed at the oven. "See that?"

"The oven?"

"Are you a smart alec? 'Cause this isn't school, get my meaning?"

"Yes." I imagined he doubled as the football coach.

"The gauge, smart guy," he barked. "On the side. Do you see it?"

I nodded.

"Do you know what that means?"

"The temperature."

"Death." He looked around the room as if to see who was listening, like he'd told me the secret of life. He lowered his voice. "If that little black needle goes below this red line, people start dying of botulism in London. Yes sirrreeee." His breath smelled of garlic. "Understand?"

I told him I did. And for the rest of the season I watched that needle like thousands of lives depended on it. I was no different from a soldier with his finger on the button of a missile aimed at China.

I enjoyed cooking the cans. It kept me away from the actual killing of the fish. I never minded hooking a fish in a stream, but whacking their heads off with a machine was different. Still, I promised myself that if I ever got to England I would take a few days to stand in front of shopping centers explaining to people why they might want to consider eating something other than canned fish.

Then one day everything changed. Everything. It was in Naknak that I fell in love with Corrina, a nineteen-year-old college student who sat in the back of the lunchroom eating green apples and reading. Her skin was pale from the lack of sun and her eyelids were slightly puffy from the long hours of work, and she laughed to herself as she fingered the pages of her book.

So many lunches I wanted to walk over and tell her I couldn't remember what it was like before her. I had never been this nervous, this mixed up. Ever since we made eye contact for the first time my stomach had been in knots pushing up under my ribcage. If the eyes are truly the windows to the soul, I could only imagine that her soul must be slightly almond-shaped, calm, honest, and dark as chocolate.

There was one boy, about her age. Sometimes he sat across from her and stared while she ate the apple. Sometimes he talked, but I couldn't hear what he said. The bastard. She didn't look up from her book much and I, being the kind that watches out for these omens, took this as a sign.

Of course, as things tend to go, she worked at the opposite end of the compound from me. She was at the beginning of the conveyor belt that carried the fish from one building to the next, and I was at the end. She was one of a dozen people standing on small stools working at a station known as the "slime line." Slime-line workers were the first into action after the fish had been decapitated and gutted by a massive machine. She stood there, alongside a dozen others, whacking off bits of leftover salmon heads, and pulling out any lingering guts.

Each time the whistle blew for fifteen-minute breaks I'd sprint to the other end of the compound and jump on the pallets next to the window for a better view. Her tool was a small knife, which she liked to cup in the palm of her hand. I imagined she hid it like that on purpose, as the Balinese do when they cut the rice during harvest; they hide it in their palm so the rice won't be scared of the blade before it gets whacked. I would take her to Bali. Hell, I would've taken her across the river for a slice of pizza if I could.

But we were on the shores of the Naknak river in Bristol Bay, which is close to absolutely nothing, but home to one of the largest salmon runs in the world. On our side of the river, besides the cannery, was a single bar, run by a local Aleutian

Indian. Across the river was a pizza shack and a few bars, but the only way there was to pay a bush pilot ten dollars for the three-minute flight. It wasn't the money that was in short supply, it was time. The fish were beginning to make their heroic run up the river, warriors on their way to die in order for the young to live. Or, in our case, so we could put them through a large machine that would behead them.

Then one night the conveyor belt stopped early, around nine o'clock. The rumor was that the peak was over. The fifteen-hour days we had been used to would soon be ten-hour days and then it would be finished. The salmon had either moved on to the next river mouth or found their way upstream, safe from the nets. Either way my days were numbered. But, more importantly, it was announced that there would be no morning shift the following day, which meant everyone was to meet at the bar, for the first time this season.

Around midnight, in my room in the workers' barracks, I locked the door and propped the mirror on top of the bed. To keep it from falling I wedged it against the wall with a towel. The damn mirror weighed almost as much as the bed, which had box springs punching through the mattress. Outside, even though it was midnight, the piss-yellow sun was still hanging around the Alaskan horizon. I stepped over to the window and adjusted the black blanket to keep out the light.

Back to the mirror. I pulled on my Levi's and tucked in my blue cotton shirt, the one I'd bought in Hong Kong a year before. It was a little worn and had some sort of peanut sauce stain, but it would do. It was the jeans I was worried about. I had one pair of Levi's. They weren't all that dirty but they had a rip in the backside, and when I bent over a bit of flesh tended to stick out.

In a state of panic, I put on my yellow work pants, cinching the belt well above the waist. They looked fine but they reeked of salmon guts. I sat down on the bed and quickly changed into a pair of sweats, the standard uniform of the Alaska fisherman. No chance, but I was running out of time. Down at the bar, the other bastards and perverts would be swooping down on her like bees to honey. I put the Levi's back on and left my shirt untucked. As long as I didn't bend over, no one would ever know.

This is ridiculous, I thought. I hadn't spent this much time in front of a mirror in my whole life. But then again I hadn't been bitten in the jugular by the love bug like this before. Don't get me wrong. I was not immune to the dreaded exotic disease known as lovesickness, but this was different. I could tell. The grumbling in my stomach and the fog in my frontal lobe were more than I could bear. Besides, this was the first time I had ever dressed for the occasion.

In the bar, a plywood shack with a tin roof, the fishermen were fat with money, and the crap games had already reached $1,000 a roll. The place was cold and smelled of dead fish, spilled beer and lemon air freshener, and like a desert wind kicking up dust devils, the odor moved throughout the bar, creating drifting clouds of stink with a twist of citron. The floor was sticky. The light was a fluorescent job and the windows were covered with blankets to keep out the madness of the never-ending daylight.

At the bar I downed a bourbon and ordered one more with a beer-back before I made my way to the pool table where she was. My knees buckled and my stomach leaped in somersaults. Her brown hair hung in braids down the back of her overalls to the middle of her back. When she leaned to make a shot I noticed the delicate hair, like dandelion spikes, sprouting from the nape of her neck. I imagined it smelled like creation right back there: dirt, sunflowers, dolphin skin, a baby's butt, mermaids, and fairy dust. Her fingers, all ten of those digits made with Zeus's own personal touch, grabbed the cue. And her breasts, camouflaged by her outfit, rested on the edge of the table like goose-down pillows.

My heart was pounding so hard I barely heard Merle Haggard on the jukebox singing "Whiskey and Gin". She peered over the cue as if to challenge me. My ears were drowning in my own blood. Dizzy, I took another hit off the bourbon and decided it was time to act. I took a few steps and stood directly in front of her.

"I was thinking," I said, trying to keep my hands from peeling the skin off my face, "it's too bad the season is already over. We should have hung out together, gotten to know each other."

The two friends she was with looked at her, then at me. There was a pause in the air as if an audience was unaware the punchline had just been delivered. And then came one of those moments.

It felt like my life had left me and I was standing there watching it in slow motion through a hole in the ceiling. It was slightly sepia in my mind's eye as my body receded to the back of the bar while she stood there smiling in a pale yellow light. I felt nothing, just empty and glad to be free of the burden of living. The desire, angst, and expectation drained away as if I was just one of eight million salmon who escaped the nets only to die splashing my colors in the riverbed. I had answered the call of love and felt ready to be damned, whatever happened next.

As the yellow tint began to fade I went where I felt safe. I started traveling in my mind. I thought of times I had got lost in tiger country in the highlands of Sumatra, of the rich Taiwanese men on golf courses learning English before they took sex tours to Thailand. No matter how many lessons we had they would still end up saying things like "Give me suckee and I pay you plenty."

I had seen women pluck razor blades from between their legs in Bangkok, had ridden camels around deserts in Egypt and skin-dived in the Red Sea. I had made passionate love with a woman on the Left Bank in Paris and fallen asleep under a Monet in the Louvre. And now here in Naknak, Alaska, staring into the eyes of a college girl, I was more scared than I had ever been out there in the world.

She recoiled with a half-grin, her eyes lidded from the work but still shining clear. The black circles under them only made her seem more innocent, as if she was waiting for something beautiful to happen.

Then her friends laughed and the moment was broken without out anyone saying a word. Dejected, I retreated and sat at the back of the bar rehearsing lines. *You are the most beautiful woman I have ever seen.* Or, more to the point, *Would you like to build a mud house in Mexico so we could live the rest of our lives there? Grow watermelons and mangoes?*

"Why did you say that?" she said as she took a seat in the chair across from me.

Startled, I looked up. "Because I meant it. I think we should go somewhere, travel somewhere."

"But you don't even know me."

"I know you like green apples and books."

She smiled, which showed her teeth. They were slightly crooked and that made me want to lick each one even more.

"That's not enough to run away with you."

"Why not? I mean what do we ever know of anyone?"

"Usually a little more than what they do at lunch."

"OK. I have a plan, kind of. I was thinking we could get a car, some used monster ride. Get some blankets and start driving. Go to the desert in the southwest and then down into Mexico. Bound to figure out something, right?"

"And then what?"

"Grow watermelons, mangoes."

"Then what?"

"Then do whatever comes next."

"Why are you saying this to me?"

"I got a strong feeling about this."

"A hunch?"

"No. I can't explain it. But it's more than I thought I could ever imagine."

Did I dare tell her I'd been spending my fifteen-minute breaks standing on a pallet outside the slime-house window watching her slice salmon guts with her knife? Or that I knew from a mutual acquaintance that she rode her bike from Spain to France across the Pyrenees? Or that she liked strawberries, painting, and swimming in the nude? Or that she was a virgin?

"You're not crazy, are you?" she asked.

"Let's get out of here." I hoped movement would make this end one way or another.

"Do you think I'm going to sleep with you?"

"Now why would you say that?" I was scared she was also capable of reading my mind. "I just want to talk to you."

"You're funny," she said, laughing.

Her eyes were perfect. Circles of stained mahogany, like sacred brown earth.

She took my hand and squeezed the tip of my thumb very lightly.

Outside the sun had set, giving way to a quarter moon that looked stapled onto the rose-colored sky, and all around us the tundra fell out of sight into blackness like a piece of unfinished tarmac.

Slowly but surely, we made our way to my room. There we sat on the bed and she talked of learning how to surf. She didn't care where she lived as long as there was water and a place to ride a bicycle. Of course, I thought, that was all she wanted. What else does anyone want or need? She was a single sunflower in a field of alfalfa. She stood straight but her neck was heavy as it arched toward the sun, her yellow face pointed to heaven.

"I want to kiss you," I said.

"Maybe I should go." Her voice. As soft as snow.

I had been too forward and needed to find a way to recover lost ground. I racked my brain for all the alternatives and then, leaping off the cliff, I leaned in and she put her arm around my neck.

Her lips, luscious and pouty, were ripe with a taste of oak, pepper and sugar from the bourbon. Her skin smelled of lilacs and rose oil. I was a goner. My eyes went blurry. We were lost in the oldest ritual known to man, the mating dance. The same tradition as the wolves, the bears and, most importantly, the salmon. I forgot the name of every girl I'd ever been with before. They were just fading faces in the crowd, all moving aside to make room for her.

At first the doorknob twisted very slowly, as if the person on the other side was trying to sneak in. Then it became a violent motion of someone trying to rip the thing off the door.

"Are you in there?" a voice yelled. I caught myself staring at the mirror, which was still standing upright on the bed. The reflection in the mirror looked guilty, but happy.

"I saw you leave the bar with her," the person yelled. I wasn't sure, but the voice in the hallway seemed on the verge of screaming.

"I can see the lights are on. Don't try and act like I'm not here, you fuck."

"What is she doing here?" whispered Corrina.

I told her it was the woman who had got me the job.

"I know who it is. You slept with her, didn't you?" Corrina asked, but there was no anger, just indifference or perhaps a trace of curiosity.

"Once." I paused. "Actually twice, but that was way before I knew you."

She giggled at that one. "You still don't know me."

"Don't say that. You are in my room and I have full knowledge of your green apple diet," I said.

This time she laughed out loud, which only made the banging on the door grow louder. I wanted to kiss the person who invented locks on doors.

We sat in silence like mice hiding from the cat. With her index finger she touched my nose and traced my face all the way round. She brought her nose to my nose as the banging continued.

"You're on the list, you know?" she whispered.

Bang bang!

"What list?"

"The top five guys in camp."

"Wow," I said. Then my ego kicked in. "What number am I, on the list?"

"It depends on what girl."

"Was I on your list?"

"Maybe. I thought maybe you were too old."

"Brutal. There's a group of people in Iran who all live to be very old. Like a hundred and ten. The oldest man stole his wife when he was in his mid-twenties and she was twelve."

"So?"

"Just thought I'd throw that out there."

We fell into a kiss and the noise went away.

"Let's get into bed," I whispered into her ear, an ear perfectly molded for all the ages. She stopped the dance and lay motionless.

"Then what? You go to Asia or some other place?"

"How do you know about all that?"

"I hear stories."

"No. I'm coming to Santa Cruz," I said, not realizing I was suddenly but gladly building a box around my life.

"I am still here, you fucker, and I can hear you two talking," yelled the voice on the other side of the door.

"Why would you go back to Santa Cruz when you can go anywhere you want?" she asked. She was sizing me up and she knew I knew it.

"Because there's a little betty down there and I just may have a chance of getting into her pants."

She punched me in the chest and then pulled me on top of her. And after a while the banging on the door went away and we slept side by side, with our clothes on. Cuddling up next to her I could tell she was athletic but not obsessively so. Her muscles were tight but her belly soft. Her breasts were round and supple. Our cold toes touched and tangled and meshed together. Her breath flowed in and out, making a hushed whisper that lulled me further into her gravity. Outside, the wind howled and the rain hit the roof like shards of broken glass.

Jesus, it suddenly seemed dark and lonely out there, in the big wide world.

13

Any traveler will tell you getting from one place to another is the easy part. The hard part is having a place to land that doesn't feel like you just stepped in a heap of wet shit.

I left Alaska a week after her with a slight crack on the top of my head. Needing extra cash for my new life of love and travel I was helping the supervisor winterize the buildings, which meant draining the pipes of water and putting up storm windows. I don't know if he was drinking or just tired, but one day he dropped a wrench on my head from the top of the ladder, one of those twelve-foot ladders. Except for the profuse amounts of blood there seemed to be little cranial damage.

Even so the cannery boss tried to convince me to stay, probably worried I would sue if I left early. Dizzy and yet somehow enlightened, I backed out of the room telling him I thought it was time to go. The loneliness was crushing my lungs, my head and my heart. I thought there was a girl in Santa Cruz who just might be the one. The last thing she had said to me before leaving was "I don't expect you to come. That's not how summer flings end."

I was a fool for staying even this long. I told myself it was the residue of living like a loner for too damn long. Don't need, don't want, and don't expect.

I caught the first flight to King Salmon with two fishermen carrying shotguns and pistols. "Any luck?" I asked. They looked at me like I was Jesse James aiming a peacemaker straight at the bridge of their noses.

"What's it to ya?"

I smiled and stared contentedly out the window while we flew above the valley of 10,000 smokes, a flat green landscape dotted with volcanic mounds of gray smoke holes.

Love has a way of splitting the world right down the middle. There are those who seem to be ready to imagine all the good that might come. They have a fire in their eyes and a momentum to their actions; to them it doesn't matter so much who you love as that you *do* love.

And then there are the fishermen, with pockets full of cash and guns cradled in their laps, itching for a chance to protect what they believe is theirs. Theirs? Did they already forget that the salmon, gifts from mother earth, gave up their lives so these fishermen could go home and buy a goddamn Doughboy swimming pool for their overweight kids to sit in? But who was

I to bring that up then? I also wanted a small piece of it all, just enough for two.

The ferry to Bellingham took three days. An eternity. My only consolation was the scenery. The boat weaved down the inlet passage, between the islands and the mainland. Bald eagles cruised the tree lines and killer whales breached the water with their single fins. The entire landscape seemed to be a place man forgot to destroy. It felt whole and fresh, like somewhere that could give you hope; if this remained wild, you sensed there was a good chance man might survive his own attempts at self-destruction.

In Seattle I caught the Green Tortoise hippie bus to northern California. I don't remember much from that two-day trip, but I do remember the bus stank like sandalwood and body grease, and everyone on board seemed to be jonesing for some drug or other. I got off at a truck stop in Corning, went to my stepfather and mother's house in Chico, picked up a few belongings and caught the Greyhound to the Sacramento airport. There I bought a plane ticket to San Diego.

In San Diego I gave my brother $500 for his motorcycle, a Honda CX 500. He had a new baby boy and was starting his law career. Motorcycles were out. I had secured the first part of the plan: transportation of my own.

Near San Luis Obispo, while driving into a headwind, I was nearly blown into a tractor-trailer carrying brand new minivans. Later the same day I did get blown off the road near King City, not far from the fairgrounds, where I had once slept on the ground when working with the United States Forest Service as a forest-fire fighter.

Near Salinas the wind reversed its course and the San Joaquin valley became a giant funnel sucking me up its chute toward my final destination. I arrived in Santa Cruz just as the sun began its daily nosedive into the Pacific. The sky was a glorious pink and purple with streaks of blue and orange. It had all the shades of a recovering black eye.

Corrina opened the door wearing a blue striped shirt that fitted tight over her breasts. They rose up in all their glory and curved the lines on the shirt like a carnival mirror. She wasn't wearing shoes. Her index toe was curled over her big toe, and her hair was tucked in a bun on top of her head, held in place by a number-two pencil.

"So now what do we do?" she asked with a smile.

"Go to Mexico and have a few kids."

"How about we order pizza?" An angel, heaven sent.

We ate pizza for three days.

It went on for months, the dance. We pissed in the shower together. We snuck into movie matinees and went to the bookstore, where we each had a book we were reading but leaving on the shelf. We drank wine on the beach and went midnight bowling. One day we made love. Her blood ran and we cried into each other's tears, and we didn't ever stop to ask why.

At times, when a horn honked or a voice passed under the window, we were forced to remember that there were five billion other people wandering around out there. But for all intents and purposes we were two people, nestled into one another's sweat and crevices, desperate to keep away any dragons roaring at the gate. Isn't that what love is for? A large net to catch you when the world comes asking for more. If there was still a world out there for me to conquer I was having a hard time seeing it any more.

Yes, and down the street the waves broke in the morning and in the evening they did the same.

And the next day, it happened all over again.

14

Sarajevo. Our first day of deliveries was tense. We had awoken to the deafening crackle of snipers. A few artillery shells pounded on rooftops all around us. Occasionally a shell would hit the upper floors of the building, shaking it to the foundations. One time we all chased each other eight floors to the basement to take shelter.

A local man in charge of the warehouse nodded and said, "Boom, boom, grenade."

Filled with a few strong jolts of adrenaline we bolted from the warehouse around eleven o'clock like superheroes rising from the bat cave. We took three trucks with three tons of chocolate baby food and half a ton of pasta. Our destination was a small suburb up a hillside on the south side of the city. Freddie, the community's representative, had come to us during the night looking for food. He talked for almost an hour before he finally got Tony's attention. He hit the magic button when he said the UN refused to deliver to the community because it was too dangerous.

"That's the one then," said Tony, slamming his fist on the table. "We go where others won't. Otherwise we're just like them. Sorted." Like some conference of apes, we all nodded and grunted in agreement, and for a moment it was impossible not to feel like the lost sons of Mother Theresa.

I drove with Allen, the Australian. We passed more burned-out cars and derelict bridges. If there was any shooting going on we couldn't hear it above the trip hop playing in the cab.

"I can't see ever wanting to visit America," he'd said to me once, sneering.

"OK then." My dislike of him grew steadily.

At the foot of the village every house had a hole in it from shells or bullets. Children ran up the road after the trucks, happily yelling and screaming. They grabbed onto the back of the truck and hitched a ride up the hill. Mothers, standing in the shadows, looked out from the windows with bandanas covering their hair. Their eyes, dark circles with black coals for a center, watched our every move. There were no fathers, except for Freddie. He was frail and nervous and talkative. Before the war it would have been easy to finger him for a gambler, a conman or the village drunk. He was the only man of age in the village not on the front line.

Freddie pointed at my camera and said he had something to show me.

"You must promise not to tell any Bosnians."

"I promise," I said.

As the others delivered the food, Graeme juggled and did

magic tricks for the kids, and I took a ride with Australian Roger and Freddie further up the hill where the houses turned into piles of rubble. Freddie pointed to the ridgeline to our right.

"Chetniks are there. A hundred meters over the top," he whispered.

Fear, primal fear, the kind that makes your ass pucker, is an involuntary reflex. My chest was calm but my body was sweating. I felt cold, like someone had dripped ice down my neck. I couldn't relax and found it hard to swallow.

Once we'd parked, Freddie motioned for us to be quiet as he led us to a house in a thicket of trees. The upstairs was missing, blown to smithereens by a shell. We entered through a hole in the wall and came face to face with an elderly gentleman sitting in a chair. He wore wool trousers, a thick sweater with holes in the elbows, and a Muslim skullcap. In front of him, partially covering another hole in the wall, was a painting of a meadow with the Alps in the background. It looked like a place you'd find in Austria. The old man rose from his seat and shook our hands. His toothless grin only made him look happier in some way.

Freddie and the old man talked for a few minutes and then quite suddenly Freddie dashed for the door.

"Follow please," said Freddie as we jogged in single file behind the older man. Even though the front lines were out of sight behind the ridge, we all ran with our heads bent over as if we were in the crosshairs of some rogue sniper who had climbed the hill. The old man stopped at a small structure built into the side of the slope. It was well camouflaged and grass was growing on what would be the roof. From any angle except standing directly in front of the door it was easy to mistake the edifice for a grassy knoll.

Whizz . . . A few mortar rounds flew by on their way to the city.

The old man lifted the bolt and swung open the door. He smiled wide with anticipation. Beckoning me closer, he put his free hand on my shoulder and shined a candle inside.

And there it was. A goddamn cow with huge titties and a piece of hay sticking out of its mouth. It looked into the light with big dumb round eyes. Just seeing a beast of nature in a place like this calmed me down. We all started laughing as if the cow had just told a joke.

Freddie explained. "This man stays up here with the cow so the mafia and the army don't take it for food. They don't think anyone would live up here. But we use the milk for our babies. Only the mothers know it is here," he said. "And me."

I took a few pictures at Freddie's request. I didn't ask why he wanted pictures of the village secret. I guessed it was because when you don't have anything left to show of your life, you share your most treasured secrets as a way of confirming you still have something to give. Roger ran to the car and returned with a box of food we had stashed in the back. It had canned fruit, lentils and strawberry jam. He handed it to the old man, who made great gestures to refuse it.

"Tell him to take it. Please, Freddie," I said. "We have more."

"He's ashamed," Freddie said.

"Tell him not to worry."

"Yes, but he's a proud man." Freddie seemed pleasantly amused by the banter.

"Tell him we can't take the food back to England so he'd be doing us a favor."

The old man smiled and kept waving his hand as if shooing away some pest. I set the food on the table and left.

So what about all those Buddhist monks walking the hills of Tibet? Or the holy men sitting in the caves of the Negev desert in Israel waiting for enlightenment or whispers of God? Or the yogis, preachers, and saints? What were they doing now? Why always this endless quest for God in the silence of our own minds? Instead of seeking God inside our own heads, couldn't we look for him in something as simple as a chance meeting, a bird flying overhead, or the way the wind sings in the autumn leaves? The trick is in being open to seeing it. Perhaps it could even be a man in a crumbling house looking at a painting from Austria while he guards a cow hidden underground. Perhaps.

In the car Roger pulled out two more cans of beans. I ran back to the house. I wanted to give the man my jacket, my pants, my socks. He could have our truck. I would talk to Graeme and we'd drive up here every week to give him a box of food and maybe even some toilet paper if he would take it. I wanted to spend the rest of the war arranging airlifts into Sarajevo just for this man and his cow that fed the babies.

I grabbed the edge of the hole in the wall and lifted myself back into the house. There sat the old man, his face covered with strawberry preserve as he sat staring at the meadow.

Beyond, through the hole in the wall, the clouds were full of rain. A storm was coming in from the mountains. The sound of artillery was close. I turned to leave.

"*Zbogom*," he said and waved. I waved back.

In the car, racing to meet up with the others, I asked Freddie what that meant.

"Bosnian for goodbye."

Translated, *zbogom* literally means *go with God*.

15

The Krishnas were Graeme's idea, of course. Turns out he had met a few one day while riding the London Underground. They said the UN convoys kept bringing their brothers and sisters in Sarajevo pork and beans. Graeme, being a strict vegetarian, was determined to right that wrong.

Loaded with lentils and rice and cans of vegetables, we drove through the old Turkish quarter near the southern end of town. The pointed rooftops of Ottoman design saddled up against the large block walls of the Austro-Hungarian buildings. With the mosques and churches within a stone's throw of each other, Sarajevo had long been seen as the perfect crossroads of east and west.

The word Sarajevo has many translations but perhaps "rest stop' is as good as any. Over the centuries the city served as a place of refuge for the weary traveler. Pilgrims and merchants from Rome, Krakow, Vienna, and beyond stopped here on their way to Istanbul, Damascus, or Jerusalem. As a result of geography, the citizens of Sarajevo made hospitality their business. Hotels, bars, cafés, and stables were the commerce of the city. As for the people, this endless stream of strangers is, many believe, the reason they are so multi-ethnic and accepting of others. In a region where ethnic lines are defined by a letter in your last name or what side of the river you live on, Sarajevo is a rare gem.

The victors of wars, as they say, write history. And history tells us that the Turkish Empire, although brutal at times, was fairly tolerant of the Balkans' various religious sects. One imposition worth mentioning, though, was the rule they placed on owning land—you had to be a Muslim, either by birth or by conversion. During the current war, this centuries-old decree was coming back to haunt the Muslim Bosnians in the form of propaganda. The Serb war machine argued that everyone in Bosnia was a Serb but they just didn't know it, or wouldn't admit it. They argued that the Turks converted what was traditionally a Serb kingdom into a Muslim empire. Perhaps. Or perhaps not. As for the people, all the Bosnians I met looked a little Turkish, Roma, Serbian, Greek, Spanish, Italian, Croatian, Syrian, Romanian, Semite, Hungarian, and so on.

Graeme turned down an alley just wide enough for the car. All the homes had plastic on the windows and broken red-tiled roofs. In the middle of the road stood a white-robed bald man with his arms spread wide open. He had what looked like a white stripe painted down the middle of his face. He seemed jolly and perhaps slightly mad. This was the leader of the Sarajevo Krishnas.

We quickly unloaded nearly a ton of lentils, rice, and other vegetarian supplies. While the others were talking, one young woman led me into the main room. More than fifty people were dancing to Hindu chants and prayers. They were all wearing white robes and had squiggly lines that ran up the center of their noses to the top of their foreheads.

I wanted to ask the woman's name, but had no idea how to speak the language. I smiled, and she bowed a little from the waist and opened her hand, inviting me into the dance.

The Krishnas of India spread the ashes of the dead in the Ganges. They say it releases the soul from the body for its heavenward journey, which frees it from the endless cycle of reincarnation. The idea that I might be repeating my exact life over and over again is something that has always frightened me into reaching for a new and different life, one of no regrets. I believe this explains why since I was young the only time I have felt I was escaping the chains of the past was when I was engulfed by the exact present. The irrefutable Now.

Now I was jumping up and down singing, "Hare Krishna, Hare Hare Krishna." I bounced and bounced and bounced and sang and bounced. At that moment I was a full-blown Krishna. At one point I turned to find myself bouncing high enough to see out the window. Up, it was soggy and wet and dark. Down, it was white and festive and people had pretty painted faces. Up, a graveyard. Down, a woman lost in dance. Then the music stopped and like a game of musical chairs I was no longer a Krishna but found myself waiting for a new spiritual chair to sit in.

Back outside, I told Graeme and Tony I was going to walk home.

"Bullshit," said Tony.

"I'll be all right." I was calm.

"You know the rules. No walking here unless for a delivery," said Tony.

"I'll see you there before dark."

"Hey, John Wayne, this ain't no fucking joke here. You die, we have to deal with it. There's a ton of paperwork and all kinds of shite."

"Let him go. He's going to do it anyway," said Graeme as he shut the door. "Watch out for them snipers. They can smell a septic, you know."

I asked what a septic was.

"Cockney. Septic tank, Yank."

Spitting dirt in my direction, they ripped around the corner toward downtown. Part of me wanted to hear their conversation. But in truth I didn't care what they thought. I wasn't here to win Brownie points for my efforts or become part of anything. I was here to tempt death to show me its bastard face.

The towers stuck out of the center of town like giant chopsticks. Using them as my landmark I walked down an alley of broken buildings. Old men stood in the doorways in their pajamas, smoking their cigarettes and staring at the sky.

I passed an enclosed yard with many voices coming from over the fence. Someone was chopping wood with an axe. Chips of wood flew into the air. There was a bustle of activity. It smelled like a morning walk on a spring day in a pine forest. I found it refreshing to smell nature, anything other than the rot of a modern city. At the gate I peered in. Standing on end against the house were a dozen coffins, newly cut. The men were busy chopping what looked like a dozen more. It was the only business I passed for a while.

I walked on. Anywhere I travel, walking is the surest way of gaining access to the cultural nuances. I must see the movements of people, the shape of their houses, the way they say goodbye or hello. The way they eat or stare or laugh. In that sense it was no different here from when I landed in Kathmandu for the first time. Right then my hunger to connect with the human condition of Sarajevo was more overwhelming than my desire to help it with any amount of money or food.

As for being alone, that also came naturally. Yes, I wanted to be part of the Road Trip, but I needed some breathing room to feel this place out for myself. And, of course, as I walked I didn't feel so alone. That's one of the secrets of being alone: you rarely are. And I wasn't. I hit upon a path and fell in step with the pedestrian traffic. The locals moved fast but not quite at a run, and there was very little talking. The women wore high heels and skirts under their long coats. Their make-up was typically Eastern European—heavy on the purple and orange with tints of red. For the most part the men wore wool blazers and turtlenecks. Some of the older men wore a beret. Almost all of them carried a plastic container filled with water. Some dragged toy carts with dozens of plastic bottles in the back. Others had a bicycle as their mule. And still others had baby carriages filled with water jugs. It was true. Life at its very simplest was actually dependent upon one thing: water.

I came to a small alley. The two women in front of me stopped and spoke about something. They craned their necks to peer down the road toward the mountains. I knew enough to realize they were staring toward the sniper, who might or might not be at his post in the hills waiting for another pedestrian.

Then they stepped off the curb and into the street, just like that, with a little jog in their step. They ran to the other side and ducked behind another building. I hesitated and then bolted into the street. At the other side I felt a rush of victory. I had defied the sniper, even though there had been no shots. My group of walkers had already moved on and disappeared round another corner. The joy of making it to the other side had obviously been lost to them long ago.

I passed a graveyard.

What can I say about the graveyard? There were no flowers or weeds in the earth. How could there be? All the graves were new, with headstones that marked death either last week, last month, or last year. A couple of hundred were lined up side by side and two men were up to their eyes in one hole, flinging shovelfuls of wet dirt over their shoulders.

Near the back of the yard, next to a building, was a man in a tuxedo sitting on a stool with a cello between his legs. A small crowd stood around him. He had a handlebar moustache and slicked-back black hair. His eyes were closed and he played that instrument like the sky was going to open up and cry.

When I looked back to the gravediggers, only the tops of their heads were visible. In reflex, I bent my head and walked on, thankful I didn't know one person here.

Downtown I found a café open for business. It cost five Deutschmarks for some fruity-flavored tea. I wiggled my toes and felt my $200. Escape money, although I suspected it would not be enough to escape very far.

The tea tasted like dishwater, but it was hot and the waitress gave me a packet of honey. I can't say the locals noticed me, but those who did either smiled or had a look of curiosity.

"You are an English?" asked the waitress with long brown hair and decaying teeth.

"American."

"How do you like our city?"

"It seems like a nice place, but a bit hectic at the moment."

She wiped the corners of her mouth, which were heavy with deep purple lipstick.

"Yes, but really it is very beautiful," she said.

"Yes." I didn't know what to say. Still, I had to say something. "Can I ask where do you get your water?"

"My father gets it at the beer factory, near Skenderija. You know where Skenderija is?"

"No, I don't, but I will find out."

We sat in silence for a moment and I drank the tea. Now it smelled like dirty wet socks.

"Do you think the women of Sarajevo are beautiful?" She smiled. Those teeth were black and jagged.

"Very."

"I would like to travel to Dallas." She wiped the table for the second time.

"Why Dallas?"

"I would very much care to visit cowboys," she said.

"Well, there aren't any real cowboys in Dallas . . ." I began.

"And," she continued as if I had never said a word, "I want to see where JR is buried."

"JR?"

"You are American, you do not know who JR is? From the television program *Dallas*."

"Well, he's not buried anywhere. It's just a television program."

"Yes, of course I know that."

People strolled into the deli and she excused herself. Inside, the men bought small shots of espresso and leaned on the bar. In a few minutes they ambled back outside, the looks on their faces still the same. They all looked tired and grizzled. I stood up and walked away.

.   .   .

I had been walking again for what seemed like a few hours before I realized I was lost. Every time I caught a glimpse of the towers a local would tell me not to walk that way. They would make their arms into a pretend rifle and shoot. "Snipers that way, go another." There was even a stretch of time when the towers fell out of sight altogether. They were either blocked from my line of vision by other buildings or hidden because I was taking some back alley that had me walking through people's backyards. So many times I had traveled in order to get lost but now it just seemed like a bad idea. The thought of dying didn't bother me much, but the thought of dying because I got lost did. Besides, Sarajevo was not a war of front lines in any traditional sense. There was no front, just back. Imagine a circle, actually more like an exaggerated ellipse, like a racing track that has been stretched longer. Seven miles by one mile, and at times the front line was no more than 300 meters from the center. Safety meant retreating toward the center in the hope that the outer circle wouldn't collapse. Either way a sniper still might get you and a shell could get you at any moment, any time of day, any place. There was no back from that.

It was just before dark when I found myself nearing the towers. I came to a stretch of road with no blockades. I was beginning to think all the talk about snipers was exaggerated when a car drove toward me. I noticed the driver. A small man with a thin face wearing a beret. He was thirty feet from me when the bullets tore into the side of his door. Small holes appeared like tricks of magic, only to be followed a few seconds later by the delayed crack of a sniper's rifle. The driver swerved into a cement embankment and slid himself toward the passenger door, which was now jammed against the cement. The bullets kept coming. Five more, ten more. Three armed guards in street clothes stood by me. We were hidden behind a building, not more than twenty feet from the man. They were yelling at him, motioning him to run toward them.

He jumped out the passenger window and landed hard on the cement. He was safe from the snipers, but was bleeding from his stomach and thigh. The guards were yelling for him to come to them and he was breathing heavy with shock. Finally he crawled toward us. At some point a Volkswagen Golf appeared from behind us with the back hatch opened. Two of the men loaded him inside and just like that he was gone. The bullet-ridden car's engine was still running and it sat there like an instant relic of war. Beside me stood the only remaining guard. My hands were white and I hadn't moved in the forty-five seconds of the entire event.

Cradling a machine gun, the guard had bloodstains on his trousers and shirt from helping the man. He gestured toward me and talked a little in Bosnian, but I understood nothing. I nodded in agreement and tried to remain still. He reached out toward my face. I noticed the red stains on his fingers. I stepped back a few paces, which made him smile.

"Cigarette?" He spoke with a thick Slavic accent.

I quickly patted down my shirt and found a pack and handed it to him. He insisted on taking only one. I told him to take them all. We fought like this for half a minute before he finally took the pack and then offered me one. I declined.

We shook hands and I turned to leave. He grabbed me by the arm and I recoiled in fear. I was set to run from him when he suddenly pushed me off the main street, against a wall. It seemed I had got turned round in my confusion and was about to walk toward the car and into the snipers. He was trying to save my life. The guard pointed down a small alley and motioned for me to walk straight ahead.

What else is there to say? A few people had stopped but most kept walking. Their empty water containers clanked against the baby buggies. The clock down the street had a bullet hole through it. For all I knew it had probably been there since the first days of the war. It said eight o'clock.

Anything else? Sure. I wondered if being born and dying, by their very nature, are the messiest things we ever do in this life.

When I got home the gang was working on a second bottle of vodka and everyone was smoking cigarettes. Allen pointed at me. "Cheeky Yank, isn't he?"

"Yeah, where you been?" said another.

"I say no hot dogging allowed here," said Allen.

"Calm down, you fuckwit," said Graeme.

None of the other drivers said anything.

Tony stepped closer and lowered his voice. "You were gone four hours."

"Sorry about that."

"You do that again and I'm going to take your passport until we leave."

"No one's taking my passport," I said and meant it.

"Is he fucking mad?" yelled Tony to the room.

"I say the bloke broke the rules," yelled Allen. He was drunk. Small bubbles of drool stained the front of his sweatshirt.

"Shut your hole before I shut it," said Graeme. He stood near the stove.

I didn't move an inch.

"You see my point, don't you?" Tony asked.

"Yes. I will follow the rules while we are all together. But if I feel like going off and meeting people when the day is done I will."

"There isn't much I can do about that, I suppose," he said.

Graeme gestured in my direction. "All right then. Take off your coat, stay a while."

"Right then," said English Roger. "Whose deal is it anyway?"

The cards were dealt and the game continued.

Maybe I didn't say anything about the man being shot because it reminded me that, unless you happen to be a surgeon or some goddamn medical genius, a person is helpless to stop another person's death. It was something I was just beginning to learn: that sometimes we can't save people. A terrible thought but one that gives strange comfort as well. The upside was that it allowed for the possibility, however difficult it was to grasp completely, of learning how to let go.

In the meantime I placed the whole event in a small corner of my brain. I pretended it was a dream in the hope that it would eventually sink into that wasteland of mind-mud and disappear. Of course I knew I was kidding myself; dreams have a way of percolating in our gray matter until they boil over and have to be reckoned with.

Like Corrina. She was becoming more elusive, lurking in the shadows, the hard-to-see lines between now and then. She usually waited until I had finished my nightly dance with the vodka, when it was easy for her to wrap herself around my insides and squeeze tight. My body immobile and my brain unable to find distractions, to analyze, crystalize, synthesize. I was helpless against the other side. That's when she would wrestle me down for the night and kiss my eyelids and say sweet beautiful things in my ear. She drew me across the river, to her side. It made me want to sleep forever.

The only problem was the artillery that kept hitting the building.

16

A few words about this new home of ours, the burned-out UNIS towers. Besides being the tallest buildings in town, they had also had names: Momo and Uzeir. Momo and Uzeir, of different ethnic backgrounds, were the names of two men used in many Sarajevan jokes. Because the towers were of equal height the idea was to symbolize Sarajevo's sense of unity and equality for all, regardless of ethnic background.

Of course they were one of the first targets bombed by the Bosnian Serbs.

We weren't alone in this derelict building. There were Bosnian government offices down below where civil servants slept on cots and made each other tea to trick themselves into thinking they weren't hungry. Once a day bread was delivered from the bakery; unless the water supply was cut off, in which case there was no bread. During those days the locals lay very still, waiting for sleep to overcome them. The deal was this: we were allowed to stay upstairs if we gave them boxes of food and cigarettes from time to time.

On the first floor was Radio M, a local station. They prided themselves on being independent and free to play whatever kind of music they wished. And they did. Rock, reggae, blues, and pop. They also played local folk music, and they didn't care if it was Serbian, Bosnian, or Croatian. That is until one day when they played a popular Serbian folk song. Graeme and I were playing ping-pong when we heard a loud bang from below. We figured it was either a small mortar or possibly a gas explosion. We ran downstairs. Turns out one of the warlords in town—and there were several—didn't like hearing Serbian songs and threw a grenade into the control room.

I don't know what was stranger—throwing a grenade into a radio station because they played a song someone didn't like, or that we raced back upstairs and resumed our ping-pong game.

Two floors below us were the offices of Première Urgence and Equilibre, both French humanitarian outfits. Equilibre had a single man in their office, Wally, from Senegal. They had been running trucks in and out of the city but that had been suspended when one of their drivers had been shot and killed in no-man's-land.

The boss of Première Urgence was David and it seemed that whenever his crew was in town the office turned into a mad drunken festival, locals and foreigners dancing and drinking like it was the eve of the end of the world. Everyone got along like comrades. David's sidekick was the crazy Yoyo, who actually preferred our parties to the French ones.

"Yoyo just might make it," Graeme liked to say, "but the rest of those frogs have lost the plot."

The secret truth, the one no one in the Road Trip spoke of, was that we envied Première Urgence. Not their nationality, but their operation. They had money, large trucks, flak jackets and they always brought a little hash to wash away the drive through no-man's-land. Every week they dropped off forty tons of food, which was delivered throughout the city within hours or, at the most, days. They stuck to a schedule. They arrived late afternoon one day, spent the night, and then the next morning were back on the road to Croatia to get more aid. They were like a well-oiled machine that had a way of reminding us we were just bottom feeders waiting for things to fall off other people's trucks and then trying like hell to give it away.

But the envy was erased once we made another delivery, Trip style. For Tony and Graeme and the rest of us it was not about how much aid was delivered, but how the aid was given. If a member of the Trip befriended a local, that person, or that family, then came under the umbrella of the Trip's responsibility. Whenever there was food in town someone would make sure that the new member of the Trip family was taken care of.

In those first days there was a sense that we could never drive fast enough or deliver enough food. We were like minnows in a sea of sharks. With each trip to the city we brought about thirty tons of food from Split, barely enough to feed a small neighborhood for one month. But we didn't think about that, we couldn't. Instead we just picked several different parts of town and gave a little bit of food to a few people. It made it seem like we were doing more. Besides, most of our delivery runs became a long process of talking with people, drinking coffee, juggling, and playing with kids. Yet, to my dismay, no matter how fast we drove, it never made the faces of the people in the street looking for water or food go blurry.

And Graeme was a stickler about the black market. There were various outlets for the black market all over town, but the central market was downtown, near the cathedral. It was an outdoor area where dozens of people had tables lined up side by side. One person had Cokes stacked up in the shape of a triangle, five marks each. Another person might be selling cheese they had received that morning from a food parcel. There were screws for sale, single shoes, matches, eggs, just about anything anyone thought someone else might need. A sewing needle, a can opener, a pair of sunglasses. And food. Apart from what they grew in window boxes or in small garden plots hidden from any sniper views, all of the food came from humanitarian donations.

Graeme couldn't stop talking about making sure that none of the Trip food made it to market. The only way to ensure this was by hand-delivering the aid ourselves. So, unlike other aid groups, we didn't use locals to distribute. But stopping the black market was impossible and I suspect Graeme knew this. I think the personal deliveries had more to do with wanting to go through the act of hands touching hands. Eyes looking into eyes. The danger of this is clear. Getting too close is the surest way of going mad.

It's true, many people go mad in this line of work. Some of us would, eventually, but in the beginning everything was going as well as could be expected. We had lodging, enough food, enough booze, and, most importantly, everyone in the group felt needed, some for the first time in their lives. Colin sidled up to me one night and said, "I am beginning to believe the worst part of being here is knowing this might be the best thing I ever do in my life. I mean I'm only twenty-six. What am I supposed to do for the rest of it?"

To a bystander, a cynic, it might have seemed self-indulgent at times, but the way I saw it we weren't hurting anyone. In fact it felt holy, like we were part of something bigger than ourselves.

17

One afternoon a local named Vladimir Kajević, or Vlado, stopped by. Graeme and Christophe knew him from the first time they had visited. He was the first local I met whom we hadn't delivered food to.

When I walked in he was in the front room laughing with Graeme and some others, drinking lemonade and vodka, and smoking Winston cigarettes. Graeme introduced me as the "skidder from California."

"San Francisco . . . Jimi Hendrix . . . is the music still good there?" asked Vlado. His voice had a deep resonating tone, like he'd swallowed a Buddhist om-chant machine.

I said truthfully no, that the city had become very affluent and the artists had all fled to more affordable places.

"And the women? Are they really all beautiful?"

"Not bad. But here too," I said.

"Ah, but Bosnian women are crazy," said Vlado.

"I guess you haven't met any Scottish women," said Graeme as he poured Vlado some more vodka.

"So can anyone spare a . . . dime, oh, I mean a cigarette?" Vlado laughed. I waited for someone else to laugh along with him but no one did. I gave him a cigarette and lit it.

"Marlboro. Nice. Aren't you having one?"

"No thanks, I don't smoke," I said.

"I understand," said Vlado, with a straight face. "You know cancer is a terrible killer'—his eyes grew wide like a child holding its breath—"and the mind is a terrible thing to waste." This time his laughter set us all off. After a few rounds of vodka it was obvious that Vlado, who spoke perfect English, enjoyed using American clichés as irony.

"Vlado is the blues king of Sarajevo," said Graeme.

"Yeah, yeah, we have a show soon. Well, maybe soon," Vlado said.

"You play live music here in the city?" I asked, amazed.

"Well, actually my band, Don Guido and the Missionaries, are on a world tour. It begins in Sarajevo and travels seven miles to the end of town. The final concert is in Sarajevo."

"Keeps the costs down, eh?" Graeme laughed.

"Oh yeah, trying to increase our . . . our profit margin."

Laughing, someone passed round a hash joint, which mixed well with the vodka.

Vlado, a.k.a. Don Guido, was a dead ringer for Frank Zappa, with black hair in a ponytail that lay flat on his back like rope. By birth he was Macedonian, of Serbian descent, and like many other Serbs in Sarajevo he had chosen to stay in town when the war began. He had a goatee and perfect black eyes. Black as coal but with long delicate lashes. His voice was his trademark in Sarajevo. He was the most popular blues singer in town and before the war had been a high school english professor.

He delivered his sentences with deliberation, pausing on certain words like "well" or "maybe." The effect was comical and he knew it. He would say things like "Well . . . perhaps we should consider drinking the rest of what you have here just in case we die before tomorrow night." Or maybe, as in "Why did the man from Sarajevo cross the road? Maybe . . . because his side of the road just got bombed."

One night, which, like most nights, ended in a fit of drinking and laughter, Vlado brought his band, the Missionaries, to the office. Three thin Bosnians filed in behind him, carrying guitars and drumsticks. There was Djani Pervan, who introduced himself as Johnny. He was the drummer and the looker of the group. He was tall, dark, and spoke what he called Indian English, meaning broken and stilted. The keyboard player was Doutso Vranić, pronounced Dutzo, who was fair-skinned and balding and had a high falsetto voice. His English was quieter and limited. The last of the three was Alan Omerović, the bassist. He was also tall and skinny but pale and his eyes had sunk into pronounced sockets. He spoke very little English and became lively only when he was full of vodka. Then he would talk in Bosnian and try to get us all to jump out the window together.

Vlado and I were sitting on the sofa sipping vodka.

"OK, I got one," said Johnny. "The Bosnian army is setting up an ambush for Chetniks somewhere in the woods near Sarajevo. Well, time goes by and it becomes very late. The Serbs were supposed to arrive at the same spot every night at 2 a.m. sharp. It is 3 a.m. and still no sign. One Bosnian soldier says to another one, "I hope nothing has happened to them.""

Everyone laughed except Australian Allen, who had a way of becoming defensive when he didn't get something.

"I don't find it funny people are dying," Allen proclaimed without much mirth. Johnny explained that it was a joke on the state of the Bosnian army.

"Yeah, I knew that," he said with a self-conscious furrow in his brow.

"Vlado," I said, wanting to change the subject, "who decides who is in the army here?"

He didn't answer the question directly. Instead he said, "I am in the army. I am on the front line two days a week. I fire a mortar at the . . . barbarians on the hills. Then on my off days I play music at the disco downtown. Disco BB. Have you been?"

"No. But it sounds stellar."

"Stellar?"

"Californian."

"I see. You must come to the disco."

"I will."

"But you know about curfew."

"What time's that?"

"Ten."

"Bogus." I was feeling the vodka and my California tongue was slipping into my conversation.

"Bogus. Hmmm . . . bogus. I like that. Yes, they will put you in jail."

I laughed so hard I started crying. The hash had hit me hard. "I always found jail funny myself," said Vlado.

"No. No. No," I said. It was all I could manage. I was caught inside a laughing cycle, the kind that makes the stomach ache.

Finally the wave left and I wiped my eyes. Graeme passed the hash to Vlado, who took a drag and then said, "Haven't you heard our tourism is taking a hit? Oh . . . taking a hit, now I am cracking myself up."

At some point the room turned into a time-warped chamber filled with laughter and smoke and vodka fumes. It was loud enough that the shelling and sniping going on outside was like an annoying distant soundtrack in a different movie, being played in some far-off theater.

"Do you know the difference between Sarajevo and Auschwitz?" asked Vlado, still snickering.

Nervously laughing along, I told him I didn't.

"At least in Auschwitz they always had gas."

Someone passed me a glass of water and I drank it. I remember being quite shocked at the sensation of the water moving down my throat and into my chest.

18

One afternoon Graeme found me in the basement with a flashlight taking an inventory of the supplies. We had five tons of chocolate baby food and three tons of cardboard boxes filled with German clothes, which meant they were ill-fitting and ugly but well made and warm. There were a few pallets of diapers, some canned soup, rice, and lentils. In the far corner was a pallet of coloring books and near the gate were twenty bags of powdered milk and a barrel of juggling balls. Then there was the medicine, none of which was labeled in English. This hadn't stopped a few of our drivers from taking some yellow pills "to see what would happen next."

"Ready?" asked Graeme.

"We've got to get rid of this stuff."

"Sherlock fucking Holmes now, are you? I know we have to get rid of the stuff. But are you ready?"

"Ready for what?" I asked, ignoring his last comment.

"Going for a drive."

"Where?"

"Beer run."

"I'm there." And I was. Suddenly a beer run made more sense than sitting in a basement counting food parcels.

Graeme and I took the Land Rover while the rest of the guys made a few more deliveries, which were usually done within hours once Tony had found some group he decided needed food. In truth there was no rhyme or reason to the deliveries, no set pattern, just random acts that followed a hunch.

Graeme and I drove toward no-man's-land. We passed through the Serb checkpoints with no hassle, and by noon we were standing at the door to the store run by the old lady with the U tattoo on her forehead. I kept staring at her forehead, wondering if she was a child at the time of the Nazis or if she'd become an adult sympathizer. Did it matter?

Just like last time, I kept the old lady busy with idle chatter while Graeme stole a few bottles of vodka and a few bottles of beer. He stuffed them into his coat and when he was done he went to the car. When he came back inside I finished up by buying a few oranges and some chocolate bars. Graeme stole a few more items while she gave me change and then just like that we drove away, off to the next store, this time to buy the food.

Tony, besides being the boss of the Road Trip, was also in charge of all the Trip money. He had given us two hundred German marks to buy a box of food, some for us and some for our translator, a fifteen-year-old kid named Marco, who hung around the office in the day translating when people came to request food for their neighborhood, clinic or orphanage.

We bought a few more bottles of vodka and a few boxes of salami, oranges, soft drinks, chocolate, salt, that kind of stuff. At the Serb checkpoint a woman guard stopped us and opened the back of the Land Rover for an inspection. She was attractive, with long curly black hair and dark eyebrows. She said her name was Gordana. She wanted to know why we had so much vodka for two people.

"We drink a lot," said Graeme.

She came to the passenger-side window.

"Before the war I was a travel agent in Sarajevo. I used to fly all around the world."

"Sounds nice," I said.

"I've been to Venice and I even went to London once. Now this shit war. I am a soldier. I can't get any make-up or any new music."

"We got some music," Graeme said.

"What do you have?"

Graeme held up five cassette tapes. "You pick any one you like. A gift."

She smiled and took U2's *Achtung Baby*. "Thank you. Perhaps next time you can bring me Ace of Base." She had nice teeth and lovely thick lips.

"We'll try," I said.

"Tell me, why are they killing all the Serbs in Sarajevo?" she asked.

We didn't say anything. What could you say to a brainwashed mind?

We spent the rest of the ride home talking about women. I mostly listened to Graeme, but sometimes I would talk abstractly about the subject. How they smelled, how they could make us travel 3,000 miles just to see them smile. Not just any woman, but the one that was worming away inside your brain.

"A rave," Graeme said suddenly. "We need to throw a rave in the office. That would be wicked."

"What do we need?"

"Sound system. Techno music. Loads of beer. And girls. Mate, we need to get cracking on the girls."

"Tough with curfew and all."

"True."

In the next week we did this trip to the store three more times. Although Kiseljak was less than twenty kilometers from Sarajevo the trip usually took three hours, and once, because of a particularly long checkpoint stop, six hours. Each time Gordana took another tape and told us about not being able to get makeup. And each time I listened to her and wondered how the world could possibly know what was going on inside Sarajevo if a person standing a few miles from downtown didn't have any idea.

Then, toward the end of that week, on what would turn out to be our last trip for alcohol, Gordana wasn't at the checkpoint. The new guard was a young stern-looking man with a quick military step. He ordered us to open up the back door.

"Where's Gordana?" Graeme asked.

"She has been transferred. She was becoming too comfortable speaking with foreigners."

To be perfectly honest I had been thinking about her. I didn't want to. I already had a feeling that the Serb soldiers were slightly crazy, in a dangerous way. Still, I wanted to go with Gordana behind the shack and have a session. I was curious if she had sex the same way as anyone else. Did she make the same groans as everyone did during orgasm? Did she have the same wants and needs as anyone else? I suspected she did, but part of me hoped she didn't. Traveling the world one spends a fair amount of time at checkpoints. There, one meets mostly bored soldiers or blind patriots who shoot in the name of a flag. And with each encounter I look for the smallest details that separate them from everyone else, but maybe the truth is, no matter how hard I try to believe they are somehow different, a part of me knows they *are* just like everyone else.

The guard took most of the alcohol and food and told us to move on. Coming back through no-man's-land a sniper took a few potshots at us. It could have been a Bosnian or a Serb. Maybe someone thought we were UN, or it could have been because someone woke up and saw something moving. Either way we were getting shot at. Our breath was short and our hearts racing when we finally stopped at the base of the towers.

That night Johnny and Dougie hooked up a television to the electrical wire running to the army office on the first floor.

Everyone gathered around the toob. The hanger, which acted as our antenna, didn't do much to cut the static. The film showing was *The Blues Brothers*. The bottles moved from hand to hand, mouth to mouth. Every once in a while someone mixed in some fresh powdered lemonade. The movie was dubbed, but I knew the scene when it came up. The one when Ackroyd turns to Belushi and tells him, "*We have a full tank of gas and it's a hundred miles to Chicago.*"

"*Hit it.*"

I leaned my head toward Graeme; he looked tired for the first time.

"Graeme."

"Yeah?"

"Maybe we should stop going on beer runs," I said.

"Cheers. Waiting for you to say that."

We drank our vodka. The door was locked. We were safe, at least until morning. The static was bad, but it was nice to sit there in the candlelight watching television, drinking, and without anyone saying anything.

It was plenty.

19

With each passing day it became obvious we were a group of fledgling do-gooders, united by a common, yet unspoken awareness that we could never do much good for many people, but maybe some good for a few. And no matter what happened in the daytime, the nights were always the same. We cooked up cans of soup, dealt the cards, and drank like fish. It couldn't continue but that didn't stop us. As time went by I suspect we all knew that our growing sense of brotherhood was just as important as our futile attempts to have an impact on this war.

Then one afternoon, after being stuck inside for two days of shelling, Graeme and Tony decided to make a delivery to the Women's Center, in the old city. We had half a ton of baby food and some tampons to deliver. Dougie and Colin would meet us there with some more supplies and the idea was to unload and get back to the office as soon as we could.

At the center we offloaded the boxes of food through a window. A line of women formed a human conveyor belt. With shells falling throughout the downtown area we moved quietly and quickly.

Then four shells hit the building next door. Shrapnel and roof tiles flew across the courtyard. One man went down, but managed to pull himself into a doorway. The women calmly made their way inside the building as a VW Golf drove up looking for wounded. The Sarajevans had long since developed a lightning response for getting the wounded from the ground to the hospital. It never took longer than a few minutes before a VW Golf would show up and drive them away.

The director of the center, Yasmina, was a slim middle-aged woman with dark exotic Turkish eyes. She put her hand on my forearm. Her touch frightened me for a moment, but I didn't do anything. I told myself it was best not to move. She motioned that she wanted to come with us in the Land Rover. Instinctively I opened the door and held her elbow as she climbed in the back, next to a can of fuel.

"What's up?" asked Graeme. He drove hard and fast through a cloud of smoke into a back alley.

"I think she wants us to take her to the hospital."

She nodded yes and kept saying, "Kosevo."

Kosevo hospital was up on the hill. Slowly her English came back to her and she said something about her friends staying there.

"Is it OK if the mothers eat the baby food?" she asked.

"Whatever it takes," said Graeme. "Whatever it takes."

At the hospital it was a mess. People were dragging other people with no arms and half a foot out of cars. The screams were enough to make a person run into the hills and start killing Serbs with an ice pick.

Yasmina held the nub of my elbow with just three fingers, as if not to be too forward, and led me to a small white building just behind the graveyard. Graeme stopped where the smell began. It smelled of formaldehyde and rotten meat.

"Mate, I'll wait out here for you," he said in a voice I hadn't heard before. It was solemn, like he was expecting something bad to happen. He sat on the ground and pulled up a long weed and picked his teeth with it. From where he was sitting the view was grim: gray sky and fresh graves.

Inside, the walls were covered with white tiles. A sepia light came in through windows in the ceiling. There was an elderly gentleman sitting in a chair at the end of the hall moving a broom back and forth over the tops of his leather boots, ankle high. In a sudden wave of nausea, I grabbed my nose and closed my eyes.

I'd been here before, to this smell. It only existed in places like this. Where dead people live.

There were four bodies covered in mud and dried blood. There was no color that I could see. Instead just a black and white image of four men lying on stretchers in a white room. Their faces were stretched tight as if they'd been dead for days or weeks. One was missing his head and another had a hole in his stomach with his head sticking out of it. Yasmina pointed at my camera and made a clicking sound with her mouth. She touched the camera again. She said they had been recovered from a Bosnian Serb or Chetnik camp, earlier in the week. She asked if I would take the photos "for history." I did while she turned away, her handkerchief over her mouth.

Outside she wiped the rain off her blouse and walked away.

A picture is worth a thousand words. All my life I've heard that phrase. All my life those words sounded less like a truth than a hopeful notion. No more. I felt ashamed to be here. Ashamed to be a witness to something I had no way of stopping. Ashamed that I had no way of doing anything that could affect that woman besides taking some photographs of dead people. And who was I going to show them to?

My stomach went lopsided and I fell down on all fours. I threw up. Recovering, I grabbed a handful of stones just to hold on to something. Graeme told me to get in the car.

"Easy does it, mate," he said.

On the way home we came upon an $80,000 white UN Land Rover. A big antenna stuck up from the roof. I threw a stone at it and missed.

"Wankers," yelled Graeme and drove down the street, as always, like a madman, but a madman with a plan.

20

The debate continues. Is anyone's character traceable to his or her genetics? Or is their personality due to their environment? Will the children of the Bosnian war grow up to be vengeful or will they find a way out of the pattern? And if so, will it be due to a change in their environment or to a deep physiological and genetic code? Or both?

These are things I wondered about, always. You see, Dad used to be a company man. CIA. He worked for the CIA in the early 1960s, at the height of their far-reaching powers. He was recruited as a top graduate of the Masters programme at UC-Berkeley and quickly moved to Langley, Virginia, the headquarters. What he did for them I never found out. Did he ever quit? I have no idea.

But what happened when I traveled to Asia made me wonder. It happened while I was teaching an intensive English course in Taiwan. One of my students, a pretty Chinese girl with lovely eyes, asked me to join her for tea. I refused on the basis of the teacher–student relationship. She was quite forward and kept insisting that she should get to know everything about me. I explained that we should keep the parameters simple.

Several days later she stopped me after class and began telling me details about my life that I had never revealed to my students. Where I lived in Chico, my phone number, the name of my girl-friend in high school; her address and phone number. The reason we broke up, what sports I enjoyed, my grade point average, and a simple but basically accurate assessment of my personality.

When I asked how she obtained all this information she said she had a friend in Taipei who worked for the Defence Department of Taiwan. She said he tapped into some mainframe system in American Intelligence. True, she could have tapped into my high school guidance counselor's computer, but still the information felt too familiar, too personal, for that to be the source.

I tell this story only to try to explain, maybe more to myself, the reasons for the violence and paranoia that existed in my father's mind. I think I do this in the great hope of giving myself an escape from my own past; that it isn't so much genetic as environmental.

Still, when I was growing up, no one in my family really knew what my father did for a living. During the years on the ranch he was a real-estate agent, but not a very successful one. And then there were times when he was gone for a week or two at a stretch. Either way, the war he waged on us didn't stop just because he was gone. More than once, after my brother Cliff had finished whipping me, I would chase him with a huge knife into the bathroom. When he shut the door I would stab the wood with all my might, hoping to catch his hand. That's how the violence was in our house: like sap dripping from a tree.

But there were always truces. One spring day, playing soccer with my brother, I put a crack in the glass of the living-room window. Instead of teasing me or goading me, which was his usual behavior, my brother just sat down on the steps. It seemed for the first time that we were on the same side of some oddly shaped triangle. I kept asking him what we should do and he just sat there staring into the field. Silent. I liked him very much for that.

When Mom drove up I begged her to take us to town to get a new piece of glass, before Dad got home. She hugged me and I remember she placed her head on the wheel. She looked like she was a hundred years old.

"We can't go to town."

"Why not?"

"I don't have any money."

"So?"

"Honey, there's not enough time."

Right then I knew that whatever my future was it would be based on my ability to survive, alone.

Cliff disappeared, headed for cover at the back of the property. Mom went inside and I sat on the porch. Our dog Boomer sat at my feet, his tongue drooling and his tail wagging from time to time. I laid my head on his stomach, which rose and fell with his breath. It was a peaceful day. The blue jays were squawking and some crows sat on top of the silo near the barn. I wondered what God was doing now. Eating, sleeping, making a new ocean?

Inside, Mom was doing something in the kitchen. I imagined she was pulling pots out of the cupboard just to put them back again. Cliff was probably already in the tree fort he had built out by the eucalyptus tree.

When car tires crackled on the gravel drive I ran for the bushes. I waited there for a few seconds, but then ran back to the porch. I sat down and then I stood up, putting myself squarely in front of the cracked glass as if it were my job to inform the commandant that the crime before him had been committed by me alone and that my fellow prisoners had no hand in this. I felt a certain peace come over me. My fate was sealed. The waiting was over.

After I explained the accident, Dad patted me on the shoulder.

"Bones, you will be a future athlete," he said and handed me some papers from under his arm.

We walked up to the window.

"I wouldn't worry about the glass, after all it's just glass. A replaceable product, right?"

When I didn't answer he said, "Right?" again.

Mom put her face up to the screen door. There was her husband walking with his arm wrapped around their son. She said dinner was almost ready. The dog wagged his tail at all of us.

"Okey-dokey," said Dad, and squeezed my shoulder a little tighter. "Bill and I are going downstairs for a minute but will be up in time for grace."

My father closed the door to the cellar and went into the adjoining room, his office. The basement was like a tomb. I hated it down there. It smelled like wet cheese.

"Sit down," he said. It's not easy to describe his anger. Although his acts of anger seemed random, his methods of punishment never were. I would not characterize him as a mean or a mean-spirited person. Instead, the anger was always present but barely contained, as if he were in an epic battle to keep order in a universe that he had created inside his head. His violence simmered slowly, a big-cat predator stalking its prey, waiting for the moment to strike. I sat on my knees like a prisoner in some faraway war. I thought of making for the door, but where was I going to go? The field? The river? I'd never make it.

"Nothing is free in this world," he said, his jaw beginning to pop in and out like he was chewing on a massive jawbreaker. "That's communism. Right?"

"Right."

"We live in a capitalist world. A God-fearing world. Right?"

Dad loved to talk about God and America, his two favorite topics. He used his American-made ruler to scratch out the dimensions of a cricket bat on the plywood floor. Once satisfied he plugged in the Sears power saw, American-made.

"I wonder what's for dinner?" he asked himself.

I was shaking. I would have pissed my pants but I didn't

have any pants on. He had told me to take them off. My under-wear too. They were down around my ankles. I would have crapped, but I was too scared.

Now he was talking about how Russia was a godless country and how evil is never far away. I thought of the map on my wall. I prayed the world was big enough that one day I could get lost in it.

The blade whirred, making a deafening noise. Sawdust filled the room as he cut out a piece of the floor, creating a slab of wood, complete with a handle on it, which was nearly two feet long and an inch thick.

"Do you understand?" he asked, brushing the flakes of wood from his shirt.

I was a small kid. I didn't talk much at home. At school I stuck up for the underdog, Crecensio, the only Mexican in our class. We were best friends and every time the others called him a beaner or wetback we teamed up for the fight. We mostly lost but we stuck together. For the most part I smiled and laughed and the girls liked my dimples, especially the one by my left eye, a scar I got from being on the receiving end of a baseball bat in the backyard when I was five. But down here in the basement I didn't understand anything that was going on. That's what I remember the most. Being confused.

The first stroke of the plywood cracked against my bare skin. I didn't cry out. Crying could only make it worse. Instead I bit down hard on the inside of my cheek. The next stroke hit the back of my legs. That stung. As the strokes continued the pain went away. I imagined my body was made of wood, like the oaks in the front yard. I didn't hate him, I wasn't even sure what hate was. At times I thought he was not human, like an alien or something. I wanted him to go away. That was all. Just go away. Then I cried, more from exhaustion than the pain. I was numb but the inside of my mouth was filled with blood. I swallowed it as fast as it bled.

"Maybe now you will learn to respect the value of property," he said, taking a break. Then he went at it again. He didn't stop until the wood finally broke on my back.

"And now we have wasted more property," he said. I barely heard him.

Upstairs, through the floorboards, my mom was pacing the kitchen. I imagined her trying to put plates on the table in just the right order. Forks here, knives there. Her hands twitching and fiddling with the hot-pads as she pulled 89-cent store-bought chicken pot pies from the oven. God help her if she broke a glass. Sometimes I used to think she must have been made of wood. How else could she take it?

Sometimes now, thinking back, I can almost see her face in the window above the sink, staring into the sun as it set on the other side of the field, wondering where her children had gone.

21

The odds of it all kept Corrina and me laughing for weeks. Even though we were five years apart in age, it turned out we had grown up in the same small town in northern California. At eighteen I left for the University of Santa Cruz. At eighteen so did she. I worked as a bag-boy at the Bay Street Safeway, the 5 a.m. swing shift. So did she, five years later. I sat at the back of the Saturn café and drank hot chocolate. So did she. But she was way ahead of me on the reading curve. I had read Orwell, Steinbeck, Kundera, Dostoevsky, Twain, Conrad, Hawthorne, but only after I left university. She had read them before she got there.

Then there were the other things.

For a while when Corrina was in high school, she and her mom had lived with her mom's boyfriend, a boozer who kept hitting both of them.

What made us laugh the most was that we met 2,500 miles away from all that, on the banks of the Naknak river. We didn't talk about it much. There was no need. Shared experiences have a way of canceling out the past and making room for the present.

. . .

In bed we shut out the world. I was always hard and she was always wet. We made love in the bathroom, the car, the city park, other people's houses, and on the beaches. Give us a hidden shadow behind a building or an extra alcove just out of sight of a room full of distracted people and we'd find a way.

"I'm scared," she said one afternoon.

"I would never let anything happen to you." I clenched my biceps and acted tough.

"I'm not scared of that. I'm talking about us."

"I know. Me too."

"Where are we going?"

"Very far into something that I don't have a clue how to get out of."

"Do you want to get out of it?"

"No, and that scares me the most. I don't want out of it at all."

"Do you want me?"

Like we did so often, I put her hand a few inches from mine. We locked eyes and waited. As always, the heat off our fingertips became so intense it was as if there was one pulse throbbing between us.

Sometimes I would find her glancing out the window, as if staring herself into some other world. Her absence in those moments made me want her even more. I had no resistance toward her; her every move felt like a draft of wind pulling me along beside her. How does one describe this? At night, with her sleeping on my chest, I could almost hear the clicking noise of our DNA stretching, growing together. I wanted to become a piece of her skin.

It was tempting, the thought of grabbing her attention when she was staring out the window, but there was no point. She was magnificent even when she wasn't there.

Then one day the phone rang.

It was a man who said he was my father. He said he wanted to meet me in the Golden Gate Park.

"Want me to come?" she asked.

"No. I'll be back in time to take full advantage of you."

She kissed me and stroked my forehead. "Hurry," she said.

By then we were spending most of our time at my place on 15th and Judah, in the Inner Sunset in San Francisco, where I was sharing a two-bedroom flat with Mike Fagen, a friend from my teaching days in Taiwan. His girlfriend had recently moved out from Chicago, so even though Corrina rented a room in a flat in Santa Cruz, where she was going to university, more often than not it was the four of us in the San Francisco flat.

One month after returning from Alaska I got a job in the film business. My title was PA, better known as Production Assistant. My pay on that first job was a free lunch, which was usually bean burritos, but I was willing to do it because I wanted to learn about making movies.

Not long after that I got my first paying job, on a television movie. The days were long and the job description called on a person to do whatever anyone higher above you on the food chain told you to do. Pick up rubbish, make coffee, direct traffic. The mode of communication was a radio that blared endless orders into my ear. One time, on orders from the assistant director, my boss, I tried to stop a pedestrian from walking into the middle of the set for a Volkswagen commercial. The pedestrian started screaming, "Do you own this motherfucking street?" I told him I did not. "Then get the hell out of my way." He passed me and someone came on the radio and said the next time I let someone walk into the shot I was going to be fired. I still let everyone pass but for some reason I was not fired.

The only time I was fired was the time I picked up a producer, director, and executive producer from the airport. The coordinator of the job told me to look for three men who were overweight and resembled stuffed chipmunks. I spotted them right away, but told them that because of the security at the airport I had to get back to the car, which I had left at the curb. I ran back to the car and dismantled the dummy I had put in the driver's seat to keep away the traffic cop. I opened the back door and the three passengers put their bags inside and off we went. I was young and full of wild stories of the world. I spent the forty-minute drive talking to the executive producer, the money-man, about traveling Indonesia and hiking the Himalayas. He told me about his travels. Overall I thought we had a great talk.

Ten minutes after arriving at the hotel I was called into the production office.

"What happened at the airport?" the coordinator asked with a heavy voice.

"Nothing," I said. Maybe I was in trouble for the dummy?

"Well, you're fired."

"For the dummy?"

"What dummy?"

It seemed the director hadn't liked it that I didn't put his bags in the car for him. Or that my shirt was untucked. Someone close to the director later told me he didn't like the fact that I had talked too much to the executive producer.

Oddly enough, and in the true spirit of Hollywood, I was rehired a few hours later. Eventually, over time, I was promoted and made more money and had to turn down jobs. Corrina and I had a plan. We hoped to save enough money to leave for good. To travel as long as we could and end up in some other town doing whatever jobs we could find. It was a simple but perfect plan.

So, meeting my father.

My brother Cliff and I had seen him quite often after leaving him that September day so long ago. The judge stated that my father couldn't touch us and Mom explained that since Dad was so hot on the US constitution being the highest power next to the Bible he would never disobey a court order. And he never did.

Still, it had been three years since I last talked to him.

I walked the three blocks to the park, past the travel agency and the Mexican taco joint. There were no gardens in the avenues of the Sunset district but it seemed all the homes had flowers in the windows. For a minute, as I walked, it almost felt like I was living here, like I had found a way to be comfortable in one place, at least for a while.

Three years ago I had taken a phone call one night when I was in college.

"All I want to know is who you are working for."

"Dad?"

"By the specs of the operation it's either KGB or CIA. I just can't figure out which one."

"I work as a bagger at Safeway, the five a.m. shift. I am also a prep cook at a Chinese crap place. Making pot stickers and egg rolls."

"Interesting that you work in a Chinese establishment . . . Murder, or I should say attempted murder, considering I am still alive, for now, is a felony punishable by many decades in a penitentiary."

"What are you talking about?"

"Happy Jacks, your fifteenth birthday."

"So?"

"I ordered a hamburger. You always order hamburgers, but that day you ordered a salad with blue cheese dressing."

"And?"

"So you aren't denying it."

"Denying what?"

"The poisoning."

"This is crazy. I was fifteen years old."

"And that is why I am willing to accept you are being used by more powerful forces than you can deter alone."

"I have a mid-term tomorrow."

"Tell me about the Chinese meal a few months ago."

"On my birthday?"

"Yes."

"What about the meal?"

"I'm guessing the food was marked by the cook in such a way that you knew."

"Are you saying I knew which piece of scrap chicken to eat and let you eat poisoned food?"

"Fascinating."

"What's fascinating?"

"Your theory."

"I'm trying to understand your bullshit theory."

"Often when someone fills in blanks they are actually revealing themselves."

"If something is wrong with you maybe you should see a doctor," I said, already knowing the response that would follow.

"Specifically which doctor would you suggest?"

"I'm not going there."

"SOP."

"SOP?"

"Standard Operating Procedure. You suggest a doctor on the payroll and the job is finished."

"This is insane."

He laughed. I could tell from the echo that he was sitting in the basement at the ranch. A large bearskin hung on the wall just above his eye line. His old Regal typewriter was directly in front of him. That was where he sat tapping away at letters, which he believed to be important secret documents. That was also the typewriter he used to write letters to his sons urging them to find a way to let God into their hearts. Or at least the godlike American government. And just under his feet was the thin carpet. But if you took a carpet-puller and tore up that carpet you'd find several cricket-bat-shaped holes in the wooden floor.

There he was, standing by the brown Cadillac. Dad, whose name was Richard but who told everyone to call him Dick. The car was one of those big numbers with four doors and seats the size of couches. It had at least a 429 under the hood and the kind of seats that move up and down with the flip of a switch. He'd always driven cars like this, big and American.

He opened the trunk and pulled out a blanket and a bottle of water. There were a dozen shopping bags filled with canned food and cereal boxes. His hair was combed from one side all the way over to the other and looked like it hadn't been washed for months. He was missing a few teeth. The twitch under his right eye was popping something fierce. My guess was that he had been eating out of his truck ever since the alleged Chinese food "incident."

I asked him where he was living and he laughed deeply and

answered, "The first time it happens it's shame on you. The second time is shame on me." From the look of the deep indentations in the back-seat cushions I guessed he was sleeping in his car.

We sat on the grass and things seemed normal for a brief moment. A part of me wanted to get to know him again. I was flying high with Corrina and felt a strong urge to share this with him. That and, I suppose, my compulsion to connect with my father, even if he was psychotic, outweighed the desire to act like he didn't exist.

Watching others in the park seemed like watching a documentary on how fathers and sons were supposed to behave. Throwing frisbees, playing football, and all the rest of those Kodak moments. The sun shone but, like some premonition of how this meeting would turn out, the fog was quickly rolling in from the ocean. It always did.

"Who's the girl who answered the phone?"

"Her name's Corrina."

"Is she secure?" which to him meant trustworthy.

I ignored him.

"Are you still wearing pink shirts?" he asked.

"Only when I play golf," I said with sarcasm.

Once, when I was sixteen, we had played a round of golf. I found a ball in the bushes which was pink and said Flying Lady. I played it the rest of the round. Ever since he had been certain that I was a closet homosexual.

"Does she know?"

"Know what?"

He stretched out his legs and took a deep breath as if he'd been studying yoga for ten years or something. "Well, that's another problem."

On the blanket he dumped all the postcards I had written to him while traveling the world. He fingered through the cards— Turkey, India, Nepal, Taiwan, Jordan, Israel, Egypt, Russia, and dozens more.

"Well, where were you?" His smile was that of the detective who had finally caught the cat burglar of Monaco red-handed. He was pleased with himself and it showed.

"Turkey, India, Nepal, Taiwan, Jordan, and everywhere else those postcards say." Most of my postcards carried brief descriptions of the local religions. It was a feeble attempt to show him that the whole world doesn't think like evangelical preachers in rural America.

"Bones, you fucked up this time. Actually the person doing the postmarks fucked up." He held up the cards from Istanbul, Paris, and Hong Kong. "All these postmark circles have been made by the same person."

I took a deep breath. I felt the world shrink around the edges of my face. It was like I was a test-flight monkey doing seven Gs in a wind tunnel while some suit from NASA kept cranking up the dial and sipping coffee.

"My guess would be NORAD. It's well hidden, secretive, and has black ops," he said.

"What?" It was the best I could do under the circumstances. I was being ambushed by a pro.

"North American Air Defense in Colorado."

The scene in the park turned into a world full of people who didn't know anything about anything. Didn't they know that the Chinese eat dogs and burn cigarettes on the faces of Tibetan monks? Or that young wives in India are burned to death in their kitchens if their dowry is considered too low? Or what about the flooding season in Bangladesh? Or that in the next six months some ferry full of people desperate to leave their lives will sink off the coast somewhere and everyone will drown? I took off my shoes and stood up.

"Tell me who you are working for," he said.

I turned and walked in the direction of my flat. I remember thinking how perfectly long the grass was between my toes. I lived three blocks away. She was there, probably staring out the window. I'd slip into bed and we would slip into each other. The fog would cool our sweat. The past was a rising red inferno of tall flames fueled by bits of memory kindling and worry weeds. It was based on a child's mind no longer mine.

The fog drifted through the trees. This man, my father, the man whose seed brought me into this world, seemed like a stranger sitting on the grass in the park. I saw him now as I might a homeless man preaching about the end of the world and begging for quarters—someone to pity, but from a distance. I felt the long grass reach up through my toes and tickle the tops of my feet. He was no longer mine. He was no longer my responsibility to fix. Strangely, I had a warm feeling toward him; perhaps it was the bittersweet feeling of loss. And it was then that I realized something very important. For better or for worse, because of the way our lives had played out, he had passed on to me a rare and useful gift: survival.

"Tell me who you are working for." Those would be the last words he ever said to me. I didn't know it at the time, how could I, but I would never see him again.

What a fool I'd been. I'd always thought distance would be the way I would erase my past. Running until I was empty. Getting in a car and traveling down a back road until the road hit a junction and then take a turn and keep on driving. I always thought I'd just spin myself into oblivion, with a fat happy smile across my face, content to be lost in the momentum. It never crossed my mind that when it finally came, that moment of calm, the *om* of the Tibetan Plateau, the ability to know the infinite, that something as simple as love would bring it to me.

22

One night, toward the end of the second week, Graeme did something that showed how completely differently we had spent the last several years.

We were at a local girl's house. Her name was Natasha and she lived near the towers, and we had met her on the street near our parking lot. She had told us to come to a party that evening, when she was going to have some friends over. Wanting to keep the rowdy Australians out of it, Graeme and I decided to keep the invitation to ourselves. We told the rest of the crew we would catch up with them down at the disco before curfew.

In the flat, a boom-box hooked up to a car battery was blaring out techno music. The windows had black cloth over them and candles gave the scene a feel of some basement club in Istanbul.

Like other Sarajevo flats I had been in, it was loaded with modern-day appliances that didn't work. Fifteen months without electricity and the television, refrigerator, toaster, microwave, radio, and CD player just sat there like pieces of cheap plastic decoration.

Graeme and I took a seat on the sofa and shared a glass of slivovitz—plum brandy—that someone had poured for us.

"So tell me what you got up your sleeve, mate."

"Whadda ya mean?" I asked.

"It's in your eyes," said Graeme. "You are crazier than anyone I've met."

"Tell me how you first found out about the Road Trip," I said in the hope of getting out of an answer.

He told me that just before coming to Bosnia for the first time he had been to Goa on the west coast of India.

"I was just tripping around really, doing fuck all," he said. When Graeme spoke he looked directly in your eyes and demanded you look at him the same way. "I was taking quite a lot of K."

"K?"

"Ketamine. A nasty bit of animal tranquilizer and it was fucking me up a little so I got out of there." He needed to yell over the music. "My girlfriend at the time was quite heavily into it and wanted to stay with all the other geezers in Goa. I mean it's just a bloody English hole, terrible place."

"Then what happened?"

"I came back to London and was squatting at my cousin's house and living on the dole. He was working on these geezers' trucks, painting them and working a bit under the bonnet, and hey, I thought, this is something I could do and not feel like a cunt the rest of my bloody life. Know what I mean?"

A young Bosnian man sat down next to Graeme. His face was young and his mustache was no more than a budding piece of peach fuzz. He was drunk and had that lazy stupid smile across his face, the one you see all over the world from punks who think they know something. It didn't take two minutes before the kid pulled out a pistol. Then he pulled out a badge and told us in broken English that he was special police, whatever the hell that meant. As far as I could tell everyone in the city was in the police or special police or knew someone who was.

Graeme got up in the kid's face but kept his smile intact. "Do they train you to pull your gun out at parties? I mean is that how they do it here? A bit silly, don't you think?" He looked at me.

"I agree," I said, playing along.

Then the kid points it at me, not in a threatening way, but in a careless gesture. He was drunk or stoned or whatever he was.

That's when it happened. Like a bird of prey diving into a field Graeme snatched the gun from the kid's hands. I was watching it but I really didn't see it happen. It was that fast. The kid leaned in like he was ready for a fight but Graeme put his free hand on the kid's chest and looked him right in the eye. He motioned for him to relax and take a seat.

Graeme began in a monotone voice, like a speaker box at a museum explaining the various art pieces. "This is an example of an early Dali, from the years he spent on the beach with pets and homosexuals," like that. Like some droll bored voice repeating something he has said a hundred times a week.

"The nine-millimeter standard clip action handgun. Popular among bank robbers worldwide and police and gangs in the United States." He began to take the gun apart. "No offense of course to our septic friend here," he said, tipping his head toward me.

"None taken."

"You see, the problem with these guns is that they are too easy to get and the idiots who buy them don't know how to use them." He looked at the kid. The barrel was now disconnected and the handle on the table. "But in the right hands it's a catchy little number. In fact I've always been quite fond of it." Now, the gun sat like scrap metal on the table, in several pieces. The bullets lay on the floor, like spilled brass candy.

The kid went to speak but Graeme put his finger in the air, as if to ask for silence. Then in a matter of seconds he put the gun back together and handed it butt first to the Bosnian sans the bullets. Graeme put those in the kid's other hand.

The whole show took less than thirty seconds.

"Right then, how 'bout you get us a bit more drink?" he said to the kid. The kid stood up and walked slowly toward the kitchen. He looked back at Graeme like he'd just seen the last samurai and didn't want to take the chance of turning his back on him.

"Come on then, move about some," he said. "Don't stand there like a sorry tart."

Graeme leaned back and looked at the ceiling. "Right then, where were we? You were going to tell us a bit of your story."

"Fuck off. What the hell was that?" I said.

"The world is full of 22-year-old nitwits wanting to pull the trigger."

"I'm not talking about that."

"What?"

"You're British. You don't grow up with guns. I don't think a Nazi from Idaho would know how to do that. Not like that."

"Oh, that . . . British Special Forces for seven years," he said without hesitation.

"Oh, is that all?"

"Northern Ireland, Cyprus, Belize, and a few nasty spots from time to time. A bit of the dodgy stuff here and there. Good while it lasted. But in the end I was just a squaddie like the other punters, driving into London on the weekends and beating up faggots. So I got out."

"And then?"

"Took lots of K and found music and some higher sense of life and decided I would never let a gun rule my world. Or any part of the world if I could help it. It's love, mate. Spread love and the whole world starts to work, bit by bit."

It gave me immediate comfort that I slept three feet away from a trained killer. It explained the skill I'd noticed he had with a knife or picking locks. And when he drove, his focus was fixed and his reflexes cat-like. Strange though: like a soldier, he was better at getting the job done than actually figuring out what the problem was in the first place; that part he seemed more comfortable to leave to others. This dynamic set up a natural balance of power where, as long as he respected the person, he would follow their ideas. But if he suspected you to be anything less than forthright he would just as easily throw you off a bridge as give you another helping of chow.

We never got to the disco that night. Instead we spent the night there. Graeme snuggled up against some girl near the window. I spooned against the backside of Natasha. The girls were probably under eighteen but so what? No one said a word. No one wanted sex. No one wanted anything.

Odd how sometimes wanting nothing can be the tenderest thing a person can give.

23

I bought the van as a surprise. Corrina always talked about traveling the country and Mexico in a 1960s VW van, the kind with a canvas roof that pulled back, exposing the sky. I found one for sale in Mill Valley and paid cash. It had windows all around and there was even a bed already built into the back. So there I was with a car, but now I was broke. We fixed up the van with white curtains on the windows and put a new piece of plywood in the back for the bed. I bought a maintenance manual for idiots and some tools. I planned to be the master mechanic on the road.

"What are you doing?" she asked one day. I was looking at the engine.

"Changing the oil," I said.

"It's right here," she said, indicating.

"I know that."

I didn't and she knew it. "Uh-uh." She smiled. She drove a VW bug and knew much more than I did about the engine.

"Well . . . I was reading about it."

"Where should we go first?" she asked, running her hands through my hair.

"Wherever you want."

"New Orleans?"

"That works," I said.

"How about Mexico?"

"I like that idea."

She stood up and went inside the van. I followed her. She was lying on her back on the bed staring up at the sky. I lay down next to her.

"I like to watch things go by like this sometimes," she said as she studied the trees growing down toward the sky.

She was trembling, like she was cold.

"Hey, you all right?" I asked.

"Are you going to leave me?" She was not sobbing, not whining, just crying because of the constant unknown swirling around us all the time.

"Never."

A man passed on the pavement, upside down.

"I will never leave you. Never," I said. "You are the one who's going to leave. Find some happening dude and dump me."

She laughed, but I could see she was still scared.

"But I don't want to live like other people," I said. "I want to take a kid in a backpack and keep traveling. I don't want all the American apple-pie dream bullshit. Know what I mean?"

"Me too," she said.

"We'll keep it simple?" I asked gently.

"Yes. Simple."

We held hands, looking upside down at the world.

"So, we are stuck with each other until the end?" I said.

"OK." She smiled.

She nudged in closer. We stayed just like that, for a while.

24

Some nights in Sarajevo I'd step over the passed-out bodies in the front room. I'd stand in the window with no glass and take in that smell. It was the stench of Varanasi, where the Hindus go to die. It reeked of rotting garbage, burning can, rotting teeth, urine, crotch, and decaying skin. It all just rose up from below like heat waves flickering in the sun, or ghost thermals rising up on the warmed entrails of the day's dead. Out there was fear: wondering when the reaper would come. And hope: it was out there in the night air with the kids always playing some game, their laughter breaking through with a spirit so strong that nothing else mattered.

The distance to the lights on the hill was less than a quick ride on a bicycle to the corner store in small-town America. The snipers were there. What did they do when they weren't shooting people they didn't know? Shit, eat, sleep, fuck? It consumed my thoughts for days at a time. What did those human beings do between killing people?

On these quiet nights the city was dark, pitch black except for a few candles here and there. Satellite dishes, television antennae, skyscrapers, and four-lane avenues dark and mute. I felt eerily free of some part of civilization, as if the world had finally gone and done it: dropped the bomb, and here we were living its skeletal aftermath. At that moment I wondered whether, at the end of the war, these lessons of how to live more simply, how to exist without electricity and eat sparingly, would survive. I doubted it, and I realized it was naive to think like this. In truth, to go by past experience, when this war was over, this city would have more electricity, more food, more money, more greed, more, more, more, more, just to make up for the loss. And of course it was more than likely that these people would take revenge by ripping the eyes out of Serbian skulls.

A red flare lit up the sky, and tracer fire shot down from the hills into a flat building nearby. There was another flare and more gunfire. Somewhere below, in the dark, I heard the patter of people running. I looked up. The red glare had made the stars disappear.

In the middle of April we were on another delivery in a dangerous part of town. Graeme and Christophe were in the front of the Land Rover and I was in the back. We had all taken off the clown noses we had been wearing for an earlier delivery to an orphanage. The back road, which paralleled the main boulevard, was slow going because of the potholes and the number of pedestrians, but the high-rise flat buildings and barricades offered shelter from the snipers.

It was gray and cold and the occasional raindrop fell on the windshield. There I was lying flat on my back watching the sky pass by. It was like watching the world go by in fragments—a piece of building, the wing of a bird, puffy white clouds, and patches of bright blue. I was deep in thought: what would it be like to starve to death? A man and woman living a few buildings down had hung themselves a few days earlier. In a note left for friends they said they didn't want to starve to death.

Graeme turned into a courtyard and parked next to a burned-out Volkswagen. They were here to deliver a box of food to Christophe's Bosnian girlfriend's family.

"Two minutes," he said to me. "You stay with the truck. Don't let any of these kids near it." That was Graeme. One minute he could throw out enough love to heal the world and the next minute he was ready to fight over a single square inch of mud.

I leaned against the bumper, standing guard.

A pack of kids showed up out of nowhere and began playing war games in the derelict cars. Two boys had lead pipes and were shooting the younger kids, who took shelter behind the cars. Finally the big kids overtook the smaller kids and pretended to kill them with knives. They were all laughing and preparing for another assault on one another. It was refreshing to know that even here kid games stayed the same.

I threw a couple of juggling balls to them. They threw them back and soon we had a game of catch developing. Just then two young women crossed my path, bringing a temporary halt to the game.

"Do you want to come to our house for lunch?" asked the girl with short black hair and a cute mouth. She looked eighteen or nineteen and the taller blond with her looked the same age.

"Now?"

"Of course now, stupid!" She laughed.

I explained that I was guarding the truck for some friends who were upstairs. She turned and spoke forcefully to the kids. They ran to us and gathered around the car, forming a miniature security platoon.

"They will watch it," she said.

"I don't know—that might not be a good idea."

"Why not? Do you think we Bosnians are barbarians? Can't be trusted?"

"No. It's just . . ."

"Our mother is their teacher. Believe me, nothing will happen to your truck."

The two girls walked toward the sniper barricade. The dark-haired girl looked back over her shoulder, as if I was a fashion photographer asking for that come-hither look.

"Well, are you coming or not?"

Her name was Lejla Pajević. She had pretty eyes, dark as linseed. "Lunch at our house has always been wonderful. Even during these days."

I had no choice. Whether it was because I was curious or because I couldn't resist a pretty young girl, I grabbed a small box of food and followed them to the barricade.

Through the cracks in it Lejla pointed out the snipers' position: in the blue flat buildings, on the other side of the Miljacka river in Grebavica, the Serb-occupied part of town. At most they were 150 meters away.

"What are you doing here?" asked Lejla. Her sister, Selma, wore her long hair in a ponytail and had glasses that kept sliding down her nose, which she kept rubbing. They were both fluent in English and severely malnourished.

"Waiting for my friends."

"No, you dummy. I mean what are you doing in Sarajevo?"

"Delivering food, some medicine."

"Don't you know it is dangerous here?" She laughed.

"He's a war tourist," said Selma with a snap in her voice. She took off her glasses and wiped her eyes. She looked wilted, like a dying flower. "We don't need your food. That is not why we asked you to lunch."

"I'm not a war tourist."

"Uh-uh . . . everyone comes for a couple of weeks, sees the horrible situation and then leaves. Same boring story."

"Do you have anything wonderful in the box?" asked Lejla, ignoring her sister. "Maybe shoes from Gucci or some make-up or perhaps Levi's?"

I told her it was just the basics: sugar, coffee, flour, rice, chocolate, lentils.

"So do you have a girlfriend?" asked Lejla.

"Oh my God," said Selma as she adjusted her glasses again. "Every boy she meets she asks this question."

I ducked it by looking through the barricade once again. "What's that?" A yellow car was parked in the middle of the street.

"Do you see the driver?" asked Lejla. "He has been there for one week. No one will retrieve him." The car was at a slight angle to the tram tracks, the driver's head on the steering wheel.

"Well, you coming?"

I bent over and tied my shoes. "Right behind you," I said.

I wondered if dying while running for a bowl of rice was much different from dying of starvation because you couldn't find a bowl of rice.

"Besides," said Selma with a sarcastic but playful voice, "you can't go home without saying you crossed Snipers' Alley. All the war tourists do it." She tilted her head, taking a closer look at me.

"I'm not a war tourist," I yelled back, and for the first time felt suddenly like, well, a war tourist.

"Watch where we run and don't stop." Lejla giggled as if we were running toward lovers' leap on our first date.

They leaped into the street with their long winter coats flapping in the wind. Their hair bounced back and forth as they zigzagged across the openness. It was a four-lane avenue with train tracks running down the middle. By the time they got to the first lane a shot was fired. Then another shot. It sounded like a 30.6 hunting rifle. They cut right then left and then right once again as they made for the other side.

I thought I heard them laughing, and then realized they *were* laughing. They shouted, "Come on. Come on, don't be afraid." The children behind me stood on tiptoes looking through the crack in the barricade, yelling for me to run.

Agitated and feeling trapped by a stupid dare, I yelled at the kids. I told them that if anything was stolen from the truck I would find each and every one of them. They laughed. I am sure I looked half mad to them or, more likely, amusing. I jumped into the street as if I was on the last leg of a tightly contested relay race. The children screamed.

Crack!

A shot.

Then another shot.

If suicide was ever an option this was the time. I don't consider myself particularly brave. I don't think I can outrun a bullet or read a sniper's mind. I just knew that this day was not the day for me to die. Not yet.

But I was scared. That's something else entirely. My heart was beating in my belly button and it was as if I could feel my bones sweating. I ran like the devil was breathing down the back of my skull. Keeping my eyes on the other side of the road I didn't see the car going 120 kph that missed me by less than a few meters. The locals drove this section as fast as they could in an effort to beat the sniper's bullets.

Two more shots.

I ran until I ran into the wall next to the sisters.

"You almost died in Sarajevo because you were hit by a car." They both laughed and I wiped small beads of sweat off my forehead.

The consolation of fighting a war in an urban setting was that even though we were closer to the snipers, within a hundred meters of the front line, we were safer now, because the buildings blocked the view of the shooters.

We passed through abandoned yards until we reached a brick wall. It had a hole in it. It looked as if someone had used a sledgehammer to make an opening large enough for a human body.

"My father did this in the beginning of the war to get us out of here," said Lejla with a giggle that sounded like a piglet snorting.

Once inside the tunnel, Lejla took my hand. It was as black as a moonless night. Not one ounce of sunlight. I noticed that Lejla's hand was sweaty and wondered what that meant. We passed through a series of holes, and each time someone touched the top of my head to make sure I ducked. It was cold and smelled of mold. Blind, I ran my free hand along the walls. They were dirt but lined with sheets of plastic, which crinkled at my touch. The girls led me along with little bits of encouragement. "This way" or "Watch your step here."

I ducked again. There was a little light peaking through near the ceiling of what I assumed was a basement. We passed through the guts of one building and into the open wound of another.

Once my eyes adjusted I could see an ornate light fixture dangling from the ceiling. Dresser drawers stood near the door. In the middle of the room was a worn-out sofa.

"In the beginning this was where we slept. Then Father finished the tunnel," said Selma.

"I helped too," said Lejla with a high-pitched whine.

"Yes, of course you did. You did everything," said Selma, but with a sense of sisterly love.

Lejla grabbed my hand again and we passed through another series of tunnels until we came to a stairwell. Straight ahead was a door with dozens of bullet holes in it. Selma pushed lightly on my shoulder, guiding me toward the stairs. We walked up three flights and arrived at a door with the letter B on it. I put the box down.

They put their fingers to their mouths and made a hushing sound, as if soothing a baby to sleep.

"Do not speak here," Lejla whispered in my ear. "Take off your shoes first."

Inside was a modern flat complete with sofas, a full kitchen and three bedrooms. The mother and father were dressed like a casual European couple on holiday in Spain or Italy. They were obviously educated and, like their daughters, severely under-weight. I handed the mother the box of food and she looked away and shook her head. The shame was palpable.

"Tell her I found it in the tunnel," I said.

God, did that make them laugh. The whole family went berserk. Finally we settled down.

"They can hear us if we speak in the hallway," said Lejla.

"Who can hear you?"

"The Chetniks," said Selma.

"The guys on the hills?"

"Yes, they are across the river, just right there." She gestured toward the front door.

"Sometimes at night they call out our names. Like they want to talk," said Lejla.

"Do they?"

"They want to shoot us."

"How do they know your names?"

"A few of them used to live in this flat building."

Before I had time to understand what was being said I was whisked into the girls' bedroom. The walls were decorated with teeny-bopper pop posters. There were teddy bears on the beds and heart-shaped designs on the desk. They slept on a bunk bed near the door, well away from the window. There was a table for make-up and a closet full of clothes. The tape deck was new, but didn't work. The window was covered in scrap wood banged in with odd-sized nails.

"So tell us, do you think the women of Sarajevo are beauti-ful?" asked Lejla. Selma looked irritated; she was already tired of this conversation.

"Very beautiful. That's one of the most surprizing things, with the war and all. How beautiful the women are."

"Yes, we are famous in all of ex-Yugoslavia for that." She acted like a spoiled rich girl even though she clearly knew everyone else saw that it was just an act. I admired her pursuit of not caring what others thought.

The sniper fire was so close it sounded as if someone was shooting their parents in the living room.

Crack, another shot.

"That is damn close," I said.

"Yes. Do you have any cigarettes?" screamed Lejla over the continuing gunfire. At one point I actually flinched so hard I fell to my knees. They acted like it never happened and kept on talking. I offered a cigarette to Selma too but she said it was bad for her health.

"Yes. She is looking out for her health."

I suddenly wondered about all the other sicknesses. Do they cease to afflict people in war? Of course not. What happens to the heart-attack victims? Diabetics? What about childbirth complications? Food poisoning? For Christ's sake, what happens to people who just have a migraine? Or what about the heroin addicts, or, for that matter, the rapists and murderers? Is there a reprieve from nature's diseases during periods of man's need to slaughter? I doubted it but I hadn't thought of it until just then. It was easy to imagine that everyone in the city was aligned both in spirit and body to defeat the outside invaders, when really all the former internal battles raged on in war as in peace.

"Don't tell my mother I am smoking. She doesn't really care, but my father will be so angry with me. They think we are good girls. If they only knew." She smiled.

"No foreigner has ever visited here," said Selma with a hint of suspicion.

"I had nothing better to do this afternoon," I said.

"Oh, so you came to our house because you were bored?" joked Lejla.

"Yeah, and I wanted to see if I could outrun a sniper for the hell of it."

This made Selma laugh, which suddenly made it easier for us to talk. They asked about current movies, music, and hairstyles. They talked about not being able to go to school and about crushes they had on boys. For a while they kneeled on the floor, then one sat cross-legged in a chair.

At one point the mother knocked on the door.

"Is Papa with you?" asked Lejla.

The answer was no. Lejla kept the cigarette. The mother came in smiling and holding a small white object in the palm of her hand. She brushed off a powdery substance and lowered her palm so we could all see.

It was a small bullet.

"It was in the flour you brought in the box," translated Selma with a look of astonishment. "That was very close."

I took a deep breath and coughed up what seemed like a small phlegm of nerves from my chest.

"You really are *lud*, aren't you?" said Lejla.

"What's *lud*?"

"Crazy."

Out in the living room the family told me stories of the war as if we were at the river eating egg salad sandwiches. Laughter and tangential topics filled the pitter-patter talk. They told me of their cousin who lived in a village near Sarajevo with his wife. The two had just become doctors when the war broke out. The shelling wiped out most of the village and injured their cousin. As he lay unable to move he insisted to his wife that she leave. She was his only chance of survival but they both knew she was likely to be raped if she stayed. He pleaded with her and she ran away before the Serbs came to town. She now lived in Sarajevo, not far from here. They never heard what happened to him.

"Would you like some tea? We have coffee as well," said Lejla with a grin that made her eyes wrinkle. Thinking of the journey across the road I wondered if I'd ever see her or her grin again.

They showed me the bullet holes in their walls, all circled with the dates of impact. Then they showed me the bullets they had collected from the street and from the walls of their flat. Big ones, fat ones, squished ones. They ran their fingers through the shrapnel like digging for sweets in a bowl.

"They shoot bullets made for shooting down airplanes at people," said Selma.

"Big bullets," said Lejla.

"Great," said Selma with a laugh.

The father, who didn't speak English but was eager to make me comfortable, hooked up the VCR to a car battery and played home movies of them skiing before the war. He pointed toward the mountain overlooking the city and said, "1984." I immediately thought of Orwell's classic and nodded my head in agreement.

"The Olympics in 1984. That was when Sarajevo was just perfect," said one of the sisters.

After the ski video they played one of the family, obviously fatter and happier, sitting around this exact room drinking wine and eating a birthday cake. Her face staring at the screen, Lejla gripped my arm. "Here, here, watch."

Nothing happened.

"No, no. Here, here, watch."

On the tape a bullet came through the window and landed in the wall behind the sofa. I looked up from the television to see the hole. In the movie everyone falls to the ground, the camera shakes, but then the person filming regains their nerve and everyone else gets back up and starts eating cake again, pointing at the wall and laughing. It was a home movie of their first bullet.

It was all so damn funny I thought I might cry.

By the time the sisters led me back down to the tunnel it was dark. Again Lejla held my hand, and again it was sweaty.

"So you never answered the question," said Lejla in a softer voice, out of earshot of Selma. "Do you have a girlfriend?"

"It's not an easy answer."

"One in every country?" she asked. I had told them I'd traveled the world with a backpack.

"No, nothing like that. Just one," I said.

"Well, where is she?"

"She's sailing around the world, by herself."

"Oh," said Lejla. She seemed surprized and maybe even disappointed.

Standing at Snipers' Alley I could see the charcoal etching

of the city before us. With no lights the tall shadows of buildings blocked out the views to the mountains. It was as if someone had rubbed out parts of the horizon in black. We stood
under a moonless sky with our arms across our chests to fight
off the chill. Down the street red laser lights took aim at a flat.
I told them I was sleeping in the UNIS towers and they told me
I was crazy, for what seemed the fifteenth time.

"Really though, thank you for the food. It will be wonderful," said Lejla.

"Yes, thank you," said Selma. It was the first time they had
been serious.

Suddenly I wanted to take Lejla by the hand back into the
tunnel and make love on that old worn-out couch. I would kiss
her lush lips and squeeze her bony ass and we would go at it
until we both came in the dark of the tunnels. At the time it felt
like the only possible solution to the war.

"So who's Radovan Karadzic?" I asked instead. Their jaws
dropped as they took a few steps back and looked at each other.
Lejla, her eyes wide open, began slowly to circle me.

"You don't know who Karadzic is?" she asked, astonished.
"You come all the way here from America and you don't know
who Karadzic is?"

"No, I really don't," I said.

"He is the leader of the Chetniks, the Serbs on the hill. The
ones on the hill trying to kill us," said Lejla.

"Oh, the guy with the big hair?" I asked. "I've seen his face
on a poster around town."

"Yes, that is him," said Selma. "Those are war crime posters."

"And Mladic?"

"He is the general of their army," said Lejla, more astonished.

"Karadzic was a psychologist who sometimes held classes
at our university before the war," said Selma.

"Really?"

"And he was also a bad poet," said Selma.

"No one liked his poetry or his wife," said Lejla. "She's very
ugly. And now they are killing everyone for it, or something
like that . . . You really are a strange person, aren't you? Who
are you? Really?"

"Just the guy who crossed the street."

I told them the Road Trip was leaving soon to get more food, but we would return. They invited me to come again for lunch. They told me I didn't need to bring anything, just come back. They said that would make them very happy. After saying my goodbyes I ran across the street. On the other side I turned round to wave one last goodbye, but they had already disappeared into the tunnels.

I walked home taking the back streets. At times I jogged. I laughed out loud. I was overcome by something, something light.

Finally I had found something familiar here, something that spoke to me more than delivering food to people who were living in a seven-by-one-mile graveyard. People here were dying by the truckloads but the ones still living were so alive it was almost blinding to witness. For the first time in a long while I felt like I belonged. But then, of course, I didn't. As a traveler I had certain privileges the locals did not. I could leave, if I wanted, through the front door. If they wanted to leave they had to run across a narrow strip of the airport at night under the watchful eyes of snipers and the UN blockades.

At times it was like a sexual lusting, my hunger for their reality, their experiences. I didn't want to be them, I just wanted to feel their feelings. I wanted to crawl inside each one of them and see through their eyes, feel through their skin. I wanted to reach into their souls. After meeting the sisters I knew nothing would slow down this desire. If anything it promised only to grow. The rush of death didn't thrill me. I already knew I wanted to get out of here, but I wanted to take everyone I had met with me.

True, I felt a little odd being so happy, bouncing along a back alley in a city draped in darkness under the glow of tracer fire. But there it was. I was overwhelmed that I had finally found a place on earth where people were so busy trying to live they didn't have time to think about the dead.

Back at the office Graeme cornered me in the hallway. He was angry I had left the vehicle. I told him I was sorry but I had met these amazing sisters who took me to their house. He told me I was out of line and I agreed, but then I told him more about the sisters.

"They live in a goddamn tunnel and they are laughing and telling stories," I said.

"Are they lookers?" asked Graeme.

"Yeah, yeah . . . Listen, I'm sorry. I fucked up." I was still high on adrenaline from the walk home.

"No worries, mate. Tony doesn't know about it. I told him you were in the basement, but I wondered where you buggered off to."

"Thanks for covering for me."

"So when do we visit them?"

"Who?"

"The sisters."

"Any time."

"Cheers," he said and then we walked into the office and joined the rest for a game of cards, vodka and lemonade and cups of soup.

And the dead? Don't worry about them, they are never far. They're always around to remind us of our ultimate fate. The trick, I had learned, was not holding on so tight to life that you became too scared to live. That was the same as living to die. No. The thing was to live like you had already died.

Of course I couldn't say this to a Sarajevan. I couldn't even tell Graeme. No. What I knew was a secret. And it would take years before I realized that it was this secret that allowed me to do what I was about to do. It was also why I had no fear. And it made me very hard to kill.

25

I believe the reason the crack is still there, the chasm in my chest that seems to have no end, is that I wasn't even there when it happened.

To this day I sometimes wonder if things would have been different if Corrina hadn't told me she thought she might be pregnant. Just the word, pregnant, seems to carry enough weight to shift the course of life. In the dictionary, *Pregnant: carrying a developing fetus within the uterus.* Also, *creative: inventive.* And finally: *heavy with significance or implication.*

Looking back on it from the long telescope of life there are so many details, so many questions, and I have no clearer idea today than I did then. All I know is that something in the timeline of our lives got out of whack.

I had been wandering the hallways of the hospital in Chico for four days waiting for some sign she would walk out of there with me. When I wasn't wandering the halls I was in the intensive care unit looking into other people's rooms listening to the end of their lives. Each room was a novel waiting to be written, a sonnet waiting to be scribbled. The haikus were flooding the floor with small cherry blossoms. And the sounds. The loved ones were moaning, the patients sucking in air and exhaling memories, machines beeping and gurgling as they force-fed life, in liquid form. Flowers piled up in the windows with cards no one would ever read. The hushed screams from darkened rooms. The silent goodbyes. It was all so damn poetic but it was also so damn repetitive. Can't we die some other way than with tubes up our asses and morphine dripping into our veins? I wanted to carry every one of these people in my arms down to the river. I would lay them on a bed of wild flowers and they would hear the red-tailed hawks cry and the fish jump as they moved from Here to There.

That first day I walked the hallways searching the trashcans. Then I checked the dumpsters out back. I almost ended it right there. I had a knife and I put it to my chest. The knot in my chest was unbearable, the cracking of my inside. The only thing that saved me was that the pain was so intense I lost my energy and had to lie down, on the pavement.

I asked several attendants if they had seen her hair. "What's it look like?" Brown hair, I told them. They all said no and quickly returned to their other conversations. How can any one moment in life contain so many levels of reality, and yet when we each glance at the clock it reads the same time?

Finally I found a nurse. "Where is her hair? Why did you cut her hair?"

The nurse looked concerned for my health. "You may want to visit our cafeteria and have a cookie." That's what she said. Have a cookie. And the *hair*? She said they had disposed of it during surgery. That was standard hospital policy.

In the room the nurses were always nice, never rude, but I knew they were being careful not to say the wrong thing. They were instructed not to get too involved in their cases. They asked me about my job, or about her job, or sometimes we just went over the charts, the facts of the case. Either way I wanted them all to leave.

Once Corrina grabbed my thumb. I raced into the nursing station and yelled that she had grabbed my thumb, but they insisted it was an involuntary movement and that she had never woken up after the accident.

The police report said Corrina hit the back of a heavy farm truck doing approximately fifty miles per hour. The driver of the truck was turning left and for some reason she didn't see it. Was she reaching for the radio? Did she fall asleep? Did the brakes fail? Why did I let her drive alone? I knew she was a sleepy driver. That was what she called herself, a sleepy driver.

And where was I that day? I thought we needed some money for our road trip. She had tried to convince me we could make do with what we had. I told her I would be gone for just a month, working on a commercial. The day she had the accident, at that hour, I was on my way back to the hotel. My job that day? My duty that kept me from her? Scrubbing down cars so they would look good in a car commercial. I had told my co-worker I was so in love with Corrina that I just loved to watch her sleep. To hear her breathe herself into dreamland.

On the last night a nurse came in and took my hand. She began to cry. She was shivering. She said, "I have never seen so much love before between two people and I am so sorry." We cried together. After a few moments I asked if I could be alone. Earlier a doctor had told me it was too late to help her. He asked me about organ donations. I told him I would ask her. He seemed to understand what I was saying.

I put my face on Corrina's pale soft stomach and fell into what could best be described as an altered state. I could hear everything in the room but I couldn't move. It was as if I had been given a paralysis drug. My head was still on her stomach and everything was the same, but everything was just a few minutes different, like we were suddenly in some other time. I could hear the nurses milling about. The machines were burping. I was calm, and suddenly and without warning I knew everything. Let me be clear on this. I don't mean physics or long division or the meaning of life. I mean I could feel the world, the entire world, as if it were contained in one large raindrop that just fell on my tongue. It was like being taken through a film of all civilization in a flash of time. I saw empires rise and fall. I saw their hardships, their joys, their victories, and their defeats. I saw a million babies crying, stars becoming supernova, mountains forming, rivers gushing. I saw the first laugh.

Corrina was here. I mean she was in the room, in this other time, resting on my back. It was heavy, like she was sleeping there. And then she hugged me. My body was scared to feel her again. I was confused. Her long wavy hair fell before my eyes. It was more real than the feel of this keyboard as I type years later. She leaned over, and whispered into my ear. *"Keep traveling. See the world and come tell me stories when you are done."* Her breath was shallow but warm on my neck. I breathed deeply, trying to capture each molecule of her air.

When I lifted my head I felt my cheek. Tears streamed down. My breath was deep but slow. I was a balloon slowly hissing out air on its long journey into the blazing sun. Rising far above the earth I looked down at all the people. They looked like ants fumbling over one another, and they all needed each other more than they could ever explain. And it was so beautiful.

I walked down the stairs and into the street. It was a hot night and people nearby were talking about a movie they'd seen last night. They made plans for dinner next Friday evening. "Nothing concrete," they said, "let's just plan on something." They hugged and parted ways. Once out of sight of their friends the man took his hand away from his wife and told her to get in the car.

I was an empty vessel, a walking spirit.

Still rising. I passed the smiling moon as it peaked over the Sierra Mountains. Or was it a frown? It was like a lantern on an empty ship drifting on the river Hades. Or was it the Light, the light at the end of the world? All I had to do was reach up and go through the moonhole to get to the other side, to her.

I walked for a few miles until I reached the banks of the Big Chico Creek. It was dawn when I put my feet in the cold water and watched the sun rise. How did the sun possibly find the strength to rise that day, of all days? And the worst thought of all: how many more sunrises would I have to witness with Corrina not here and me not there?

And so it had come to be. Everything I had tried didn't work. I had begged God for days on end, but finally I couldn't stop the large hand from moving forward. Corrina Essence Barton, born under a quicksilver moon, died that morning as the sun rose.

It wasn't until weeks later when I woke up hungry and shivering in a cave somewhere in the Utah desert that I realized she had died on 19 June, exactly one year to the day from when we first met.

26

This much I know. Grief produces an abundant energy that must find a way to burn itself up. And that is the fundamental problem, one it can take a lifetime to exhaust.

And death changes things. Small things. Like the color of the sky and the sound of people's voices. At first all incoming signals are dulled as if your skin is numb. Then at some point, which I'm sure is different for everyone, all the body's senses become hypersensitive. Therein lies the paradox. Grief: the act of letting sorrow flow freely can be so overwhelming that many push it away in the hope it will just disappear, which of course it can't, won't, doesn't. Not until it has run its course. The truth, which is rarely admitted in Western cultures, is that grief has a way of making you feel more alive. Not necessarily with a shit-eating grin, but more *aware* of being alive. The only constant is the pain in your chest. A gnawing thud in the middle of your chest that feels like a soul being ripped apart. The screaming is so loud that some days I was sure people could hear my skin wailing.

Grief also has a particular weight. At times it feels like you are floating in the Dead Sea, suspended by a bath of sticky salt. You are just there flat on your back listening to the roar of your own breath, staring into the sun, watching shadows of birds cross your line of sight. At those times death feels light, as if it almost makes sense.

Then comes the advice. Family, strangers, women all told me that time was the only true healer, that in time I would move on and find another.

That's when the weight of grief feels like someone strapped a refrigerator on your back and told you to walk to Mexico, in the summer.

After six months and 6,000 miles from Montana to New Mexico I ended up at the San Francisco international airport and bought a ticket to Trinidad. There, I found myself in love with every woman, young or old, married or not. I was in love with them for as long as I sat across from them. I fell in love with men too, but I had no inclination to touch them. With women, sex was a device to connect with the promise of neverland. A way to be temporarily suspended, neither here nor there, in blissful nothing. I wanted sex everywhere and with everyone. I wanted to eat everyone alive, not to hurt them, but to fondle every part of love they had inside them. I wanted to reach up through whichever hole I could and tickle their soul from the inside out. Maybe God lived in there and if so maybe there was a way to talk with Corrina.

After New Mexico and Trinidad I wound up in the Amazon of Venezuela. I spent time at a place called the Abysmo, the Abyss. It was a cliff edge that looked 1,000 feet into the Amazon basin. There aren't many places on the planet where you can stand and feel you are on the "edge" of the world. This was one. The locals told me it was a popular place for people to commit suicide, by jumping into a pit of lush vegetation. Sure, I considered it, but I could never overcome another force, residing deep within: I had a desire to live, even if it felt empty at times. Besides, I had made a promise to Corrina three weeks prior to her death.

We were in Chico, sitting in the van, under a clear moonless night.

"Do you believe in ghosts?" she asked.

"Yeah, I guess, more like a presence, not the white sheet kind," I said.

Then she asked what would happen if one of us were to die.

"If I die," I said, "you should live a rocking life and in fifty years I'll bring you across."

She said she didn't know what she would do if I died. Then we made a deal. We thought suicide meant that the other person would have to live in a state of being able to see the one they love, but unable to touch or interact with them. Forever. So death at my own hands was out of the question. In fact any conscious act likely to bring about my death was out of the question. The only option I had was to live so fiercely that I might one day get caught off guard and slip.

In Venezuela I broke out in a rash of red dots from head to toe. My insides were coming out. After a week the rash still hadn't gone away and I hadn't slept more than an hour a night. I covered my body in various creams and lotions, none of which worked, but it did give me a ghost-like appearance. And this only had the effect of frightening the locals. In one village the police put me in a holding cell and fed me bean soup. They said I "had the curse."

Finally, with help from a pension owner, I caught a bus headed for the Colombian border. My skin was a combination of red from the rash and white from the creams. Everywhere I went, the locals avoided eye contact and kept their animals clear of my seat. It was the first and last time while traveling by bus in an underdeveloped country that I had a seat to myself.

Months later, after flying to Miami and then driving the southern route across the States, I found myself standing on cliffs in northern California looking into the Pacific Ocean. More than a year and a half had passed since I had spread Corrina's ashes here. I arched my head up toward the foggy gray sky.

God. This is Bill here. So, now what? You give us life so we can love, then lose it and live with the pain? That's it? I mean if that's all you got going on down here it's a pretty fucking raw deal. I have an idea: I'll quit bugging you if you send Corrina down. We'll call it all square.

There was no answer, but . . . there was an old woman.

Walking along the cliff edge, she stopped twenty feet behind me. There it was again. That same feeling I had in the hospital, when I knew everything, felt everything. Again, it lasted only a few seconds but it was utterly complete. I turned and the old woman was trembling. She was crying.

"I lost my husband of fifty years last year to cancer."

"I know." And I did. There are but a few times in a life when we see everything in perfect clarity, like when the desert night slips into a perfect blue dawn or being the sole human watching humpback whales cruising a Mexican lagoon at dusk. I felt everything she was going to say ahead of time. Except this.

She took my hands in her hands. She stared straight into my eyes.

"Even though I was with him for fifty years, him dying

wasn't the hard part. We were prepared. The hard part is to keep on living."

"I think that is my problem," I said.

"All I can tell you is this: to keep on living one must keep on loving," she said.

Her eyes were sparkling and her face was fragile but strong, like she'd been staring into the wind for a lifetime. Smiling.

"Don't ever stop that part of you. Love is the only thing we have to connect us to everything here and beyond," she said.

Then she turned and walked back up the coast. She did not turn round. The sunset stretched out like a bruised tattoo on the horizon. Sometimes happiness comes in hushed colors. And when it does there's no way to explain it.

It was then that I spent the last of my money on a ticket to Europe.

I had a friend, Jason Aplon, who was working in Split. He was involved somehow in the Bosnian war. On the phone his voice was depressed. I asked him what was going on.

"It's completely insane here. I feel like I can't do anything to change anything. The powers that be know what is happening but no one will do anything to stop it . . . Bill, what are you thinking?"

"Nothing."

"This isn't the right place for you."

"What do you mean?"

"Don't come here. You are not in a good place to be here."

"Don't worry. I'm fine."

"Promise you won't come here."

"I promise," I said with a deep sense of calm.

A month later, after landing in Luxembourg, I hitched across Europe and caught a train in Salzburg. I crossed the Slovenian border some time after midnight and woke up on a bench in Zagreb when an armed soldier poked my stomach with his rifle. "Off," he said.

The temperature was just below freezing. From there I caught a ride on a bus with American Christian missionaries on their way to deliver medicine to Bosnia. But first they were going to pray at Medjugorje, a pilgrimage destination in Herzegovina, traditionally a Croatian part of Bosnia. They said that at Medjugorje there was a mural where blood flows from the eyes of Mother Mary. They tried to preach to me, but I acted like I was asleep. I knew the bleeding Mary was all tricks and gimmicks set up to sell Christian kitsch, but it made me wonder. Why would God create human beings only to watch them destroy each other?

In Split the rising sun cast an orange glow on the Adriatic Sea. Standing on the seashore it felt like I was looking back at something. Something over there. It was cold but I felt good, like I was doing the right thing.

Jason drove up, got out of the car, and shut the door. He walked over and extended his hand.

Shaking his head he said, "What took you so long?"

27

It was toward the end of April, three weeks since we first arrived in Sarajevo, and I wanted to leave the city for the simplest of reasons. I wanted a shower. I wanted water with ice. I wanted a steak and a cold beer. I wanted not to have bullets hitting the wall above my bed. I wanted complete silence. And perhaps most of all I wanted not to look into the eyes of people I couldn't help. The reasons to stay were fewer but much more compelling, the main one being the feeling that I was living in a place with a lack of linear time.

This was the secret of Sarajevo. In Bosnia there was no past and no future. The past had been blown to smithereens and the future was only as long as the present moment lasted. Buddhists would call this living in the Bardo State. Christians might say you have attained spiritual oneness with the Holy Ghost. Sufis may determine you have finally eliminated the barriers between you and God. And that was the odd thing. In the middle of death there was a calming presence. One cup of coffee. One liter of water. One spoonful of rice. Her smile. His jokes. Simple acts, simple pleasures and then blow out the candle, the day was done.

So, with the erasure of time the outside world began to slip away and the timelessness of the many had erased the death of the one. It's not a lie. There were moments I envisioned living here, in this suspended time, the rest of my life. But I knew that would take some planning.

Meanwhile the warehouse had become empty. It was time to leave.

But leaving wasn't going to be simple. By mid-April 1993 the war in central Bosnia had changed. Since our arrival in the city central Bosnia had been turned into a killing field of its own. In the beginning of the Bosnian war, fifteen months prior, the Croats and Bosnians had fought side by side against the Serbs, but in April 1993 the Croats opted out of the alliance and decided to get a piece of the land pie for themselves. They turned on the Bosnian army.

There were reports that the Croats were rounding up men by the thousands in Mostar and other towns across central Bosnia. Camps were set up, and this was about the time pictures began arriving in the Western media of emaciated Bosnian men clutching barbed-wire fences. Meanwhile the Serbs must have been laughing as they watched their two enemies burn, rape and kill each other with a brutality they thought only they possessed. They had become turkey vultures on a busy desert highway, perched on a tree branch waiting for the inevitable road kills.

Seeking information on the status of the roads, Graeme and I drove out to the UN headquarters at the airport. The United Nations officer, Reinaldo from Colombia, laughed when I asked him the best way to travel back to Croatia.

"Oh, I don't know." He offered Graeme coffee. "It seems that staying in Sarajevo is now safer than driving in Bosnia. That is something, no?"

I had to admit it was something.

"But, friends, let me tell you, please don't come to Colombia, it is even more dangerous," he said.

The plan was simple. We would divide the convoy based upon fuel supplies. We siphoned petrol from Ragga, our Land Rover, and gave it to the trucks, which would give those drivers enough to make it to the high road, through Zenica. This was a safer route. There they would wait on the side of the road until they could tag along with a UN convoy escorted by British Warrior tanks. By doing this they could bypass Prozor and Mostar, towns which were reportedly in chaos. With just enough fuel left to go back to Fojnica, Graeme, Tony, Christophe, Josh and I would take Ragga and drive to the home of Achman, the teenager we had befriended on our last visit there. His parents were the ones who had allowed us to put our fifty-gallon drums of fuel in the basement. We would fill up and be only a day or so behind the others. We would meet at the pension on the beach.

The going-away party was ripping. Vlado and the Missionaries showed up with beers and guitars and played Frank Zappa tunes. We opened the last of the vodka and the French brought a couple of balls of hash. We lit enough candles to make the room look like a Chinese opium den. Everyone's faces were full of life, as if we had just been shined and polished and were now basking in a sepia glow. It was glorious. The buzz was on and from time to time guys from the Trip would hug some of the locals and tell them, "We'll be back as soon as we can." The Australians tried like hell to get a couple of local girls high on booze and steer them into the bedroom. But no luck there. It seemed that even in war there were standards.

At one point Vlado pulled me into the hallway.

"So when are you coming back?"

"I'm not sure, but we will."

"I think you will come back."

"Why do you say that?" I asked, curious as to what Vlado could see. Because good or bad, drunk or sober, people near to death see things. It might be a two-headed monster or some evil unknown, but they see something.

"You are comfortable here."

"I'm thinking of bringing a video camera. Maybe make a documentary. Stay alive and you can be my first subject," I said.

"Cool," he said.

Before we went back into the room I asked, "You want anything from outside?"

"Just make it back. That is the most important." He turned toward the door. But before he had taken two steps he stopped and turned round. "Actually, maybe you can bring me a guitar pick. I am down to one."

Heading back to the party I let Vlado walk through the door first. I stopped and slipped into the cover of the dark stairwell. I held my hands to my eyes. Tears were bursting out. In all this, the only thing he asked for was a single guitar pick. I really hope the meek do inherit the damn earth. But sometimes I'm afraid they will get bought out.

The next day we loaded up. There was only one remaining question. What were we going to do about the Jews?

28

"What did the Jews say?" asked Graeme as Tony returned from a meeting with someone representing a Belgian Jewish organization operating in Sarajevo.

"Only their people," said Tony.

"Fuck 'em," was Graeme's reply.

"Mind you, we could use the money, mate," said Tony.

"Fuck 'em," yelled Graeme. "Either they are in for everyone or they are fucking liars and skidders. Fuck 'em."

The Belgians had offered us a wad of money and fuel if we smuggled out five Jewish Sarajevan citizens in our trucks. They told us they had already paid off the Serbs at the checkpoints and there was absolutely no risk. Of course these same people were the ones who flew in and out of Sarajevo on UN blue cards, avoiding the checkpoints.

In the true spirit of the Trip the counteroffer to the Belgians had been quid pro quo. We offered to take their five people as long as they also arranged the escape for two Muslims, two Serbs, and one Croat, roughly equal to the ratio of people living in besieged Sarajevo. It had been Graeme's idea. Of course. Our moral warrior. He was always looking to "find out where everyone stands on this." With Tony still stammering on a solution, Graeme jumped in Ragga. Everyone followed, climbing into the trucks. No one dared question Graeme's lead. We'd leave the Jews behind.

Anticipating a search at the checkpoint, I had hidden my film in various places over several vehicles—under the steering-wheel column, in the seat liner, in the bottom of dirty socks. I had shot seventeen rolls and figured if they found it the Serbs would take the film just because it was there.

Stopped on the road going into Sarajevo was a white UN-PROFOR Land Rover and several UN aid vehicles. Behind them were armed UN soldiers in armored cars. Behind them was a car which had PRESS written across the window in black duct tape. We stood on the side of the road while soldiers searched the interior of our trucks. They didn't search very hard and seemed bored, as if everything had lost meaning.

They took some of our bags and put them through an X-ray machine. A skinny young guard took my camera out of the bag and held it up like he was carrying the Olympic torch.

"Why do you have this camera?" he asked.

I figured since it was so obvious, lying would be pointless. I told him I was taking pictures in Sarajevo.

Another guard, one of the ones who had checked out our trucks three weeks ago, told the skinny guard not to worry about it. This only pissed off the young man further. He stormed out of the building and returned accompanied by a fat guard with thick jowls and a bushy beard. His hair was long and by the looks of him he was a classic example of what Bosnians called a Chetnik.

Three guards gathered around the fat one, clearly indicating that this man was the head honcho at this checkpoint. It seemed like a moment for a speech. Through an interpreter, the fat guard spoke.

"This camera is not allowed in Sarajevo."

"I am not taking it into Sarajevo. I am taking it out of Sarajevo," I said. Note: logic, man's last defense against insanity, is useless at most of the world's checkpoints.

"You must declare this camera when entering Sarajevo in order to take it out."

Tony produced a copy of our manifest. The camera was on the list, indicating I had declared it on the way in. This seemed to confuse them, so they had a short meeting among themselves.

"You must leave it here. This can be used for spying on Serb positions," the man said. Meltdown. I wanted to point out that logically it was the film he wanted, for it was the exposed film that might be dangerous to the war effort. Not the camera. But I knew he really wanted the camera to sell. The film and the spying were of no interest to them.

"So you are a bunch of fucking thieves, is that it?" Tony yelled. "You tell us to declare it, he did, and now you want to steal it. You don't care about the manifest. It's all bullshit. You just want to sell it on the black market in Belgrade. You fat fuck thief."

The interpreter stopped translating after the first few words. There was, as they say, a pregnant pause. Then the interpreter quietly asked Tony if he meant what he said. Tony said, "You're fucking right I do. He's just a fucking thief."

"Do you want to go to jail?" asked the interpreter, who by this time had stepped closer to us, so his eyes and mouth were out of sight of the commanding officer. "Because if I tell him everything you just said you will all be going to jail."

"He's a thief," said Tony, losing steam.

"I don't recommend our jails."

The officer barked out something and the meek translator turned to us. "We will take you to the office and give you a receipt for your camera."

We followed them across the road, crossing in front of the

UN troops and their 50-caliber machine guns. We weren't UN-accredited human beings, and thus we weren't covered by the UN mandate of protection. How odd that the Serbs knew they could massacre us in front of them and the only thing that would happen would be some Geneva bureaucrat would make a report on the incident. Of course an official complaint would be registered with Karadzic's office in Pale. The US embassy would pass on condolences to my family and there would be a small story in the local paper of how a local boy trying to make good died in an accident in Bosnia. Pathetic.

The officer put the camera and an extra lens in a shoebox while he made out a receipt. "You may reclaim this camera in Banja Luka," said the interpreter. Banja Luka, located in the northern part of Bosnia, was the stronghold of the Bosnian Serbs. It was like a Mexican cop at the border taking your valuables and telling you to reclaim them in Mexico City. The camera was already gone. The officer smiled and waved us out of the office.

I crossed the road, still looking in curiosity at the UN soldiers. Tony dropped a camera lens in my hand. "Just a little souvenir I picked up when I was shopping recently," he said. It was my lens. He had stolen it back from the box in the officer's office.

Although it was still early in the afternoon, by the time we stopped in Kiseljak the clouds were hovering on the horizon and the day was slipping into a veil of darkness. There was the smell of smoldering smoke and fuel in the air. In town a Canadian UN tank rumbled in the other direction. Then another. It was ominous and felt like something was going to go very wrong. All the stores were closed but we did spot an armored BBC truck parked outside a shut-down café. Graeme jumped out and went inside.

"This doesn't feel right," said Christophe.

"It feels like shit hitting the fan," said Josh.

"I wonder if Fojnica is already history," I said.

"Then we are royally fucked," Tony said.

"He's probably drinking a goddamn beer in there," said Christophe, looking impatiently at the café.

Graeme walked out the door. A girl followed him.

"He can't even wait until we are out of this mess," said Tony.

Graeme opened the back door.

"This is Valerie. She's French, but don't hold that against her. We're giving her a ride," said Graeme, throwing in a handful of double-A batteries. "They'll never miss them."

Turned out the Frenchwoman had been traveling with a German humanitarian group that had been robbed by the Serb guards at the checkpoint that morning. For some reason she had got out at this café as the Germans drove into central Bosnia looking for something to do. She didn't say much, but she did say she thought the Germans "were a bit strange." Later, after some vodka, she corrected herself, saying the Germans were "absolute fucking crazy fucking stupid fucking idiots."

At first sight Fojnica seemed just like we'd left it. The streets had innocence to them, as if Christmas was just around the corner. The snow fell in soft bunches and people's breath floated away in gusts of white mist. Of course no one knew what was about to happen. How could they? How could we?

At Achman's house his parents brought us beers and cooked us chicken and prepared cabbage salads.

"Well, it looks a bit dodgy," said Graeme as we sat around the table breaking bread. "The BBC bloke said Kiseljak is going to blow before nightfall. If that happens we won't have any way out of here."

We talked about our options. The French girl said nothing. She had a long nose and dark eyebrows. She smiled from time to time, but otherwise she stared beyond any of us, toward the window. Her lower lip was slightly bee-stung swollen and her eyelashes were dark.

That night we filled our whiskey glasses and ate like warriors back from the fields of Sparta. The world might have been falling down outside but that night we owned our existence in totality, not something most people do but for a few times in their life. That feeling that every cell in your body is tingling with electric awareness. The sips of red wine felt like our own blood dripping down our throats. The incidental touch of another against your skin felt like the rawest of emotions being transmitted through the tiny hairs on your arm. An itch became a sudden acute awareness that we were still alive. It was the same feeling as grief, alive but with one foot in the grave. Every word crackled with reminders that it could be the last word ever spoken.

And yes, all of us were keeping an eye on the French-woman.

The radio squawked from the corner and Achman translated for us. It said the Croats had taken Kiseljak and were now advancing toward Fojnica. By ten o'clock that night two more villages were on fire. The killing wave was now seven kilometers away and closing.

In this war, as in most wars, it mattered where you were standing. In Sarajevo the danger was every second, every minute and every hour of every day, but it was from an external threat. The person next to you was in the same danger so there was a common bond, regardless of ethnic background. In central Bosnia towns were decaying from the inside out. Towns were being divided up overnight. It mattered who was a Croat, who was a Serb and who was a Muslim, and what mattered most was where you slept. That was our problem. We were in a Muslim home on the Croatian side of town. Since the Croats had the upper hand this house would be among the first to burn.

Yet the night passed without incident. The next morning Christophe and I volunteered to go to the amputee hotel to see if the phone still worked. The locals told us to be careful. Croat snipers were rumored to have taken positions on the hills.

On the way out of the door Graeme gave me a long strong hug.

"Not like running for vodka, is it?" He laughed and held on to me for several seconds. His face seemed sad, a child lost in a railway station. We had shared blankets, chocolate, baby food, and our booze. We had shared secrets and a couple of moments of absolute fear, when a man can be excused for wetting his pants.

I came here thinking I just might die by mistake, which would have been acceptable, but now I wanted to live. It had started with meeting Graeme. Then the rest of the Road Trip, because even though I didn't get along with all of them there was no doubt that we were in this together. Then Vlado. Then the sisters and their family. Caring: it can get in the way sometimes.

For some reason, still inexplicable, the phone in the hotel worked. We connected with the UN security forces in Sarajevo. The man on the other end spoke English like he was Danish or Dutch or maybe Norwegian or Swedish.

"No. No, we are not in Sarajevo," yelled Christophe. "We are six internationals in Fojnica in a soft-shelled car."

"Why are you driving a soft shell?"

"What?"

"That is an improper car to drive in this war zone."

"Yes, I know. Can you come and get us today? The town is beginning to divide."

"You shouldn't be in Fojnica. The only road in and out has been taken by HVO. All the villages have been compromised and they are advancing."

"Yes, yes, we know. We need you to come in an APC and pick us up. I don't think we have long."

"You are right."

"You will come?"

"No. We cannot do that."

"Why did you say I was right?"

"I was confirming you won't have long. My advice is to obtain a hard shell and drive away from the area as fast as you can."

That was, as they say, that. The United Nations were doing what they do best, avoiding confrontation. Next plan.

We decided it was time to negotiate with both sides. Tony went to the local Croatian army headquarters and I agreed to visit the Bosnian army headquarters. Our idea was to talk to the commanders, who probably knew each other from the weekly soccer matches, who sat in buildings within sight of one another, but who were now fully prepared in the next hundred hours to decimate each other and each other's families.

Two soldiers with machine guns, dressed in army trousers

and thick winter coats, showed me into the commanding officer's quarters. I was in a large ornate square room with tall ceilings and tall windows. Of course there was no electricity. The sunlight was dim at best and threw a gray pallor over the room. It looked like it might rain inside. The desk was the size of a small car. The commanding officer had a thick black mustache and long skinny fingers. On the table were charts, maps, and what looked like a long list of phone numbers. He spoke English so I told him our situation and asked for his advice on the best way to leave town.

"You of course understand that Tito was a great man," he said. Marshal Tito, the revered leader of former Yugoslavia, seemed to have had an ability to hold together this region plagued by intra-nationalist hatred.

"Yes. He was a car mechanic in Vienna when he was twenty," I said, hoping to disguise what little knowledge I had. "And Stalin, Lenin, Trotsky, and Hitler were all in Vienna at the same time, all as young men."

The commander stared long and hard at me. He screwed up his face and cocked his head to one side. Then whatever it was passed.

"Do you think we are barbarians?" He had a thick accent, which made him sound like a drunk Russian speaking English.

"Not at all. I think you are very normal people living in abnormal times."

He poured himself a cup of coffee and made me one. I told him I didn't drink coffee but he put the coffee in front of me anyhow.

"I believe the Chicago Bulls will win. Do you agree?" he said and lit a Camel cigarette.

"Who?"

"Michael Jordan is too good for anyone right now."

"He does seem to be the man right now."

He motioned at one of the soldiers, who left the room, leaving us alone. We talked of sports and the movies. He talked about *The Godfather* and *Scarface*. He especially liked Al Pacino in his role as the tough Cuban drug lord.

The same soldier who had showed me into the room returned and spread out a map on the desk.

"Please, my American friend, come and I will show you something," said the commander. I moved around the desk until his pistol grazed my leg.

"Do you see this?" He pointed to a small red line on a topo map. "This is what the United Nations call Salmon Run. It is a dirt road that runs from the back of Fojnica, behind the Muslim quarter, and over the mountain pass."

"I see."

"It is a dangerous road," he said.

"I understand."

"Do you have the appropriate car?" he asked. "The pass is covered in snow."

"We have a Land Rover."

"Then there is only one problem left. I can tell you our guards are at the pass so you will have no difficulty there. But after our checkpoint the Croats are five kilometers down the road. And of course I do not have any control over their actions."

"Thank you for this information. I wish there was something I could do for you."

"Well, there is nothing," he said. Then he corrected himself. "Actually there is something."

"What's that?"

"Tell your President Clinton we don't need his army. We don't need anything, but we need the world not to help the Serbs. Do you understand what I am saying?"

"I can't promise he'll listen to me, but I'll try."

He laughed. "Yes, promise to do your best."

"I promise."

After dinner we gathered in Tony's room for beers and chocolate. Josh rolled drum cigarettes for everyone. The conversation focused on the guns and grenades Achman's father placed near our doors. He had said we might need them this night.

"We gotta get out of here," said Christophe. His voice was full of fear. All of ours were.

"I didn't come here to kill people," said Tony. "I already got a bloody war back home."

"I didn't either. But if some Croat bastard comes in here to kill us then I'm going to defend myself," said Graeme. I agreed with Graeme. I said I didn't come here to fight, but I wasn't going to die at the hands of some nineteen-year-old soldier who wouldn't even bother to turn the lights on before he put a dagger in my liver.

"I do not believe I can fire a weapon," said Christophe. That was believable considering he was technically AWOL from the French army.

"I do not believe dying here would be useful to anyone," said the Frenchwoman.

Christophe said something in French to her. They argued.

Josh was talking to Achman and I noticed his demeanor had changed. Josh was acting like a mental patient on lithium. His smile wasn't the usual smart-ass crack he walked around with. He was actually smiling like he cared, but more likely he was just scared. He kept asking Achman questions like "Have you ever been to the ocean?" Or "When's your birthday?" I suspected it was Josh's way of ignoring the quickly arriving future. Achman, a smart kid, sat at the end of the bed, near the radio, interpreting the news. An HVO roadblock had been set up one mile from town. They were now 1,500 meters away.

The family who had given us shelter hadn't traveled outside this village since the war began, almost two years before. They didn't know what was coming. They couldn't know. That's how war is: the people in the center of the war are quite often the last to grasp what is happening to them. We weren't so lucky. We had driven all over the country and in and out of decimated villages. We were the travelers in this village and therefore had tales from the outside world. The question was, would telling our stories do any good to the locals?

All of us knew that this village was going to be ethnically cleansed within days.

"We can't leave this house," said Josh. He nodded his head toward Achman. "What about the family?"

"Listen. We all want to help but if we stay and kill people

then there's no going back. We would have blood on our hands. That's not why I came here. It's not why you came here. Besides, if we fight we might all die," said Tony.

Achman spoke. "He is right. This is not your war."

I have thought of that statement and Achman many times in the years that have passed. "This is not your war." If this was not our war, then whose was it? His? A sixteen-year-old's? As far as I could tell it was less his war than it was mine, or more accurately all of ours. I, and so many from the outside world, had had the opportunity to see the UN not doing their job, and had watched the press spin stories for the best headline, and watched politicians hem and haw over what the best "course of action" would be.

Achman was right, it was not our war, but it would still be our disgrace, our shame. The West was willing to declare war over the price of oil, but when it came to the wholesale slaughter of human beings we folded our hands across our chests and tapped our heels, with great anticipation that Sunday's sporting events would be wonderfully entertaining.

In the morning, before the sun had crested the mountains, we packed the Rover and said our goodbyes. It was still below freezing but there wasn't a cloud in the sky. We gave Achman's father a hundred German marks and what was left of the fuel after we had filled the tank.

The road up the mountain was a rugged dirt track that eventually turned into a thin layer of snow. Thick forests of pine trees crowded both sides. The only conversation was Josh explaining why we should have stayed and fought. And that somehow got him onto talking about hunting deer with automatic weapons.

"Someone ain't gonna tell me what kind of gun I can't own. Who says I can't hunt deer with an AK-47?"

"Shut up," said Graeme, reflecting the tension in the car.

Once we reached the pass the problems mounted quickly. The snow was three feet deep. At the checkpoint the Bosnian guards greeted us by running out from behind a tree and pointing their guns in our window. When they learned we were foreigners they invited us to join them around their fire. They were drunk on brandy and eating some kind of charred meat. Still, the real problem was at the peak of the pass, where, in the middle of the road, two trucks were stuck in the snow. We walked down the road to get a closer look at the trucks. The first one had brandy in it, the cargo covered by a canvas tarp. As we approached the second truck, further down the road, it was moving, rocking slightly from side to side. We approached slowly.

It was full of pigs, their snouts and asses squeezed against the railing.

"Right, Tony, you talk to the geezers." Graeme pointed at me. "Bill, drive me down the hill. I saw something back there we can use."

I drove down the hill to a farm. Graeme convinced the farmer to let him borrow his tractor. It was a sight . . . An Englishman with earrings and electric orange hair driving a tractor up the hill in central Bosnia. The Bosnian guards up top grabbed their guns and ran, ready to shoot at the noise coming up the hill. Maybe they thought it was a tank. When they saw Graeme they buckled in laughter. One motioned that he was going to piss his pants.

We hooked up the tractor to the brandy truck but ultimately it was no use. The snow was up to our knees. Then for a few hours the tractor was stuck and we had to hook up the Rover to the tractor to pull it out of the snow. This took all day and we only managed to move the truck a couple of yards. With just a few hours of daylight left we agreed to go back to town and spend another night. The gamble was this: were beds and blankets worth dying for? At this point, in freezing temperatures, they were.

In town we rounded up Achman and his friends and had a soccer match on a small patch of grass down by the hotel. As we ran around the field, parents stood by half smiling with their arms crossed. They seemed relieved their kids were having a laugh. The noise echoing in the background was the rattle of artillery coming from over the hill in Busovaca. It wasn't a threat, yet.

We beat the kids 8–7.

That night we didn't discuss the pros and cons of shooting people. We took shifts standing guard with Achman and his father downstairs by the door. They gave us machine guns, shotguns and grenades. I drew the long straw and was elected to sleep the first shift.

I quickly fell into a dream of Corrina down by the river. She was washing her face in the water but I couldn't see her irises. Her eyes were just solid black, like mirrors.

Sweating, I propped myself up. I had forgotten where I was. The windows had small flakes of ice crusting at the edge of the glass. Somewhere in the house I heard laughter but didn't recognize the voice. There were heavy steps on the wooden floor downstairs. I lay back down.

Someone sat down on the end of the bed and began caressing my leg. The hand moved up my thigh.

"It's me," said the voice.

"Corrina?"

"Who's that?" the voice asked. It was Valerie, the Frenchwoman.

"Oh. I was dreaming."

The moon was bright and I could see her body as she took off her trousers and sweater. Her waist was thin but she had a round bottom, and she had small but full breasts that curved upward. She crawled under the sheets. She lay against me for a few moments. Her sweat smelled of lilacs and fear and alcohol. In the silence I could hear her breathing. Fast, through her nose.

"Do you wish to fuck me?" she whispered with tenderness.

I muttered something.

"If this is the last night of my life I want to make love," she said.

"Why me?"

"'Cause your eyes. They don't look scared. They look calm."

In the moonlight the whites of her eyes looked like hot steel.

"Make love to me," she said.

Her on top, me on top, from behind, from the side. We rode each other as if our lives depended on how furious our passion was. We held each other tight and called out names that were not each other's. Names of past loves? Perhaps of loves meant to come. It wasn't perfect, but it seemed like what people are supposed to do when they reach the end of their world.

Afterward we fell asleep. I woke a few times to hear cocks crowing, but it wasn't daylight. It almost seemed like I was a boy again, back on the farm waiting for first light so I could walk into the orchards and water the trees before school. Later that night the door opened and a candle entered the room. I saw a figure with a gun. I reached for the machine gun next to the bed.

"Easy, skidder," whispered Graeme. "Your shift."

The French girl was asleep and for the briefest of moments her breathing seemed like the one I had lost. I put on my coat and walked to the door.

"Well then," said Graeme, raising his eyebrows, "that's cozy."

For the rest of the night I leaned against the front door watching cars with Croatian license plates cruise the street. I had a shotgun against my leg and in my pocket two grenades. Achman had the machine gun; he swapped once I told him I didn't know how to fire an automatic weapon, but had hunted with a shotgun as a kid.

To keep awake, Achman told stories of fishing in the mountains and asked question after question about America. No matter where you travel in this world, no matter how bad the war or how dark the jail cell, they all want to know if America is really everything it's supposed to be.

"You are from California?" he asked.

"Yes."

"Do any movie stars live on your street?"

"No. They live somewhere else. It's a big state."

I told him I once lived in a place where I could surf in the morning and then drive four hours to snow-ski before the sun went down, which I figured was enough to let his imagination take over.

Soon the blue sun crept over the hills. Achman said the danger had passed, at least for now. Finally I shut my eyes.

"Maybe one day I will visit America," he said.

"You will be welcome."

"Are you going to leave now?"

"I think so."

"OK," he said. "Good luck." He turned and walked away.

That next day, just after the break of dawn, it was strangely quiet on the streets. No one was outside except soldiers, some in uniform and some not. Some carried machine guns and others carried bazookas. At this point the only way of telling Croats from Bosnians was if they were driving a car. Each group had their own colored license plates. As for distinguishing the people in the street, there was no use in trying. Tony put the Rover in gear and the rest of us, still covered in dried mud from the day before, stared out the back window.

The sight was innocent but sobering. Achman running after us in his pink high-top basketball shoes, with the laces untied. He was smiling, waving us goodbye. That was the last night before the war arrived in his hamlet. His face seemed so innocent, so ready for what might come. I looked at Graeme. Both of us had tears in our eyes. So did Tony and Christophe and Josh and Valerie.

We all wanted Achman to get in the car with us. Tall for his age and slightly round with baby fat, Achman didn't have that hyped-up desperate energy that the teenagers in Sarajevo had. For him it was always good enough to tag along a few steps back. I imagined I was having the same nightmare as everyone else: Achman with his throat cut, lying on the ground like a bloated pig, with his pink Chuck Conner high-tops perfectly still.

Graeme yelled at Tony, "Come on then, turn up the music." Tony turned it up full blast. We passed children along the road in the Muslim sector of town. Some waved and some chased after us yelling for bonbons. We just stared out the window and drove like scared schoolboys up Salmon Run.

Using the tractor and the Land Rover, it was noon before we pulled the brandy truck out of the way. But we still had the pig truck. Josh and I had begun feverishly cutting down branches and collecting fallen timber to build a sort of bypass bridge over the snow, around the truck. At one point a Bosnian guard came running down the road waving his arms. He was yelling something but we couldn't make it out. We kept grabbing large slabs of wood.

Finally the guard got close enough. "Mines. Mines. Mines," he yelled. We had been stomping around in a minefield.

After slowly retracing our steps back to the road we kept scraping for lumber, but were careful to keep our feet on the track. We reached for any wood within arm's length. Finally we had a small covering of wood in a bent line around the truck. Graeme drove the Rover around it, over the logs. As we left, there were the pigs, their heads resting on the back gate and squealing at us, as if begging for a lift out of there.

Ten minutes later we passed through the Croat checkpoint but there were no soldiers. It took us less than a minute to drive through a camp full of fuel tankers and large artillery guns. We passed jeeps, armored cars and rocket launchers. Still not one person. Later we would joke that we had driven through during their lunch hour.

There's still a part of me that believes we were granted a temporary suspension of time that afternoon. What else could it be? Luck? Of course not. I've never believed in luck. All I know is that for a window of forty-five seconds on that mountain ridge, everything around us stopped and we slipped through the hangman's noose. To this day I laugh to myself when I realize all this happened on a dirt track called Salmon Run. Was She involved? One can never be certain, but it sure felt like more than luck. It felt like we had ridden on the wings of an angel.

After several more hours of driving the weather turned hot as we dropped over the geological divide between Bosnia and Croatia. Down the hills into Croatia, the land of leisure and tourists. Just over the border, roadside cafés had lamb carcasses turning on spits over open fires. The blackened bodies suddenly looked like dogs or small humans. Families gathered around the tables drinking red wine from Šibenik and fish from Dubrovnik. Trees were blooming and flowers sprinkled the roadside with dots of orange, red, and yellow. It was the beginning of spring here. If you stopped for a conversation someone would tell you how hard it had been since the war ended.

The war had ended here a year earlier. What about the war in Bosnia, less than seventy-five miles away? "Oh, that war," they would say and wave their hand above their hair as if shooing off an annoying insect. They didn't want to hear about it. They had their own problems. One in particular that kept coming up was how the war next door was going to scare away the summer tourists.

Tony didn't let up on the gas until we reached the sea. With water in sight we cheered and gave each other high fives as if we had just won some competition. But hadn't we? Hadn't we beaten death and spat in her eye?

And Valerie, the Frenchwoman with whom I'd spent the last night on Earth? Occasionally, over the months to come, we'd pass one another on a dirt road in central Bosnia or on the highway in Split, but we never spoke again. You can only fuck once with a person like it's the end of the world. After that it all seems somehow less. You have to find another scared soul to share that time with if it should come again.

Over the next few days we ordered more cases of beer and sat in the sun. One day, while swimming in the Adriatic, I told Graeme of my idea.

"I own a video camera with a friend in California. If I can get it here we can make a documentary in Sarajevo. Vlado, the sisters, the disco."

"I'm in. What do we do first?"

"We need UN press passes," I said, knowing I would never get an expensive camera through the Serb checkpoint without it being stolen. "If they took that still camera of mine they will definitely take this bastard."

"I got a pass," said Graeme.

"How?"

"The first time I was here they were giving them away like candy, mate. Now they are tough."

"How about forgery?" I asked.

"Tough on those passes."

"Right."

"You know how to do all that filming thing?" he asked.

"Used to assistant-direct some films, commercials."

"Oh yeah, when was that?"

"Before."

"Before what?"

We opened another round of beers.

"Before now," I said.

"Here's to the making of it." He laughed.

We clanked bottles and each took a healthy gulp.

And Fojnica? The last any of us ever spoke of the place was several days later when listening to a BBC radio report. The reporter was yelling into the microphone, appalled. He recounted walking into a building, described as some sort of medical institution, on the hill above Fojnica. He spoke of how the disabled children had been left behind, tied up by sheets to the beds, while the adults ran for their lives into the hills.

That week we tried everything to bury our heads in the sand. But the problem remains the same the world over: the sand is never quite deep enough.

Part Two

29

As much as I would like to say I began this journey with an agenda in mind, a fixed purpose I was working toward, I cannot. The truth is, up until this point, I had never thought very far ahead. It was in my training as a traveler: live in short spurts until the next portal opens up.

Yet there would be no turning back. Not now. Not after meeting the people I had met and seeing what I had seen. It would be like hearing a woman scream rape and going for a drink just to get out of earshot. No. It was too late for people like Graeme and me, suckers who believe that if we give a little more it will all turn round for the better. It wasn't that I thought I could save the world. At this point I would have settled for erasing my memory. Once memory gets hardwired into your brain it gets more difficult to erase your sense of responsibility. Why else do we have that cancer called television? Why are we inundated with sound-bite news, and infantile politicians making promises they never intend to keep? Low ball, baby. Keep it simple and stupid. Keep the masses doped up on false expectations of lower taxes, second mortgages and entry into the country club and you've got yourself a happy society ready, willing and able to ignore those cries of rape. No one can hear them—the TV is too loud.

From where I sat the worst thing was that the world leaders, drunk on French wine and Danish pastries in Geneva, knew the right and wrong of what was happening inside Bosnia. They just didn't want to address it. One time in Sarajevo, three-quarters into a bottle of Jack Daniel's, Graeme and I made a promise to hitchhike to Geneva and yank one of them from his limo and drag him into the tunnels that led to Lejla and Selma's house. We promised each other we would deck any one of the officials if we ever saw them. I thought of this promise when a few years later I did see the Japanese official, Agashi, who for a time was the UN politician in charge of Bosnia. I spotted him as I double-dipped into the buffet at the Intercontinental Hotel in Zagreb. He had no bodyguards and I had a clear shot. I could have floored the bastard before anyone could gag me and throw me in The Hague with the rest of the war criminals. Instead I sat in my chair eating plate after plate of food on some rich magazine's expense account and told myself that hitting him would prove nothing. I opted out. I'd give anything to see him again. I'd floor him. At least that's what I've told myself every day since.

No, the leaders knew. They knew these people weren't dying for some ideology or religious cause. They knew that all the UN "safe zones," with names such as Zepa, Goražde, Srebrenica, and Sarajevo were just reservations where the Serbs were allowed to kill, so long as they didn't overdo it. They knew because they had their lackeys driving up and down the road in white Land Rovers with the word *Observer* painted in black. They wore white lab coats and white helmets and spent their days counting how many bombs had fallen and how many were dead. They buddied up with commanders on both sides by giving them whiskey and food and promises of getting them out. Just them.

One night in Sarajevo, during the war, I was invited to attend a dinner in the house of a wealthy Bosnian. His guests included a UN monitor. This man was from Madrid and had slicked-back black hair and a goofy thin moustache. He had just got in from "the field" and was still wearing the UN-monitor uniform—the white lab coat. When he spoke he had an air of snobbery that had nothing to do with money. It was snobbery based on the power of being able to dole out life and death. He stuffed his face with steak while going over the numbers. This many dead, this many wounded. There was not a shred of concern in his face and he seemed perfectly content to be void of irony or conscious thought. I could only wonder how long he had been dead.

No. The war was much simpler. I suspect most wars are. These people were dying as they tried to get a glass of water, a scrap of food. They were dying in their homes, their schools, their mother's arms. They were being killed because they were quite literally alive. I had only $100 left in my shoe but I had a growing desire to record a wrong that needed to be righted.

And that's how the idea of getting a camera came about.

In Split the weather turned even warmer. Tony had some money wired from the Road Trip's head office in London. It was enough to pay for pizza and our rooms at the pension for a few more weeks on the beach a few miles south of town. The three Australians met three Austrian girls, down from Vienna for some humanitarian business, and they went at it in the rooms above the garage for nearly a week. It was almost unbearable to hear them screaming as they leaned out over the balcony half-naked. Some of the other guys found French girls, Croatian girls or even Bosnian refugees.

I usually took the local bus to town in the afternoons to drink beer in the pub and read the *Herald Tribune*. It was the same. Always is. The news from America concerned the price of fuel. The headlines in Asia said something about China ignoring human rights in Tibet, and Indonesia was slipping into astronomical inflation. Soccer scores and talk about a European Union dominated the news from Europe. And the rest of the world? There were plans for a space station. Nothing different, it was all the same as before.

But enough of that. We can't pay attention to everything all the time. After all, we are just humans; born blind, slapped on the bottom, and released into the world where we learn how to swim, eat, sleep, dream, and make love. With our feet in the Adriatic and the wind from Venice blowing in our faces there wasn't much to complain about. Surviving has a way of making you feel like you've earned the right to be lazy for a while.

"Well, give me the short version," said Jason Aplon on the veranda of his pension.

"Surreal," I said as he poured the wine.

The sun was warm on my skin. The chicken on the rotisserie was almost done and the smell was giving me small stabs under my ribcage. It was in his pension that I had taken my first shower in weeks. His girlfriend, also his translator, a local named Ivana Sirović, had told me to please go back and clean up the crap in the shower basin. She was smart, beautiful, and business-like and right. The basin was brown with filth and there were piles of hair in all the corners. I apologized and Jason said, "Don't worry about it." She said nothing as we ate our food.

Jason was telling me how the roads going into Bosnia would be jammed for the next two days. Seemed there was a large convoy of cargo trucks hauling water to Tuzla, near the eastern border of Bosnia and Serbia. The Pakistani UN troops, who were there to "keep the peace," insisted on having water from the Ganges to wash their feet in before prayer. So, after a couple of weeks on board a cargo ship, paid for by the world, the water was now en route to Tuzla on the back of a massive truck convoy, also paid for by the world's taxpayers. And while the Pakistanis prayed in comfort, several more Bosnians would die of dehydration or starvation or from the lack of a medicine that could have been on an aid convoy. At times I found myself remembering that ridiculous question I'd pondered the day I met the sisters: was it better to choke at the end of a rope or starve to death?

"I think Ivana and I are going to take a break this summer and get a boat to sail the islands. If you're around you should join us."

"Sailing," I said, with a hint of sarcasm.

"We've been at it almost a year straight," he said, pleading his case.

"Sounds great. But really I don't know where I'll be by summer."

"I think they're going to promote me to head of country."

"Run the organization?"

"Maybe."

"Christ. You've done that many things wrong. That's not like you."

"Yeah, well . . ." He laughed. "I can probably get you a job pretty soon. Have you decided what's next for you?"

"I'm going to call Bob and see if he can send over the camera. Take it into Sarajevo."

"What's going on in there?"

"It's hard to explain. But in the city the Serbs, Croats, and Muslims are all living together. They don't identify themselves as Serb, Croat, or Muslim. They say Bosnian first. No one asks what another person's ethnic background is, although they always seem to know. And they are all fighting against the Chetnik Serbs on the hills. Even the Serbs in Sarajevo are fighting against the Serbs on the hill. They just won't give in to Karadzic's idea of a nationalist state."

"And you think you can shoot something there?"

"Hell, I'm not sure how I'll be able to charge the camera batteries."

"And what will you do with your film?"

"I don't know. But how many times have you seen the press interview some old lady with sticks on her back? All the time. That's all we see in these wars. But all the people I met were hipsters who spoke English and partied like freaks. The place is filled with great people. And it's a killing field."

"You know I can't do much to help you from out here."

"You're feeding me chicken and wine and giving me a hot shower. And you are going to help me get the camera from Bob," I said.

"But when you're in there . . . Listen, I want you to take my old UN blue card. It's expired and has my photo but in a crunch a UN soldier might let it slide."

"Thanks for that."

"Don't let it out of your hands."

"I won't," I said. "I'm working on a press pass."

"That will be tough." He watched me rip off a chicken leg. "I also think we're going to the U2 concert in Verona in July. We got tickets."

"What are you talking about?"

"The U2 concert."

"Oh."

"You don't understand," he said, slightly defensively. "Paperwork, delays, accounting. Nothing happens and nothing gets done. Money gets thrown around but the results are so far away. What if we build 200 new homes in Jablanica and then the Croats burn them all the following month? I mean we are supposed to help people rebuild, not build in the middle of a war."

Jason was a brooder, a natural-born worrywort. In college, where we met in our freshman year, he over-studied for every exam and questioned every angle. Even then, after acing the test, he wouldn't relax until the summer vacation had fully arrived. But for all his brooding, his surface pessimism fooled no one, including him. I suspect it was all in the hope of hiding the eternal optimist he really was. His intelligence was overshadowed only by his ability to worry about achieving his own high standards. That was why I liked him. He never stopped short of reaching for the unobtainable. He was doomed to a life of suffering and longing but at least he was smart enough to realize this.

Since his arrival in Croatia his intellect and ambition had taken him far. He landed in Split with no job but armed with a few phone numbers of international aid groups. Within six months he had created a job that no one in the UN or NGO community could imagine hadn't existed before he arrived. Together with Ivana, Jason had created the bulletin board in the war for humanitarian aid. No humanitarian aid moved in Bosnia without Jason and Ivana knowing about it. Their office, at the end of the hall in a UN building in Split, had become the traffic cop of all food from NGOs going into Bosnia. When a group of German Mennonites brought ten tons of clothes, they were directed to see Jason. He would know who would move them upcountry and where they should go. When an American Christian group showed up with medicines that were out of date he thanked them and told them there was nothing more they could do. They went home happy and Jason found a quiet way to dump the medicine, making room for the fresh batch a Swedish women's group was bringing the following week.

As is also his nature he began toeing the line, taking the official stance on safety and keeping realistic expectations. Of course he was suspicious about the Road Trip and our cowboy ways. On many occasions he tried to talk me out of returning to Sarajevo.

"So do you want to go to the show?" he asked.

"What show?"

"The U2 show in Italy? Ivana's sister is going too. Maybe we can try to buy another ticket. Although I think it's already sold out."

"Don't worry about it, but have a good time."

"You sure?"

"Yeah. I can't plan that far ahead. And I hate big shows like that."

"So, what do you think is going to happen here?" I asked.

"Where?"

"Bosnia."

"Most likely nothing. There's no political will from the West."

We drank some more wine and my glazed eyes turned toward the sea. I watched some refugee kids swim. They are easy to spot. They are the ones whose mothers stand on the shore watching the horizon instead of their child.

"You mind if I have another piece of chicken?" I asked.

30

The waves gently lapped against the rocky shores of Dalmatia. It had been almost two years since I had thrown Corrina's ashes into the Pacific Ocean, on the other side of the world. In the end, she weighed just over three pounds and fitted into a square box. On that day I had sat on the edge of the ocean and run my fingers through her. She felt like dried coral, smashed seashells, and sand. I ran the white ash of her over my face. I put some on my tongue. It tasted like chalk. So that's it? After we leave this tiny round rock, a dot in the Milky Way, we turn into dried-up sea crap. I wanted to add water and watch her rise up out of the sea like a rehydrated mermaid.

Here, at night, like a sea breeze flooding into the room I could taste her saliva in my mouth. I could hear her whisper in my ear. When I closed my eyes I could see her hair in front of the window in San Francisco. I kept telling myself that the consolation of losing someone I loved so dearly was that life would be a cinch from here on out. All I had to tell myself was that I had a purpose for still being alive. No giving up. I figured all the questions in the world couldn't undercut the sense of being here, doing something. Whatever happened next, I could always say I'd been here. Besides, I had not told anyone about Corrina, and keeping this secret to myself, for some reason, made me feel invincible.

As for the UN press office? All I had to remember was that I was a famous journalist from San Francisco here on urgent matters.

I already knew I didn't want to be at the mercy of the Road Trip's schedule, which at times resembled Grateful Dead fans outside the show waiting for their miracle. I had to get back into Sarajevo, but I didn't want to cross Serb lines with my new camera.

But there was a problem. To get on a free flight on a C130 UN military cargo plane in or out of Sarajevo you had to have either a UN-certified blue card or a UN press pass, given only to certifiable members of the press. You had to be legitimate or connected. I was neither.

Here was the con. My friend Bob Phillips in Berkeley, an assistant director in the film business, wrote a fax on a piece of headed stationery that said I was making a documentary on the Bosnian conflict for a fictitious company we named Moondog. He listed his home phone number as the office number. Then he changed his answering machine to a standard corporate message giving the office hours and to please leave a message.

The whole thing relied on a sure bet: that the United Nations has the least efficient bureaucracy on the planet. I knew I could count on them to work exactly nine to five and no longer. California was nine hours behind Croatian time, so if they stuck to their schedule they could never reach Bob's house during office hours. The key was for Bob never to pick up the phone.

A young English sergeant was in charge of all press passes for Bosnia. His boss at the airport was a Frenchman who wore a white scarf around his neck and spoke English, although he loved to speak in French, especially when he knew you couldn't speak his language. Naturally he hated my long hair and American clothes.

"Zhy don't you purchase some zeal clothes?" he would say to me.

But he wasn't my problem. It was the sergeant, who spoke with a south London accent. I asked him if he'd had any luck calling my corporate office in San Francisco.

"There was no answer."

"That's odd. When did you call?"

"Today."

"Yes, but when?"

"Before lunch."

"Ah, see, there's the problem."

"It don' matter. I 'ave to speak to a ac'ual person, you see?"

"Well, I think the problem is you are calling when they are closed."

Success is always in the simplicity.

He continued, "I mus' speak to someone to give you the pass."

"Fine. There are fifteen people in that office during office hours. Someone from here has to call by seven a.m. or stay late, until around midnight."

"We 'ave hours, you know," he said.

"Yes. I am sure you do."

This went on for days. Back at the beach Tony had heard good news from the Trip's head office in London. It seemed they had secured a new load of food to transport into Bosnia. The donating group was a German charity whose supplies were already in Split but they were having trouble getting the

UN to take the goods across the border. Jason had helped hook up the two parties. For petrol money and a little bit extra Tony had agreed to take the load.

Around this time Graeme had started seeing a Frenchwoman by the name of Brigitte. She had sky-blue eyes, burned red hair, and a healthy sway to her hips. She enjoyed the company of men and could talk anyone into a corner with her ideas of how to solve the crisis in Bosnia. Her eyes latched onto yours until she was convinced she had persuaded you. Most of her ideas revolved around having control over an organization, which one didn't seem to matter. And then all would reveal itself.

No one had seen Graeme for days and for the most part everyone was jealous. She was a looker. Some said he had disappeared for good. After about a week he surfaced one afternoon and insisted on driving me to the airport to see the sergeant.

"Well?" I asked.

"Well, what?" he snapped.

I said nothing but started humming out the window.

"Ah, not you too," he said.

"Just the basics."

"She's relentless, mate."

"Yeah?"

"I can't shag that much."

"What's next?"

"She wants to come with us."

"And?"

"I told her it wasn't possible."

"What she say?"

"She wanted to know if I ran the Road Trip."

"And?"

"I told her Tony did."

"Well, you really run it."

"Don't matter. She started shagging Tony."

"Where is he now?"

"AWOL, mate. But I have a pretty good idea."

"Oh. Sorry about that."

"No. She was too much. I don't need that shit."

"Still, it was probably nice. Better than hanging around the rest of us," I said.

"You got that right, mate."

Graeme parked near the entrance to the airport. "I'll wait here," he said.

I walked into the office like I didn't have a care in the world. Another key to success: don't act, but actually believe you belong wherever you are. Given half a chance people want to get out of the way of someone with ambition.

"Still no luck, sir," said the sergeant. I had to play my last card.

"The President of Bosnia is speaking on Friday morning," I said. I stood up and put both my hands behind my head in frustration. "If I miss that press conference then my documentary is shot. The whole fucking thing has been a waste of time. We've spent a fortune on cameras, interpreters, cars, lights, and plane tickets. It's now or never."

He hesitated for a moment, and then the magic dust settled. He shrugged his shoulders and pushed my card through the lamination machine as if he had just been waiting for a reason to say yes.

Just then a large rotund man with a photographer's jacket and scruffy beard came and stood at the door. He smelled of sweat and pasta. He wore a round-brimmed hat and had several passes round his fat neck. He looked like some hack covering backstage at a Rolling Stones tour. When the sergeant handed me the pass the fat man raised his eyebrows and gave me the once-over. Yes, I thought, I am now one of you.

The entire time I walked down the hallway I searched and searched my brain for the answer, but it just wasn't there. No matter how hard I tried to remember I didn't know the name of the Bosnian President. Not even a clue.

Graeme was in the Land Rover playing GameBoy. I flashed him my press pass.

"Bloody hell! The English are a stupid lot, aren't they, believing a stupid fucking Yank," he said. "Right then. We fly tomorrow."

"Good. I'll get some rations from Jason. You talk to Tony?"

"If I can find him."

"I got guitar picks for Vlado. We need some food for the sisters and booze. And I'll get some popcorn. What else?"

"We need to make a stop on the way home," he said.

"What for?"

"We need to pick up some morphine."

31

The amount of morphine taped to my groin was worth much more than the contents of my duffel bag, which had a state-of-the-art High 8 Canon camera, a hand-held microphone, ten two-hour tapes, a tripod, two lenses, and a battery charger. Bob had also sent along a $100 bill stuffed in the toe of a new pair of boots. Already I felt the morphine was worth more than any footage I could capture on tape. Besides, how would I ever get anything I shot to be more than a home movie? The morphine, on the other hand, could erase pain, at least for a while.

It turned out Graeme had run into some doctors with Médecins Sans Frontières and they had asked us to take some morphine to Sarajevo by plane. The UN and the Serbs were having a disagreement about allowing certain medicines to come into Sarajevo by land. They said it didn't fit the strict humanitarian guidelines. I don't think they had visited the hospitals in Sarajevo where doctors were busy cutting off people's shattered legs and arms with no anesthetic.

This was how it came to be that we each had two sardine-can-sized containers of morphine strapped to our crotches with packaging tape.

Walking across the Split airport tarmac, wary of the company we were keeping, we stayed far behind all the professionals—the reporters and humanitarian workers. They walked with jackets slung over their shoulders, carried PowerBooks and joked about time zones and their jet lag after returning from Paris or London. It was at times like this that Graeme was at his harshest.

"Wankers get paid bloody money to fly around and find fucking tragedies."

I agreed with him about certain individuals but not about the media in general. In fact it could be argued that media exposure was Sarajevo's only chance of survival.

"You know," I said, "if they don't report it no one knows. If no one knows then there isn't a chance in hell this is going to end."

He agreed, but usually ignored me when I talked like that.

At the huge French military cargo plane, the luggage was laid out in a line just under the propeller. It was the last flight of the day. Already the light was turning bronze and golden.

A German Shepherd, held on a leash by a French soldier carrying an automatic rifle, sniffed each bag. I slipped into a daydreaming nightmare. It went something like this: the German Shepherd would smell the drugs between my legs and rush toward me. I would run toward the main building. The soldiers would chase the dog, their guns raised and ready to fire. Just before I reached the doors, my hands on the handle, the dog would grab a hold of me by the balls. As they dragged the beast off he would be eating my cock. The soldiers would pat his head for being so darn good.

Meanwhile, back in real time, at the plane, the dog was tearing a hole in my bag. His jaw was locked in a death grip. I slipped my hands in my pocket and felt under my butt crack to make sure I hadn't left the morphine in the bag. Graeme looked at me and took a small step backward.

"Whose bag is zis?" yelled the French commander. He threw the dangling part of his white scarf flamboyantly over his shoulder. I, like everyone else, looked around the tarmac waiting for the guilty party.

"I zee," he said as he pulled the dog off the bag. The soldiers' guns were now in lock-and-load position.

The commander leaned over and reached into my bag. He then stood up and thrust his right arm over his head. He was holding a large clear ziplock bag full of C4 explosives. There must have been three pounds of the stuff. Enough to blow up a bridge. Maybe even two.

"And whose is zis?" the Frenchman barked.

"Oh Christ," said Graeme under his breath.

I raised my hand. "That's my bag, but I don't know anything about that." My tongue had no more spit. Everything was going up in flames. The guards leveled their rifles and walked toward me. Sweat poured off my forehead and I said something to Graeme about contacting my mother. I hadn't finished rattling off the phone number before the French commander was standing in front of me. He made little sniffing noises, as if he was testing the air for garlic.

"*YES*, American! We know it is yours."

I searched my brain for the correct words to begin my defense. It was *Midnight Express* and somehow I had been cast as the lead actor. Already the words sounded hollow, falling upon can ears: "I was framed."

The Frenchman laughed so hard he started choking, but then quickly recovered. "It is ours. *Ha!*" he said. "*Ha!*" He was very pleased with himself. "We put it in your bag. Just checking our dogs. *Ha!* My friend–" he wrapped his large sweaty hand around my shoulder—"the dogs are good, no? No hard feelings?"

As usual in situations when an authority lets me off the hook, even though I'd done no wrong I said thank you. And then hated myself for saying it. I should have sucker-punched him and taken my chances with a UN court. The guards laughed as they corralled everyone to the rear of the plane. Graeme walked by.

"That git gets on the plane? I will throw that fat fuck out the window," he said.

I stepped up onto the rear cargo entrance. Only one thought came to mind. I would never be getting on this plane or, for that matter, be here at all if she was still alive. I would be making love under a palm tree somewhere deep in Mexico. Maybe we'd be making our second kid by now. These thoughts always came in flashes—death, grief, and a realization that we are truly alone. I didn't know whether to be angry with her for leaving or thankful my life had become a very different trip. For the moment I was at ease enough to wait to see where it took me.

The flight was short. It took just over forty minutes to cover the distance we'd made in thirty hours by truck. The mountains of Bosnia, snow-capped and jagged, floated below the window like island volcanos rising out of a sea of pine forests. I thought this really would be a great place to go cross-country skiing. French soldiers with headphones on stared out of the side windows, listening for the radar-lock sound that indicated Serb surface-to-air missiles. With my hands gripped tightly around the camera bag, I rested my head against the cool shell of the plane. I fell asleep to a low humming noise. The next thing I remember is one of the French crewmen pulling off his headphones and yelling above the roar of the propellers, "Welcome to Sarajevo."

32

We handed the morphine to a Canadian doctor at the hospital. "Any problems?" he asked.

"Not really," I said. What was I going to say? I almost had my dick chewed off by a pack of dogs?

At the office Graeme and I busied ourselves rearranging the layout. I made a shelf for the camera equipment in the bedroom. We placed our sleeping bags in the same room but separated our sleeping quarters with a filing cabinet. Graeme organized the food rations and checked on the propane tank. We had enough fuel to last a couple of weeks, which we thought would be when the rest of the Road Trip would return with a new load of food to distribute. On the shelf we had dozens of bottles of chocolate baby food. That and some canned soup. In the warehouse there was still more baby food, rice, and some powdered milk we had left behind. The toilet was clean and the lock we had installed was unbroken; no one had been inside and messed it up. We made candle-holders out of the empty vodka bottles, swept up the floor and secured the barricades. It looked like there were a few new bullet holes in the kitchen wall. In the ping-pong room, which we also called the sniper room, seeing that it was exposed to sniper positions, the table was untouched. We set up the net we had brought with us and played the best three out of four.

Because we had no access to satellite phones, once inside Sarajevo the only way for us to communicate with the outside world was if the French group Equilibre allowed us to use their marine hand radio. And the only way for the Road Trip to communicate with us from Split was by the same method. So, in my mind, I was here for the duration. Either until the end of the war or until I couldn't take it any more. I had few physical needs. I could eat baby food forever. I had new friends. I had lost all connections with the outside world and with them my own personal history had slipped under my mind's shag carpet. All that mattered now was that I was true to myself, and even though I was feeling slightly lost, I had great certainty that if I followed my intuition, in time I would know what to do.

That first night, lying in our sleeping bags, we passed a bottle of vodka, around the front of the cabinet, to each other in the dark.

"You got dolphins in California, right?"

"I've seen surfers ride waves with them."

"Wicked. That's a dream of mine. I think that's like talking with God. Surfing with dolphins."

The filing cabinet hid our faces from each other but I could imagine Graeme smiling. He was throwing number-two pencils into the ceiling, where they stuck lead first.

"Where should we start?" he asked. "Who do we film?"

"Don't know."

33

After we'd been back a few days, the weather turned cold once again and the rain returned. With it came a fresh scent, water on pavement. The city was quiet, almost calm. At times like this it was like the stubborn eye of a swirling hurricane, refusing to blink.

Seated on the couch, in front of my camera, was Mira, the mother of two children, a daughter and a son. She hadn't seen them since 14 May 1992, when they had escaped from Dobrinja, a heavily besieged suburb of Sarajevo. Dobrinja was one of the first parts of the city to be surrounded and cut off from the rest of the world by the Serb forces. Her children had escaped in the first months of the war, on a convoy sponsored by an international aid group. Because there was no means of communication with the outside world she hadn't heard from them since. Now she lived in a friend's house near the UNIS towers. It also happened to be the home of Fadja, a thirteen-year-old boy who helped us around the office from time to time.

It was Fadja who suggested we film Mira.

I steadied the camera, leaning the long lens on my forearm. Graeme held the microphone near her, but not too close. We had done only one other interview so far and were still getting used to working together. I told Graeme we should refrain from talking during an interview because it might interrupt the interviewee's momentum.

Mira had been telling a story about living with twenty people in her basement for one month. It was at the beginning of the war, after her children left, and food was running out. Mira cleared her throat and stared out the window, toward the clouds, then continued.

"I am sitting with my friends near the steps. It was my neighbors. They have names. Mirsada, Rada, Dinko, and Rashida. It was a very quiet day and then I heard one sound. It was the sound when you put metal on stone . . . And then it was dark. Totally dark, but the sun was still shining. A grenade had fallen. When it exploded I became unconscious for half a minute or so. Rashita was killed. Her husband was wounded. Rada was wounded. I passed through without any problems. And Mirsada too. When we got up we ran to a flat and then another grenade fell. And we heard only the voice of my neighbor, who was calling out for his wife. But his wife was dead. That voice, I can never forget that voice ever, ever. It was very sad. I can cry at this moment."

And she did.

I kept the camera rolling, but through my headphones I could hear a crackling in the sound. I tapped Graeme's leg and he readjusted the baby diaper wrapped around the neck of the microphone.

You see, when the camera arrived, along with the spare shoes and the money and clean socks, there was also a microphone and a bag full of baby diapers. And a note from Ellen Devine, a friend from the commercial film business. The note said that, although it was a good microphone, it had a slight wiring problem—the only way to keep it from crackling was if we held a diaper round its neck.

"OK?" asked Graeme, getting a better grip on the diaper.

"Good."

"Got the kid in the background?" he whispered, referring to a teenage girl smoking cigarettes near the kitchen table.

"Got it," I said. "Hold the diaper still."

"Nappy, you eejit."

She continued. "And then we had to make a grave. My husband and neighbors did this behind our building because we haven't any special land for burying her. We can't go anywhere else because of the shooting. And we don't have any wood for her box."

"Coffin," said Graeme.

"Yes. Coffin," said Mira. "And then we find a piece of furniture and put her in that furniture. And we make the grave. And when we are making the grave they are shooting."

"At you?" asked Graeme.

"Yes. And after that we are leaving."

She looked directly at me, and nodded her head up and down.

I nodded too, as if I understood what she was saying. Of course that was a lie. She had just told me she had buried her best friend in her dresser. Was there anything *to* understand?

I put the camera down and Graeme lowered the microphone. We were now just two strangers in her living room.

"Do you know what I am most afraid of?"

"What?" I wanted to grab the camera, but it was too late.

"I am afraid that I will forget to miss her. That one day I will not miss my friend any more."

I could hear my heart crashing downward through my chest cavity, sinking all the way to the base of my stomach. That fear devoured me alive and kept me projecting the film of Corrina on the wall of my eyelids night after night. The title: *Never Forget*.

Mira offered us each a can of tuna. We refused but she insisted. She began talking nervously about the condition of the house. She was embarrassed that we were witnesses to the mess.

"The tuna would be great, thanks," I said. Graeme took his can.

"Eat, please eat," she said with a smile reserved for the truly hopeful or the naive or perpetual dreamers. She got up and stood near the window and lit a cigarette. She rubbed her hand up and down her thigh really roughly, as if the itch was not on her skin but under it. Outside the rain returned in a sudden gust, spattering drops against the window, like the sound of drying sheets flapping in the wind.

She turned round and said, "It's strange. Before the war I never thought so much about eating." She almost stopped herself from giggling, but a few trickles of laughter leaked out. Then she reached down and let out a deep belly laugh. A real howler that made her double over. We joined her. We couldn't help it. Man, it felt good. When we finished she wiped her eyes and took a long drag of her cigarette. Whew.

Graeme and I looked at each other and scraped the bottom of the cans, until there was no tuna left.

34

It was now early May and the weather couldn't make up its mind. Some days it was warm, others there was a chill in the air.

As for me, my butt cheeks were sticking together and my trousers chafed against my thighs. The cloud of body odor moving in front of my walk had become a noticeable reaction on people's faces. With that in mind I became curious how people here took showers.

That was exactly what I was thinking about when I bumped into a man on the staircase of the UNIS towers. His appearance shocked me. In his early thirties, he had all his teeth and his hair was perfectly healthy, maybe even bouncy. His clothes were American preppy: Levi's, short-sleeved polo shirt and a sweater tied around his shoulders. With his movie-star looks he seemed like someone who would be comfortable heading for the country club for drinks or perhaps yachting in the afternoon. Most of all he looked like a man who showered regularly.

"Are you American?" he asked.

"From California."

"California. That must be very nice."

"It's got some nice spots."

"Is the fishing good?"

"Great. The streams in the Trinity Alps way up in northern California are the best."

His face reacted to my every word. He seemed pleased with the fishing report.

His name was Ciba, pronounced C-H-E-E-B-A, Karisik. He asked me to visit his office, downstairs. Inside his office were plenty of people, maybe a dozen, maybe more. He sat me down at his desk, which was covered in sketches showing Serbian tanks running over people or American fighter planes flying low and dropping bombs. This was the Bosnian army press office, in other words the Bosnian war propaganda office. Well, good luck, I thought.

"A painter," he said, pointing to his desk. "I am a painter."

"I see."

"I do this sketch work for the army. It is a requirement," he whispered and forced a smile while looking around the room. "But it is stupid shit I do here. My real work is at my studio."

"I would like to see that," I said.

"Yes, of course."

He was so well groomed and impeccably dressed I asked him my burning question, not caring how ludicrous it sounded. "Any chance you could tell me how you take a shower?"

He laughed and while doing so he moved his hand over his body, acting out the part of someone washing.

"Yes, shower," I said, laughing at the whole thing.

He led me back out the door we came through, where a man sat at a desk doing what appeared to be nothing. We walked down a hallway to the toilets. There Ciba dipped a one-litre plastic Coca-Cola bottle into a large drum of water. Then another bottle. He placed a cup of water in a coffee pot over a propane flame. When it boiled he funneled the hot water equally into the two plastic bottles, bringing each of them to a lukewarm temperature.

"How full were the rivers on the way into Sarajevo?" he asked.

"They seemed full to me."

"Probably too high for fly fishing." He was correct about the river being too high, to say nothing of the effects that dead cows, dogs, and humans can have on the fish population.

"OK, this should make the water warm," he said, smiling. "You are American?" he asked again, with noticeable excitement.

"That's it."

"How uncommon," he said. "OK. Rinse some, then wash with the soap and use the rest to rinse. I will stand outside the door and make sure no one bothers you."

Naked, I stood in front of the mirror. I could see the three stalls and two urinals behind me. The tiled floor was cold and I realized I was shivering. I ran my hands through my long ratty hair and soaped myself. I guessed I had lost five, maybe ten pounds. Under the bright bathroom light my body shone like a beacon of raw flesh. It seemed so tender, so vulnerable. I imagined a bullet tearing it to pieces. Sometimes I think it is easy to forget we have blood in us until it starts to leak out. I rinsed and dried off with my shirt. It was the best shower I had ever had.

A couple of days later, Ciba escorted me to his house for lunch. He lived within minutes of the office in a typical Austro-Hungarian building with tall windows and high ceilings. He explained that, as with many people in the city, this wasn't actually his home. His flat was in Grebavica, the Serb-occupied area of Sarajevo. At the beginning of the war, when they found themselves living on the front line, they quickly left the flat for the middle of the city. This flat he was living in was that of a Serb friend who had fled. By all accounts hundreds of flats were vacated in the middle of the night at the beginning of the war as people tried to escape.

As we approached Ciba's flat there was a cou-cou sound from above. A blond-haired woman leaned out of the window and waved.

"Amra, my wife," he said. His eyes danced a little when he said that.

A young girl, I guessed about seven years old, and also blond, ran up to Ciba with a group of friends. She started to make a fake cry, the kind kids do to get attention. Ciba stopped and ran his fingers through her hair. He flicked a knuckle on her head and talked sternly, but she knew he was joking. She smiled and ran away.

"Anja, my daughter," he said. "She already knows how to get what she wants from me."

Ciba's wife wore Levi jeans with a white cotton blouse. Her hair was blond and cut in a hip European style. In short, they were people who might easily be spotted in Nice taking snapshots of their holiday on the riviera.

Lunch was a spring onion for each of us and rice. The onion was from a small wooden box full of dirt sitting in the window. I had seen many window boxes but I'd never guessed they were tiny vegetable gardens. The rice was from a humanitarian package. Amra spoke English fluently, and over the course of lunch she helped translate Ciba's broken English.

"Tell Ciba all about fishing in America," she said. "He was once the fly-fishing champion of all Bosnia."

We passed the afternoon talking about fishing and travel. Ciba talked of living in America one day while Amra shook her head and said things like "I don't believe I would like America's life. Too busy." I kept out of it and saw my role as that of the ancient traveler, the one who brings news from the outside.

Amra was an economist—but "That was before the war," she said with a defeated but gracious smile. "I hate to admit it but I like this life we have now. I don't mean the war, I mean Ciba, Anja, our daughter, and me. We are just three. We live for each other. We are a family."

She was thin, graceful, a survivor from head to toe. Ciba was a painter but he also had the strong and agile body of an athlete. Amra said Ciba was the best soccer player in all of Sarajevo. He liked that and kissed his wife on the cheek. His paintings covered the living-room wall. He was a realist painter trained in attention to detail: flowers, landscapes, the leaves in the wind were his art. And it was easy to see they were in love.

Amra stood up and walked to the window.

"Bill, tell us all about your adventures in other parts of the world," she said. Ciba inched up in his chair, smiling and eager to understand every sound of the English language.

"Where do you want to know about?"

"Have you ever been to Alaska?" she asked, leaning out the window. Ciba glowed at the word Alaska.

"I have," I said. The lump in my chest wasn't fear. It was more a nervous reaction that had a way of shaking me to the core. A shiver rippled down my spine. This always happens when I am reminded that, inevitably, we meet the people we are supposed to meet.

She called down to their daughter, who was playing in the street with some other kids. The noise from the children was heart-warming, calming.

"Everything OK?" I asked, suddenly worried about every-thing.

"Yes, of course, but sometimes I worry about the snipers." Slowly, as if gathering her emotions, she ran her hand along a crease in her Levi's as she sat back down.

"Bill," interrupted Ciba with the excitement of a child, "tell us about Alaska. Is it like it is in the pictures? Big? And the wilderness?"

I thought of telling them everything. But how could I? I de-cided to keep it simple. I told them about the salmon fishing.

35

The only true constant in this war was the same as in peace: the need to get a glass of water. All else, when forced to prioritize, was secondary.

One time late at night Graeme suddenly said from his bed, "If I ever write a book about this place I will dedicate it to 'complex simplicity.' "

Each day we set aside some time in the mornings to find water, which could take up to six hours for two gallons. This was a change from the last time we were here. Then there had been a source of water in the basement of the UNIS towers, but that source had since dried up. Throughout the city water was becoming scarcer. The sources of water could literally shift each day, from block to block, neighborhood to neighborhood. For a while there was a house down the street that had sprung a leak in the basement. That queue was sometimes six to seven hours long, but it often seemed less because there was a ping-pong table in the alley made from a door, with torn shirts as the net. One of us would stand in line while the other one played table tennis with the kids.

Then there was the pipe across the river under a destroyed building complex. That queue was short but seemed to last forever. This was probably because it had been shelled in the past.

There was the beer factory but that was a long haul across exposed alleys. There were other places where the water would be on for a day or two and then gone for a week or more. There were also water trucks that drove around town and hid behind buildings, but we never used those. That would be taking from people who couldn't travel outside their neighborhoods. There was also the river, but besides being an easy target for the snipers, it was heavily polluted with the occasional dead body, animals, and rubbish. In addition, it was the source of a popular doomsday scenario for Sarajevans. They imagined the Serbs would slowly poison the river, thus killing the whole town. I never believed it because it was clear the Serbs wanted the town alive, as a political grape to squeeze in the Geneva peace talks.

Sometimes in the mornings we would hold meetings in the office with community leaders who were requesting food from the Road Trip. After all, even though we had little food to give away there was a certain obligation to our official titles: Sarajevo Station Chief Officers for The Serious Road Trip. Badges that stated this hung on shoestrings round our necks. Badges we had made ourselves.

The visitors were usually the same. Dressed in their best suits, the ones they had saved for special occasions. They came bearing large smiles of hope. The men would wear a tie with a pin of the Bosnian flag. The women would have on a suit, the kind women politicians wear, and with their high heels we could hear them approaching from the floor below. They were almost always in their late thirties but looked sixty, their eyes sunken and skin a light shade of gray. They were always parents of kids aged between seven and thirteen. These were the adults desperate either to flee the country or to secure a consistent food supply. Their children were old enough to be left at home while they did business and yet young enough to remind them their children's childhood was being stolen.

Usually they would arrive before 10 a.m. with a fistful of paper. We would take their paperwork from their long skinny fingers and tell them we'd do what we could. This was the truth. Usually what we could do was put them in a stack of papers that was becoming quite a pile. The hard part was the knowledge of how long it had taken for them to complete the paperwork. Before they arrived at our office they would have already suffered several days of defeat. First they would have had to find a typewriter, a monumental task in war. Then there was the ribbon. One that worked. And the paper. This could take weeks. Then they had to translate all their information into English and pray they didn't mess up along the way. They had to make copies, meaning retype it, because only the large foreign aid groups had the electricity to operate a photocopier. Everything was hard enough in a war but trying to get anything done in an ex-communist country, a place designed to be buried under hills of paperwork with official-looking stamps and signatures, was enough to make a person die of starvation waiting for the process to work.

So we would make them coffee and all of us would sit in the dark and talk about the war. And the food. For the most part we told the truth: when the Road Trip convoy returned we would see how much we had and give to the most needy. We would tell them we couldn't promise anything but that we'd try. What we didn't tell them was there was always a chance the Road Trip would be delayed, which often meant the crew would be stranded for days back in Split, drunk and hungry, eating off the trucks.

When the coffee ran out the conversation often shifted to politics or news from the talks in Geneva. Everyone would shake their heads and curse the politicians until someone mentioned the peace plan. It could be them or us. This signaled that the purpose of the meeting was over. We'd linger in conversation a little longer. Then we'd stand and shake hands. I always felt humbled that I belonged to an organization they took seriously enough to visit. (It wasn't until years later, after speaking with some of these people again, that I realized many had come to our office because the rumor was that we always made coffee for visitors.)

And then there were times I just wanted to lock the door and hide. Sometimes that was exactly what happened.

I remember one day in particular. The batteries for the camera were being recharged by a friend of Vlado's over at the Holiday Inn, which always had electricity for the press corps. The routine went as follows. Film for two days and then take three days off to recharge the batteries, get water and sleep.

Anyhow, on that day there was a soft rapping of knuckles on the door. Some days we just didn't have the food and couldn't look into another mother's eyes—sharp and determined but full of pools of water. Their lives were being torn to hell but they never cried, at least not in front of us; their pride was still intact. That day neither Graeme nor I got up. We just lay there on our separate sides of the filing cabinet throwing pencils into the ceiling. There were large holes in the corner of the ceiling, as if someone had stood on a chair and punched it in anger. Eventually the knocking stopped. There was a pause and then the tip-tap of steps as they walked back toward the stairs.

Graeme got up and stretched. He went into the main room to put on hot water. "I gotta find a dentist," said Graeme.

"Yeah, it's starting to smell pretty bad." One of his teeth had already crumbled into his coffee cup. Not all at once, just bits of enamel over a week. We had spent a few days asking around for a dentist. We even found an office with the drills and everything. But without electricity it just looked like tools from a torture chamber. We scrapped that idea.

In total six teeth were rotting and needed to be pulled.

"What about we take some food over to the sisters today?" he said. We had set aside boxes of food for Vlado, Ciba, and the sisters.

"Sounds good," I replied. "But you gotta eat some gum."

And that was how we cured that ache.

36

Some days later, just before ten o'clock, the curfew hour, Graeme and I arrived at the disco. At the door a guard with a machine gun patted me down and gave a little nod of his head to another guard. The other man looked at the camera and checked my backpack, which had extra batteries and tapes. "MTV," he said and we stepped inside.

The stairs led down, down, down to an underground room that smelled like hot sweaty sex, but sex in a petrol-station bathroom that hadn't been cleaned in months. Although it was pleasantly warm outside, in there it was hot, very hot. Everyone was smoking and if they weren't smoking they were preparing to smoke. There were no windows, no air ducts in sight. To move I had to turn sideways, forcing myself between people who had resorted to yelling in one another's face, above the music. It was hard to breathe. There were just too many people sucking up the oxygen.

The room was divided into two sections. In the front was a bar serving local and foreign beers and spirits. The dance floor was directly off the end of the bar. There, soldiers high on something, hash, alcohol or maybe just one more day of being alive, bounced up and down while their trophy girls tapped their high heels to "Sex Machine" being played up on the stage by Vlado's band—Don Guido and the Missionaries. The lighting was dim and purple and currents of smoke passed from one room to the next. It was the gay days of Berlin 1932, but without the Germans.

We were ushered into what seemed like the back room.

Here there were two tables. At one, two vivacious women in low-cut dresses sat either side of an outrageously large man whose face was the same as in the oil painting hanging on the wall directly behind his head. Just as in the painting he wore gold chains round his neck and several gold rings and a gold bracelet. And as in the painting a pit bull sat on its hind end under the big man's knees.

At the other table sat five Bosnians, men and women, all

wearing designer clothes. The women wore make-up, but not too much, and they all had wonderfully sly smiles on their faces. Visibly tired, most likely from hunger, they were emaciated but stylish. They resembled a bunch of Manhattan hipsters out for the evening . . . in a concentration camp.

A tall, thin man with square black glasses stood up and extended a joint. In perfect English he said, "Don't just stand there. Buy us a round of drinks."

I had twenty German marks in my pocket, enough for five beers. I ordered. He introduced himself as Shibe and said, "I am a surrealist." He pointed his long finger in my eye and asked, "Are you a surrealist?"

I told him I was from California.

"Ah, California. We don't get many Americans here. So how do you like your Indiana Jones adventure so far?"

"I'm not here for an adventure."

"Of course you are. Why else do people come to the center of the universe?"

I hated that it felt like he was right, that I was here to have an adventure of some kind. Whether it was a spiritual, political, or moral quest, I was still in someone else's backyard.

I turned the camera on from time to time, but no one spoke when it was on.

Now Graeme was rolling a joint and talking to a woman with large round eyes and licorice-black hair. They were laughing at something but I couldn't hear the conversation.

Shibe introduced me to his fiancée, Amila. She worked as a translator for a UN officer. When I asked how it was working for the UN, she shrugged her shoulders, more from boredom than as a response.

"This is all a test," said Shibe.

"What is?"

"To see if you are real or surreal."

When he spoke he had strength about him, as if in all this chaos he had a handle on the real truth. He was bold, loud, and funny.

He turned away to laugh at someone else's joke. Graeme passed me the joint. Suddenly Shibe turned back to face me.

He was laughing and yelling in his language at the top of his lungs. People all around clapped.

"Trust me," he said to me in English. "Everyone is coming. The poets, the artists, the politicians, the authors, the important, the parasites, and the bored."

I took a long deep hit of the joint, like I was sucking the plant down into my belly.

"So which are you?" he asked.

"None of them, I hope."

"Are you sure?"

"No."

"There is a price for everything you do here, even if it is free."

"Yeah, but what can I or Graeme or anybody really do?"

He leaned in and for the first time looked directly into my eyes.

"Indiana. Tell me. Everyone in your home city is sleeping in their large beds with the alarm set to wake them in time to go to a job they hate. But you are here, yes? They are the ones that are truly dead."

Vlado sat down next to me and lit yet another joint. "Let us all joint together," he said. Everyone raised their glasses in a salute.

"I see you have met Shibe," said Vlado.

"Yes. I think he thinks we are shit for being here," I said.

"No. He wants to know why people come. If they have an open heart then he welcomes them, always."

"He is crazy, man! Totally crazy. And he is my brother," said Shibe.

"Vlado's your brother?" I asked.

"Everyone at this table is my brother. To sit here means you are my brother. Or sister," he said, looking at the women. "Except Amila. She is my wife-to-be." He gave her a big sloppy kiss.

More hash. More beer. More laughter. This constant state of living in the present moment was overwhelming at times. This was what I wanted to capture on film. This was the marrow of a life worth living. At times it felt so rich it made living in peace seem like very hard work.

"Hey, Indiana Jones, here's a story for you," said Shibe. "On the hill they have the electricity but still they play music on a one-string bullshit guitar. We have no electricity and Vlado plays the blues on a six-string electric guitar. He plays on catguts. They have no rock 'n' roll and we are rock 'n' roll."

Now he was shouting like an evangelical preacher on the road. "That is the difference between us and them. Please don't bore me with any other differences. They are bullshit. That is the real difference between us. Rock 'n' roll and one-string hillbilly music."

The large man from the other table was standing at the edge of our table. I was stoned and it seemed everyone else was too. The man's crotch was level with my forehead and that's how I noticed he had a 357 Magnum in his waistband.

Someone passed him a joint and he shook Vlado's hand before retreating to his table.

"That is Celo," said Shibe, "one of the warlords of the town. He runs this bar. Big guns but small mind. Very useful in war." When he said this he leaned his head down and pushed up his glasses. "Yes?"

Everything blended into something else. Time passed but I don't know when. I filmed some of it, but when I watched it later it made no sense. All I learned was that before the war Shibe had been one of the city's most popular comedians, belonging to a group known as the surrealists.

By four in the morning the lights had dimmed and there were shadowy movements in every corner. In one it looked like a woman had her dress hiked up and was riding a man sitting on a chair. In other dark corners piles of people, six, seven or more, were asleep. They just lay there as if hit by some poison gas that had knocked them out mid-conversation. Graeme had his head on our table while a woman rested her head on his back. On the floor near the door a woman slept sitting up while her boyfriend drank shots of vodka and danced solo to a barely audible Prince song: "1999."

"Indiana," said Shibe, waking me up from my daze. "Do you know what is happening here?"

"How so?"

"Are you in the real or surreal?"

"Well, real. But this is surreal."

"You are in the center of the cosmos. Outside, in London and New York, they believe their lives are real. Feed the dog, say nice things to the neighbor, act like they understand everything. That is not real. They think they are real, but nothing is more real than what is happening here."

"So they are surreal?"

"No. They are unreal, the non-real," he said. I nodded my head, too buzzed to disagree or agree. "Non-real are people who watch other people die on television and then turn it off to go eat dinner."

"But," I said, "I have met people here who told me they were still trying to get to the beach when the Serbs were attacking the Croats."

"Then they are also unreal. Being here doesn't make you real or surreal, it makes you decide who you are."

"So who are the surrealists?"

"We all are," he said, swinging his arm around the table. "When you leave this place and enter the non-real world you become a surrealist. You will have no choice. And then no one can touch you because everything they say is unreal and you will be so real you will glide through all the layers of bullshit. And that is the definition of a surrealist. Gliding through the unreal life."

I told him I thought it was a sound philosophy, one I tried to adhere to.

"So we drink until dawn?" he asked.

"I'm in."

At dawn the men at the top of the stairs opened the doors. We stepped into the light and heard the sound of early morning gunfire. At least it was consistent. The cock keeps crowing, rain or shine, war or peace. People kissed each other on the cheek and made dates to meet up later.

Shibe offered his hand to me. "Indiana, I hope to see you once again." I told him I would see him at the disco again soon.

"Yes. Yes, of course. Be careful. If you stay too long you will never want to leave."

One by one, two by two, everyone quietly disappeared into the long early-morning shadows of the city. They didn't walk, they trotted, something faster than a jog but slower than a run. Someone would later tell me this movement was called the Sarajevo shuffle.

37

Over the next couple of weeks it seemed we could film anyone we wanted. Perhaps it was because people had got used to seeing Graeme and me around town. After a while we were known as the crazy strangers who lived in the UNIS towers. And it didn't take long for us to slip into the role of the crazies. One time we raided the basement and found some new clothes. Graeme found a leather duster coat that fell to his ankles. I found a wool jacket that went down to my knees and a pair of orange corduroy pants. We both wore funky thin glasses we found in the box that wrapped around our eyes. If nothing else it made a change from our one set of soiled clothes.

Then one day we wore the outfits to drink tea at the café near the UNIS. There, a beautiful woman, older than both of us, sat down at our table.

"Why do you wear such clothes?" she asked.

"It's laundry day," said Graeme, trying to be funny.

"Those clothes are quite ugly," she said.

That was the end of that. We changed back to the clothes we came in.

There was always enough to film. Occasionally there would be a gallery opening. Or a fashion show, or a modern art show, and of course there was the production of *Hair*. On most days actors performed the musical *Hair* downtown at a theater and people always came to the show. And there were other shows as well. Like the time Susan Sontag came to Sarajevo and directed Samuel Beckett's *Waiting for Godot*.

And once there was an art opening that featured local artists who had created something from the aid donations. Models walked a catwalk in "United Nations dresses," made from the plastic the UN donated for people to use in their windows. A stack of empty feta cheese boxes that went from floor to ceiling and water canisters stacked on top of one another formed another modern-art piece. I wondered whether in twenty years there would be a museum with a stack of bones from the floor to the ceiling.

Once while wandering the streets with my camera I found Shibe and his surrealist troupe working on a film down an alley near the hospital. There was a camera on a track and someone had a boom microphone. There were people applying make-up to actors and getting them dressed in their wardrobes. The sketch was something about a vampire sucking the blood out of people in the city. But the vampire was then donating all the blood to the hospital. When I walked up, a man was crawling on the ground. The scenario was that the vampire sucks the man's blood until he is so weak he ends up crawling. But then the man sees a piece of cheese on the ground. Dying, he eats the cheese, but really all he is worried about is his canister of water, which he left behind when the vampire sucked his blood.

Something I learned in Sarajevo was the role of comedy in the art of survival. Someone once said that ironic comedy is the public version of private tragedy. In Sarajevo the private tragedies were everyone's public comedy. What one person was experiencing, everyone was experiencing. There was no time for grief or complex thoughts of why this was happening to them.

And the comedy was everywhere. One day I took the camera to film one of Ciba's soccer games, played inside a gym. The game was played with professional deftness. There were four men on each side and each was capable of precision passing. One of Ciba's teammates was Paya, a player for the Yugoslavian national team in the 1982 World Cup. Also on Ciba's team was Celo, the warlord from the disco. The game was relaxing to watch, as if I was in any city on a Sunday afternoon, but after it ended something a bit odd happened.

A man walked up to Celo, who stood bare-chested and sweating, and put a gold chain round his neck. Celo, now talking to several other people, who all laughed at everything he said, put out his hands and the man placed gold rings on his fingers and bracelets on his wrists. Once dressed, he walked into the bleacher seats where he stood directly in front of a thin woman in a short dress and high heels. She handed him, butt first, two 44 Magnum pistols. He put them in his holsters. On the way out one of the men he had been talking to came up and began speaking to him; by the way his eyes were squinted and his hands in the prayer position on his chin, it looked like he was begging. Finally Celo whipped out a wad of money and gave the man some. The man reached up and kissed Celo on the cheek and thanked him what seemed a hundred times.

I followed him outside. With the girl riding shotgun and the dogs in the back seat he roared off in a Mercedes Benz. Before the war he had been in jail for rape. Now? Now he was running a small army of men and controlled a large portion of the black market. He was the king of the street, even if the street was in a prison seven miles long and one mile wide. And if someone didn't realize who he was he made sure they remembered.

There's a photograph of Celo at a checkpoint. In it the guard has his mouth open, and Celo is thrusting a pistol into it. The message is clear: never stop Celo. And then there was the time he rode down the street on a horse, fully armed with a rifle and pistols, and his pit bulls all tied on long leashes to the saddle. But that's another story.

The camera became my way to begin a conversation. Sometimes I would walk the streets with it. There I found kids playing basketball, men playing chess and women reading the coffee beans. I'd walk into a café and talk with the owners, who would laugh and tell me stories of when they were younger. I would ask about the war and they would say, "Ah, I'm tired of this shit."

But the truth is I didn't want to hear their war stories. I only wanted to hear their stories of day-to-day living. What they did for fun. Did they still believe in anything? What about sex? How come everyone laughs so damn much? Soon I came to realize that everyone wants to tell a story. When the camera was on, people would pour it out.

I interviewed Lazy, the lead guitarist for the musical *Hair*. I asked him to tell me his biggest fear in the war.

"When the war started I put my guitar down and went downstairs and asked the soldiers for a gun. When I joined the army I wasn't afraid of being shot, I was afraid of losing my touch for my musical instrument if I didn't practice a lot. That was my biggest fear. After some time I was able to trade shifts on the battlefield so that I was on the front line at night and in the day I could practice the guitar."

I asked if he felt anger toward the Serbs on the hill.

"No. I do not feel hate. I never have felt hate. I think it is because I played my guitar and kept my mind clear."

"Why did you stay in Sarajevo?" I asked. "In the beginning you could have left."

"Yes, I could have left, but like Vlado, like many other people, I stayed. Our people need hope, good spirit, music. Many of us artists thought we had to stay and do our jobs to help save the soul of this city."

"What do you think this war is about?"

"To fight against this primitivism, whether it is from ourselves or from the other side."

"What do you mean by primitive?"

"I mean stupid people are the most dangerous people in the world."

I asked Lazy to tell me the strangest thing that had happened to him in the war.

"Strangest?" he asked.

"Surreal."

"Well, one day I had a grenade in my flat, in my bedroom, but it did not explode. It happened the same day I discovered that my favorite guitar had been stolen. I came home in a horrible mood. Then I entered my bedroom and saw a hole in my closet. It was just like the cartoons. There was the shape of a grenade on the door. It was like a message from God: don't bother about your guitar, you are still alive."

"What happened to the grenade?" I asked.

"My mother came into the room and saw my clothes all over the floor. She was scared to touch the shell. It was big."

"How big?" I asked.

"Well, it was big, an 82 millimeter."

"How big is that?"

"Maybe a meter long."

"Then what?"

"Well, I took it to friends of mine who cut it up and made three grenades from that one. That is the way we get our ammunition. We sent it back to them."

"I heard people sometimes send messages on the bombs. Did you?"

"No. But sometimes the Chetniks do. They say things like 'regards from.' You know, we know many of these people. They were our neighbors."

"This is the craziest thing to understand. How did this happen?" I asked, confused.

"I don't have any explanation. It's part of this primitivism."

38

After almost three weeks, the Road Trip returned with twenty tons of food. And Brigitte, the Frenchwoman with sky-blue eyes and scorching red hair. The maneater. Already the guys followed her orders as if Tony himself was speaking. By the looks of it she had taken over ten men and there was no end in sight. The friction between Tony and Graeme was building.

They weren't staying long, just enough time to deliver most

of the food. In Split Tony had made a deal with the Belgian Jewish group and had arranged some deliveries up north in exchange for petrol money and supplies.

Brigitte stood in the doorway. "We are desperately trying to inventory the supplies. I don't know what you two have been doing this whole time, but the place is a mess," she said with a flair of French accent.

"Bugger off," screamed Graeme. In the front room people shuffled supplies but kept silent.

"I would do it myself but I am busy with Road Trip business," she said.

"What fuck-all business is that?"

"I am going to speak with the French commander at the UN headquarters about getting a secured passage through no-man's-land."

"I've seen you *talk* before. I bet by the time you are through talking with him he'll make you a fucking general or something," said Graeme.

"Oh shut up," said Brigitte. "This is getting old already."

She turned to me with those big blue eyes.

"Bill, can you help us?" she asked.

"I don't mind helping the Road Trip, but I'm not going to help you."

"Well, I am now Tony's assistant," she said.

"Bollocks," said Graeme.

"Brigitte, maybe you should leave us alone and we'll do what we want," I said.

She was furious at that. She put her hands on her hips and looked away and then back again. "I am asking you both to help out the Road Trip and you say no?"

"Come on, bury the shite," said Tony as he put down a box of paperwork. "We need everyone to help. Let's go."

I grabbed a box and started for the door, but she beat me to it. She went ahead of me down the hallway, her red hair swishing. There it was. In Levi's her ass made the shape of a perfect half-moon. There was no way round it. You wanted to give her the business and throw her out the window at the same time.

. . .

On the Trip's return the mood wasn't nearly as friendly as on our first journey into Sarajevo, but for the next three days we got on with delivering aid. We dropped off food and clothes at the hospitals and clinics. A few of the guys dressed up as clowns and delivered goods to a refugee camp near the edge of town. We also hit a few spots from the stack of requests we had taken over the past few weeks. We took more vegetarian food to the Krishna center on Sunday, but, with the heat becoming unbearable, there was no dancing this time. We gave some more baby food and women's clothes to the women's center and delivered some powdered milk and toys to the orphanage. It was better than anything else I could imagine. No matter what else was going wrong, every delivery felt like clean work, like polishing the dust off your soul.

Wanting to take advantage of the transportation while it was here, Graeme and I took Ragga, the trusty Land Rover, and headed out to Dobrinja hospital with the camera. Marco, a teenager who was acting as our translator, came along for the ride.

Graeme drove and I filmed. Near the cut-off to the front-line neighborhood sat a minivan. Attached to the sides and top of the car were two sheets of steel that draped the vehicle, acting as a sort of homemade armor plating. On the side it read *Dobrinja ambulance. One Way. Fare: Your Life*.

Out here several ten-story flat blocks stood like abandoned pieces of a giant Lego set. A few of them had half of the building torn away, blasted apart or riddled with so many bullets the damn thing was on the verge of collapsing. On the way we passed through what was known as "death alley," a series of barricades that ran along the road. There was a large pool of blood off to the side of the road. A woman's shoe lay nearby with the strap dangling. Adrenaline began coursing through my veins.

At the hospital we each carried a box of medicine and some food for the doctors. Inside they had no light, just headlamps and candles. Somewhere in a room someone was screaming. It sounded like that person was being dipped in boiling water. I held the camera and talked to a doctor. The only light was a small light I had attached to some batteries on my belt.

"Would you like some coffee?" the doctor asked, in a steady voice.

"No thanks, mate. We've already had some," said Graeme, being polite, but I could tell he was nervous.

"It's a bit dodgy here, isn't it?" Graeme asked.

The doctor smiled as he tilted his head toward the screaming. "I do not know this word dodgy."

"A bit hectic."

"Do you have any morphine?" the doctor asked.

"No, we gave it all to Kosevo hospital," I said. "How long have you been operating without lights?"

"Yes," he said, as if I'd made a statement and not asked a question. The screaming was getting louder. The whole place was beginning to feel like a Hallowe'en party gone terribly wrong.

"Do you have water?" asked Graeme.

The screaming was now hysterical. And then it stopped. The doctor's eyes looked somewhere over my head. As I focused the camera lamp on his face he rubbed his chin hard with the back of his hand.

"Finally," he said. "Will you excuse me?"

"I don't think I got any of that. Too dark. The microphone was crackling. Where's the diaper?" I spoke urgently to Graeme.

"For fuck's sake, how many times do I have to tell you it's a bloody nappy," he said. "Not a diaper, a nappy."

"Fuck off and give me the goddamn *nappy*."

Bodies bumped into other bodies in the dark. Muffled voices echoed against the tile floor. Someone slipped and fell against my back. It was like walking around in a morgue that had suddenly come to life as a room full of zombies. Then a flood of light from down the hall revealed the zombies. A door to the outside had opened.

Graeme said we had to leave.

The shelling, from the nearby Bosnian Serb forces, was heavy as we ran for the car. A few small mortar rounds hit a flat complex across the street. Most of the people were running or jogging for cover. One man, who looked very sane and peaceful, was standing still, as if waiting for some signal to give him direction. A part of me recognized that stillness. What was it? He was in the bliss of speaking with death up close.

"This man needs a ride to town. Is that OK?" asked Marco, who had his hand on the man's arm.

"Get in, mate," yelled Graeme.

Of course the man had a story. Marco interpreted for us, Graeme drove and I sat next to the man in the back.

"This morning this man's woman was hit by a sniper bullet in the spine. She is now in Kosevo hospital. They think she will live but it is a very serious wound. Perhaps mortal," said Marco, speaking clearly and loudly, as if narrating the nightly newscast.

The man, balding, was in his fifties. He wore a buttoned-up sweater and a white shirt buttoned to the top. He looked straight out of the front window. Calm. Serene. It was the same look I had had when I lifted my face off Corrina's stomach in the hospital. No fear. Nothing to fear. No time. No nerve endings. No life beyond this numbness. He fumbled with his wedding ring. No one spoke until we reached the hospital car park.

"He says thank you. You are so very kind," said Marco. The man walked straight to the front doors, never wavering from his path. Everyone who was in his way moved, not so much because they noticed him, they didn't; it was more like he was a force that moved everything silently. He had turned into a ghost. Graeme looked over at me.

"This place," said Graeme.

I was lost in that man's ghost trail. Like an addict needing a fix from the other side, I wanted to fall in and catch a ride.

"*Spam!*" yelled Graeme.

"We're going to have to get to Italy and fly the F-16s ourselves."

"What you got in mind?" asked Graeme.

"Bomb the bastards."

"Could be a bit dodgy, don't you think?"

"You got training."

"I skipped the class on flying fighter jets with one-ton bombs on the wings."

"Marco, what do you think we should do?" I asked.

"Maybe we should go back to the office and play a game of ping-pong?"

Back at the office the day's events quietly slipped into memory's mud. There was no time. Right? No time. Only the present and today, while the sun was still up, but now that was already long gone, a distant event. Peace at last. And there, in the main room, sat Vlado, Johnny, Alan, Shibe and his girlfriend Amila, and the Road Trip drivers. Shibe was telling a story.

"I was at the border trying to leave," he said.

"Where were you going?" asked someone.

"From Algeria to Morocco."

"I was there once. Bloody forward lot, aren't they, up in me face about this and that," said one of the drivers.

"So I got there too late. I had to stay the night. A man in this small village takes me in. Great. I am tired from all this heat and desert shit. I lie down and he brings me a pound of hash. I smoke and then his daughter comes in and we screw all night. It was like an Arabian fantasy."

A joint landed in my fingers. I toked. "The next day the man sews the hash in a pillow for me as a gift and I drive to the border. So there I am with a pound of hash in my pillow on my way out of Algeria. This is a country that kills people for fucking."

"Crazy Muslim people," said Johnny, the drummer.

"Oops." Graeme was laughing.

"Oh, I see," said Johnny, exaggerating in jest. "Yes, many Bosnians are Muslims too. So, OK, how about 'Oh, those crazy Algerians, killing people for fucking?'"

"What happened at the border?" I asked, getting back to the story.

"Nothing. I was invisible. I am a surrealist. They didn't see me coming."

Someone else spoke, the beginnings of another story, but I don't remember what it was. I went for a piss break and when I returned I sat next to Tony. He asked, "So how's the filming going?"

"Tough getting the batteries charged but we're getting some stuff," I said.

"What are you going to do with it?"

"Don't know. I have a few friends on the production side. But editing is expensive as hell."

"Well, I think it's all shite, but I wish you the best of luck," he said.

Graeme handed me a warm beer and sat next to us on the sofa.

"So you got it all worked out, have ya?" said Graeme.

"Na, just flying by the seat of my ass as usual . . . You staying here or coming with?" asked Tony.

"Staying. I'm into the filming thing. Besides, you got Brigitte copiloting so you don't really need much help."

"Not that again."

"Tony," I said, "she is telling Graeme and me what to do like she's the boss. I listen to you, but her? No way. What's that all about?"

"Careful, mate. Soon enough she'll make the Trip her idea," said Graeme.

"She's just trying to help," said Tony.

"She's not worth it, mate," said Graeme.

"Yeah, well, this is the way it is for now," said Tony.

"Right, mate, whatever you say," said Graeme, his voice changed from laughing to scornful.

Tony mumbled something under his breath.

"What's that you say, Paddy?" asked Graeme.

"Nothing," Tony said.

The next day things calmed down between them. At dinner Tony called a meeting and said that Graeme was number two in the organization and that I was to be second in charge of the Sarajevo office. Of course there were only two of us there so this wasn't much of a promotion. Still, Brigitte looked disappointed.

The Road Trip left town with promises of returning with more food, propane gas, and popcorn. They said it might be three or four weeks. It could be longer if they ran out of money or had mechanical problems. But I had to forget about them for a while. It was easy. I just fell further into the people I was meeting in Sarajevo. Each one seemed to be a small shard of glass that added up to the whole shattering of Corrina. Almost. And then there was Corrina. She was always there, just over the hill, in the house with the lights on. Sometimes I could almost hear her calling me to come find her. At other times I could feel her hand on the small of my back, pushing me further into this place.

39

In the middle of May Ciba's art show was almost ready. It had taken the better part of a month to gather enough wood for the frames. We got most of it from a friend of Ciba's who had owned a framing business before the war. Then we borrowed a car and brought the framing machine from his house to Ciba's office in the UNIS towers, where there was electricity a few hours a day.

The day of the opening it was heavy outside. Lots of snipers and shells. The venue was a store owned by Paja, another friend of Ciba's. It was located on a street that ran perpendicular to the snipers. So a person could walk safely up a side street and see the gallery twenty feet away, but to get to the front door they would have to cross a street with no cover. I was certain no one would come, but Ciba didn't seem to be bothered by the prospect.

He kept smiling and walking around the gallery adjusting his paintings. Amra beamed a proud smile and greeted people as they ran in the door as if they were rushing to take cover from the rain. Head and chest first, followed by the feet, as the whole body tried to slow down once it crossed the threshold. Paja put out wine, biscuits, and cheese. And of course the place filled up so much you could barely move from one end of the room to the other. I put the camera on a tripod and let it run.

Later, when I watched the raw footage, the most noticeable thing was what people were wearing. Everyone had on suits and ties and when they entered the door they took off their stylish hats. It could have been a gallery opening in Prague, Manhattan, or London. The only conversation I could make out on the tape was Celo, the warlord. He saw Graeme and me in the corner behind the camera and walked right up and said, "You have any hash?"

There was a frail but happy old man standing in front of a painting. He had wrinkles that dug into his skin from his forehead down to the tip of his nose, no teeth and a large bump protruding from his right temple. And he just kept smiling like an idiot who was glad to be out of the cold. He and I got to talking. His name was Leonardo and he was telling me about the time all his Jewish friends were put on the trains. I asked him when this happened and he said at the beginning of the war. We talked about a few other matters before I returned to the trains.

"The trains were destroyed in the beginning of the war. The Serbs couldn't have shipped people out," I said.

"No. No. Not this war, World War Two."

So there it was. Two wars, worn deeply into the face of one man.

In the end Ciba sold several of his paintings, which were mostly landscapes. The goldsmith bought one and so did Paja, the gallery owner. Celo, decked out in his gold chains and burgundy suit, bought the biggest one, a field of pastel-colored wild flowers. He put it in his restaurant, Bohemia. Later, when I asked why he bought this particular print, he said it made him feel calm.

Outside? It was still raining steel.

But all in all the day ended better than most.

40

After a month I had a routine and Graeme had his. I got up, dabbed a little water on my face and pissed. I checked to see the toilet was still clean and took a dump, if I could. Travelers all know a feces examination is the surest way to check your health. I was in good color but I had lost ten pounds by now and was having irregular bowel movements. After cleaning myself with scrap paper I'd blow out the candles and lock the bathroom door so that no one could use it unless they came to the office for the key.

After the bathroom ritual I would first put on my shirt, which reeked of me. Then I'd put on my pants, sweaty, but they still worked. A few weeks back I had to put a hole in the belt above the last notch to keep them up. Some days there was no shelling, and some days, when the shelling was heavy, I didn't get dressed at all. I stayed in bed and read. I was engrossed in the thick magical textures of Gabriel García Márquez's *Love in the Time of Cholera*.

Gradually Graeme took to sleeping later and later in the day. Occasionally he would sleep through until dark. The stink from his decaying mouth got so bad I eventually moved my sleeping bag to the other room. Our conversations became short and simple.

"You getting water today?"

"Yep. Soccer?"

"Three o'clock."

"See ya."

Soccer with Ciba. Tea and beers at the café next door to the UNIS towers, and socializing in the office in the evening. Vlado was there more often than not. As were Johnny and Dutzo. But Alan, the bass player, was there less and less. To escape from being drafted into the Bosnian army Alan had decided to pose as a schizophrenic, but he had become too good an actor. It seemed his schizophrenia had taken hold in a way he couldn't shake. He disappeared for a while into some mental black hole.

Graeme brought home a cat one day. We named it Bonkers. Then not long after its arrival it had a litter, and we began feeding the small ones the canned milk we had in the basement cage. Our ping-pong games were fierce and we would invite local talent just to whip their asses.

Then there was Ivan. This was the name we gave the sniper across the street. Like clockwork we could rely on Ivan. Every day at 11 a.m. he would start blasting away. It took a week or so to realize that he never hit anything except rooftops and walls, down by the school. We figured he was either new to the gun or very young. I asked one of the locals about Ivan.

"I have this fight with some of the others at least once a week. I think he is forced to," she said. I asked her what she meant.

"He never shoots anyone. Maybe he is missing on purpose. You know there are many young boys on that side who are forced to fight," she said.

I tried to imagine it. Ivan took the shift when the kids were in school to keep the murderers he had lunch with at bay. He shot at the kids to save their lives. It was possible, I suppose.

That was what I learned in Sarajevo. Everything is possible.

From then on, Ivan became a back-handed hero. His secret was safe with us.

And that was how Ivan became part of the day. There was cooking, retrieving water, feeding the cat, crapping, playing soccer, sleeping, pissing, laughing, drinking and then there was the sniper who was secretly shooting high from the other side of the river.

And so it goes.

41

It was hot and almost the end of May, and I was staring at the ceiling wondering what the name of the girl lying next to me was. Graeme and I had been at the disco until three in the morning, filming Vlado and the band. It had been so crowded at the disco and there was so little air that my camera had literally begun to sweat. It had lain in the corner, near the foot of the bed, temporarily out of order with a fever.

I looked at the girl and we started kissing. Soon after that we were panting and tearing at each other's clothes. My head was still full of the night's indulgence. Then, like always, I had to start with the guilt. I had a hard time being with women even though I always wanted to. I just didn't see the point sometimes. When I made love it was as if I was crawling up the ladder that led to Corrina. But after, when the buzz of passionate possibility wore off, I would roll over and not sleep, somehow wishing to be anywhere but where I was, next to another woman. It drove the women crazy wondering what I was thinking. In the end they usually left disappointed. What I really wanted was to fall asleep with someone. That would be a step in the right direction. Besides, I didn't want to get mixed up with any girl from here. What if I became some pipe-dream way out of this place? The truth was even I didn't know if I was going to get out.

Still, this time I was overcome by desire and wanted to have sex until we both screamed so loud the snipers would be roused from their naps. Instead, she backed off, saying she didn't want sex. "Everything is too shit to do that," she said. Then she quickly unbuttoned my trousers, fished around my crotch with her hands, and, like one of her cigarettes, she proceeded to take me inside her mouth and smoke me.

After she fell asleep I lay there wondering if Corrina was watching all this. Was she a part of it? Was she somehow moving people around down here to give a signal everything was all clear on the other side?

Then, or just about then, the world erupted.

The building shook from the first direct hit. Then another.

Dressed in my pants, I walked into the office and out into the ping-pong room. Bombs were hitting every fifteen to twenty seconds. Downtown, uptown, midtown, on the outskirts of town. Another one hit the building. Rockets spitting red tails of exhaust blazed down from the mountains. Tracer fire erupted from the sniper positions on the hills. The big guns firing from several kilometers back hit the city with the boom of a marching band's tune.

I hadn't noticed Graeme sitting in his underwear next to me.

"This is it, mate," he said in amazement.

"What's happening?" I asked.

"The end."

"You think?"

"I think they are going to try and take the city."

The shells were now landing all around us. We ran into the office and put on our shirts. The two girls were up and dressed. They were screaming at each other about something. They made for the door.

"Where are you going?" I asked.

"Home," she yelled.

"You sure? It looks bad out there."

"Yes. I am sure."

After they left the bombing got worse. Our building was taking hits every other minute and the view outside the window was like a fireworks factory that had just blown up in some western province of China.

The hours turned into more hours and after a while we found ourselves lying on our stomachs in the office with our hands over our ears. In the afternoon the camera began working again. I set it on a tripod and faced it out the back of the building, toward Ciba's house. I was filming when Wally, the French-Senegalese running Equilibre downstairs, walked in. He was wearing his bulletproof Kevlar jacket.

"Real shit, eh?" he said.

"I'd say," said Graeme.

"I think I will see *Hair* today," announced Wally with a smile.

"What?" Graeme yelled.

"I can't stay here. I'm going crazy. *Hair* will be good today."

"Wally, maybe it's been called off," I yelled above the shelling.

He laughed. "Bosnians would never call it off because of shelling."

"You aren't walking, are you?"

"No. Taking the hard shell."

So Wally left the building, but Marco, the young kid with horn-rimmed glasses, came in. He asked if he could stay. Graeme said yes, as long as he made some tea.

Graeme and I went into the ping-pong room and started a game. It was strange playing ping-pong while bullets flew through the office, into our bedrooms. In fact it was mad, but it seemed like a good idea at the time.

"How's the hot water?" yelled Graeme.

"It's ready," Marco answered.

"Well, come on then. Let's have us some tea!"

It was really coming down now. The sniping was a constant but random patter. Glass was breaking everywhere. The shells were landing two every minute, but they seemed to be concentrating mostly on specific areas, further away from us.

"Right. You lead 7–3," he yelled. "My serve."

"It's my serve, you ass," I said. Our brains were beginning to rot. A lack of sleep and poor nutrition combined with the stress was beginning to make us act like we weren't getting enough oxygen to the brain.

Marco walked in with the tea. Graeme tasted it.

"Oh bloody hell, this is absolutely horrible tea."

Wham. Wham. Two shells landed just outside the window. Laughing, I filmed Graeme and Marco.

"What did you do to my tea, Marco?" asked Graeme. "Marco," he continued, "if you can't make decent tea then I'm not sure you can be in the Road Trip." He wasn't angry at all, just losing his grip like the rest of us.

It went on like this until nightfall and then it continued well into the night. At one point I interviewed Graeme in the ping-pong room. His face was gray and he was in a state of shock. Whatever was happening to our nervous systems was starting to show up on our skin. The adrenaline was beginning to rot us.

Words fall well short of describing the primal fear that takes over your body when you are the recipient of an incoming artillery attack. And it's not the explosion that you remember; it's the sound of the shell hitting concrete, something like a metallic scraping of pavement. That sound quickly turns into a thud in the thick of your groin that stays with you for some time. Years later, after a bad dream, I can still sometimes feel this thud just below my waistline, like someone tugging at my small intestine with needle-nose pliers. The strange bit is that it has a taste too, like chewing on mercury flakes from an eroding cavity.

As for the sniper? That monster works on another part of your body entirely. The crackling of the 30.6 sends a steel rod through the spine and pushes the vertebrae flat. And then there are the sniper's cross-hairs, from his scope, on the back of your skull. You always feel them, no matter how dark the room or how deep the basement. You feel them especially when you are asleep in a room with no light. They are always there, an X on your leg, arm, forehead.

Either way, artillery or sniper, when you survive another attack you are left with a fresh injection of adrenaline percolating in the pit of your stomach. Soon the chemical courses through your veins to every organ and limb. It reaches your gums, your tongue, your heels, your crotch. If you stay long enough, and aren't ripped apart by a shell or shot in the head by a sniper, then it will be the adrenaline that begins to kill you. You can see it most pronounced in the young. Premature wrinkles show up and the hair begins to fall out. Nerves are shot and eyes begin to twitch. Teeth rot, skin turns gray and sullen. The mind becomes mush.

I asked if this was the worst Graeme had seen it.

"Yes."

"Are you afraid for your life?"

He didn't answer.

"What do you want to do?"

"I'm not sure."

"So, Graeme Bint, why are you here?"

He locked his jaw down tight and stared over my head.

"What was that?"

Wally returned later that day and said the performance of *Hair* had been great. Of course, Wally was going mad too.

The war never seemed to let up after that. And Graeme was never quite the same. He made a decision to return to London to fix his teeth. When? He didn't know, but soon. In the meantime he started sleeping even more, for days at a stretch. And his teeth kept crumbling into his morning coffee. Piece by piece.

42

It was around mid-June when I thought of the idea.

Graeme and I were in the Sarajevo television station when my eye caught a television monitor. This was one of the few places in the city where you could get satellite television and have a constant source of electricity. We were there to talk with Senad, the producer of the offbeat and surreal programme *Rat Art* or, translated, *War Art*, which sometimes parodied Serbian television programs. And there was always plenty to parody. At that time the latest Serb music video was of Serbia's most popular girl pop star, who was dating Arkon, one of Serbia's most prominent war criminals, sitting astride a tank turret with her legs dangling on either side. The title of the song: "My Lover is a Chetnik".

So there we were in the *Rat Art* studio when my eye caught the monitor. It was an MTV program and someone was interviewing the Irish band U2 about their upcoming European tour. The host asked a question I didn't catch, but the answer from one of the band members was something like "A great deal of what's behind this tour is the idea of addressing the idea of a united Europe."

What Europe were they speaking of? Europe was ignoring their geographical ass down here in Bosnia. And, I thought, while we are on the subject, whatever happened to Bob Geldof or any of the other outraged artists out there in the world? Isn't it the job of the artist to light a candle to show the injustices of the world? Probably not, but it seemed like a good notion. Still, I became obsessed with the idea that Mr. Geldof and many others had raised a load of money and a great deal of awareness with Live Aid, and yet as far as I could tell no one was talking about Bosnia, even though it was being beamed live to the world via CNN. We were reminded of it constantly. Like the time we were watching CNN on the local station and they were showing the UNIS towers being bombed. Nothing unusual in that, except we'd been in them at that moment.

So it was about this time I had the idea. I asked Graeme about it as we stood on the side of the road preparing to run across Snipers' Alley to the sisters' home with some food.

"What do you think of trying to interview U2 about Sarajevo?" I said.

"What for?" His eyes were focused on the sniper locations across the road.

"I saw them on TV talking about a united Europe."

"That's a load of bollocks."

"I know, but an interview would be a connection of some sort. Right?"

"Never happen."

Graeme ran across the street with a box of food on his head. I followed with the camera. There were no shots today. It was a lovely day with cumulus clouds and a hot sun. A breeze carried the scent of leaves. Maybe elm? On the other side we caught our breaths, which I noticed were getting shorter and shorter by the day.

"All right, let's say you arrange an interview with these wanker posh boys," *huff huff*, "and they say things that make them look cool, but it doesn't do squat for here." *Huff huff*. "Then what? You look like the fool."

At lunch I told the sisters, Lejla and Selma, about the idea and they laughed. They told their parents and they laughed. No one was making fun of me, it just sounded ludicrous from where we were sitting. They said I was becoming crazier by the week. But Lejla did say, with great drama and great sarcasm, "If you do get the interview, darling, please do invite Bono for lunch at our home."

Feeling inspired, I went back to the TV station and asked Senad for two pieces of paper with the Bosnian station letterhead. Then I walked four kilometers across town to the headquarters of the International Rescue Committee, IRC, an NGO. This was the outfit my friend Jason worked for in Croatia. Jason had told me about the Sarajevo chief, John Fawcett. He said he was the most level-headed and possibly the most informed person in the city about what was happening here.

On Jason's name I was allowed to enter. Fawcett's office was in the back of the UN headquarters, past armed guards. We introduced ourselves and I proceeded to tell him my idea. John was an ex-hippie who had migrated to Vancouver in the early 1970s. He was five foot eight and wore Levi's and a red flannel shirt. His walrus moustache drooped down the sides of his chin. His face, pale, long, and drawn, looked tired but calm. He wasn't the kind that got too excited or too dejected. He stayed the course. I could tell by his smile there was no doubt where he thought I was coming from: a little out there.

I sat in his office, surrounded by a refrigerator full of Coca-Cola and juice. There was bread on the table and cheese waiting to be eaten. I hadn't seen this much food in more than a month. Our food had long run out and I was eating a steady diet of chocolate baby food and rice. I smelled a little and my hair was dirty and uncombed. The locals in this office, even if their situation at home was desperate, still took great pride in their public appearance. It was a pride that came from living an urban cultured life. In public they dressed up, did their nails, wore perfume and made certain to act like nothing ever affected them. They might have been standing in long water queues before and after work, or fighting the local bureaucracy to remain in their homes, but in public, especially around foreigners, they stood tall and proud. Me? I had spent too many years traveling out of a backpack. Dirt and filth were part of my background.

I told John my plan. Jason and Ivana were going to the U2 Verona concert, so transport would be taken care of. Once there I would interview the band about Bosnia and return to deliver the tape to the television station. The idea was so simple it might work: to remind Sarajevans that there were still cultural icons who had not forgotten them. I figured that if I wrote the letter on Bosnian stationery it would catch the attention of a secretary, who would be too frightened to dismiss it out of hand. If logic prevailed she would give it to someone higher up who would feel the same impulse not to take responsibility for assuming this was a hoax. Ignoring a fax from a place that is dying would be a daunting decision, I thought. The only thing going for me would be this piece of paper with the letterhead of the Bosnian TV station on it. If I wrote the same letter on a piece of white paper and signed it "Bill Carter" I was sure I would hear absolutely nothing back.

He agreed to let me use the typewriter to write the letter and when I had the correct number for U2 management he said I could return to use his fax to send it. Somehow this all led to a conversation about the artists of Sarajevo. John said, "When this thing is over, and it will end one day, the artists are going to have to take the lead in getting this city rebuilt, emotionally." This man was light years ahead of anyone else in the humanitarian aid business, which as far as I could tell was littered with people worried that if the war ended they would be out of a job.

RADIO TELEVIZIJA BOSNE I HERCEGOVINE
RADIO AND TELEVISION OF BOSNIA AND HERZEGOVINA

To: Paul McGuinness
Cc: U2 band members   June 25, 1993
From: Senad Zaimović/Bill Carter

Dear Mr McGuinness and the Band Members,

Bosnian television, based in Sarajevo, is very interested in doing an interview with the members of U2. We understand that the group will be in Verona, Italy, July 3, and think this is the perfect opportunity to do this interview. Verona is one concert in Europe that will have the largest ex-Yugoslavia crowd due to the fact that it is the only U2 concert that tickets are being sold for in Croatia. Plus it is the only concert we can possibly attend.

Sarajevo, in former Yugoslavia, was the center of its art and rock and roll culture. It still has an art scene trying to survive, but it lacks creative input, due to the obvious physical and information restraints. To many people here the true tragedy of the war is the lack of personal and creative freedom. The television is constantly showing the war that exists directly outside their windows and what people really need is some fresh input.

We think a direct interview with the band from our TV would be very special. We would invite you here for a concert but due to the obvious numerous reasons that can't happen. Showing the interview with the group would be a phenomenal uplift for the Bosnian spirit. There are thousands of U2 fans in Sarajevo and this is the next best thing to seeing a live concert.

U2 is the perfect group for having an interview about both their music and their homeland. In addition the Zoo TV concept seems perfect for addressing issues such as Bosnia and a united Europe. We realize that the band must have done hundreds of interviews by now but Sarajevo and Bosnia have not been privy to those. This interview would be exclusively for Sarajevo and Bosnia. This is the chance to speak directly to Bosnia.

Since communication and travel is extremely limited in and out of Sarajevo this fax has taken a substantial amount of time to get to you. Due to the fact that there is a new Serbian checkpoint at the entrance to the Sarajevo airport, travel for Bosnians is next to impossible. Our foreign associate, Bill Carter, who has been in Sarajevo for months working on an independent documentary and working closely with Sarajevo TV, is coordinating the efforts and is the one who would come to Verona. The taped session would be put on Bosnian TV when the electricity comes back on. Due to the difficulty in communication and travel arrangements it is hoped that your response is speedy.

Good luck with all your efforts.

Thanks,

Senad Zaimović, Director of *Rat Art*, Sarajevo TV

Bill Carter

43

It took a few days to find a fax number for the band. I found it by going to the town's alternative radio station, Radio Zed or, translated, Radio Wall. It operated out of an office well bunkered with sandbags. Hip, aloof and a bit pretentious, the DJs were perfect for an urban youth station. We scanned a few U2 albums but couldn't find any numbers. But I found what I needed. A name: Principle Management.

"It won't work. No one cares about this place," said the DJ. "I don't even care any more."

I thanked him and promptly left, more determined than ever.

Now my problem was the phones. The only working phones in Sarajevo were satellite phones, gadgets that come in small suitcases with tiny umbrellas sticking out of them. At $25 a minute, it was primarily news organizations that used them, although I did meet a Dutchman once who'd sold his car in Amsterdam and borrowed money from friends to buy a satellite phone for $25,000 and a train ticket to Poland. There he bought a red Zvasta, a plastic car. Once in Bosnia he drove around the country looking for the front lines. When the fighting started he would park the car behind a barn or on the side of the road, open up his truck, set up his umbrella, and rent the phone out to the highest bidder. By the time I met him he had made his money back three times over and was in the final stages of buying an armored car to rent out to news organizations on a weekly rate.

George Soros, the billionaire philanthropist in New York, paid for the only other phones that worked in the city. These were landlines and were found only in what were deemed to be priority buildings: those of the army, the Presidency and various aid groups, including John Fawcett's group, IRC.

"It's actually a local call from Pittsburgh," said John the day I asked if I could use his phone to call Dublin information.

"What do you mean, a local call?" I asked, wondering if John was screwing with me.

"Somehow, and don't ask me how, the call goes to an operator in Pittsburgh. That's how it's set up. So theoretically if you called someone you knew in Pittsburgh it would be charged as a local call."

This made no sense, and I never met anyone who could explain how or why this worked. And if it worked so well and so easily, why didn't anyone connect the entire city to these landlines?

John gave me the use of his phone. The Dublin operator quickly gave me the number for Principle Management. When she'd finished reading it off she thanked me and wished me a "good day".

I called the number.

"May I help you?" the voice said.

"Yes. Hello. Is this the correct number for Principle Management and U2?"

"It is."

"I need to send a fax from Sarajevo. Could you give the fax number to me, please?"

"Certainly," she replied and gave me the number. She thanked me and hung up. Click. My first contact with the outside world in months had been a lovely Irish woman for less than twenty-five seconds. It felt like a splash of the Adriatic on my face. The voice was soft and polite. I was saddened and excited in the same moment. I wanted just to sit and talk with her a while about what she'd done that morning, what she'd had for breakfast and what she was going to do after work. Take a walk along the river, have a beer, or maybe make love to her boyfriend? A thought crossed my war-racked mind: would she consider marrying me?

After sending the fax I called Jason and Ivana to tell them their office number in Split was the one I had used as a contact for U2.

"What are you doing with U2?" Jason asked, sounding a bit stunned.

"Well, nothing yet, but if we're lucky I might get them on tape about Bosnia."

"You know Ivana and I are going to the concert in Verona?"

"Yes. I'm trying to make it happen at that concert."

The hard part would be contacting me if U2 called back. We agreed the only way it could happen was if U2 contacted Jason in Split, and then Jason would contact John in Sarajevo, who would then somehow get a message to me at the UNIS towers.

Feeling dazed by the communication with the outside world, I sat down with John and the other expats in the coffee room. It was the social hour and people were talking of nothing in particular and gossiping about other organizations or certain political figures. It was strange; it resembled any office lunchroom anywhere in the world. Small talk to fill the time. I found it comforting.

There was one man who stood out. His name was Fred Cuny and he towered over the others in the office. He spoke with a Texan drawl and I guessed his cowboy boots were size fourteen. He was talking about bringing in gas pipelines from Texas via special air force planes, and he was angry about the Pentagon holding up his requests. He had an intimidating presence but at the same time his smile was genuine and by the tone of his conversation he was perturbed because he couldn't help the people here as fast as he wanted.

On the way out I put two Coke cans in my trouser pockets and a couple of fountain pens in my shirt pocket. John stopped me at the door. I apologized for the Cokes and pens.

"Don't worry about that. Come on by the IRC house for dinner Friday. Living in the UNIS can't be all that great," he said.

I thanked him for the phone and the typewriter and told him I'd be there for dinner. It was nice to know I had a place to go, even if there was no way to fill the hole in my chest that constantly reminded me of the only thing I knew for certain. That in this journey we call life, we are all ultimately alone.

44

Graeme's departure had a mixed effect on my state of being. He caught a ride to the airport with the French and said he would be back soon. He was returning to London to take care of his teeth. Besides, I had to admit, the place was getting to us.

For instance, that day when the shrapnel hit the room, we had gone to the top of the building. Who knows why? We'd taken the camera. On the top floor Graeme filmed me tiptoeing toward the front windows.

Bang, bang, bang. Three shots. They sounded like they were coming from inside a room just in front of us.

"I don't like the looks of this in here," I had said.

"Open the door," said Graeme.

"Dude, I'm not opening that fucking door."

"Come on then."

More shots were fired.

"It's either a sniper shooting out, meaning he's Bosnian and that's cool. Or those are bullets being fired into that room."

We crouched low to the floor and crawled toward the room. For a few minutes there was no sound.

"Maybe they got bored," I said. I was now filming Graeme, who looked as scared as I felt.

Bang. A bullet burst through the wall just above Graeme's head, sending pieces of metal everywhere. He caught a small piece in his back.

"Go. Go. Go."

Whoever was shooting shot at us the whole way down the stairs, which were exposed at each floor. We jumped stairs and delayed our descent hoping the shooter would get off rhythm. He did.

In the office I used tweezers to get the piece out of his shoulder. We were breathing hard and our guts were light.

"OK. No more of that bullshit," he said.

So Graeme left. Besides the madness, his rotting teeth had decayed to the point where you could smell them from anywhere in the office. I was glad to be free of that rot.

Still, it took only one night alone for me to feel his absence. The office was empty. There was no laughter echoing down the halls. No one here to spontaneously make fun of the guards or the Frenchies. When I called the French "frogs" it just sounded mean. When he said it everyone laughed, especially the French. He was more than my best friend. He was someone I had bonded with through all that we had seen here. Sure, I had people back home that I'd known for more years, but Graeme and I had shared this time, this place, this space. As I lay on top of my sleeping bag the sky was filled with stars and no wind. I was sweating in a June heatwave and for the first time I felt like leaving. Not because the city had finally got to me, but because my friend had left. After all, what was I doing here? Handing out food packages to people who had become my friends. Why not just give them the keys to the office and warehouse and get out of the way? And what else? I was filming people, interviewing them, in an attempt to capture something of the spirit of life among the rubble. The truth was I had $100 to my name and that wasn't even enough to mail these tapes home to someone who could edit them. Still, I couldn't leave quite yet. I told myself I would wait to hear the answer from U2. At least that was a reason to stay.

All I knew was I didn't want to stay here so long that I was like Graeme's teeth, rotting away, waiting for someone to pull me out.

45

The heat affected the city as it would any other modern city without services, electricity or sewage. Everything about Sarajevo felt like walking into some past century where the plague was in full epidemic and it stank like human grease and decaying dog dirt.

Earlier in the day, downtown, I had run into Johnny and Dutzo—from Vlado's band—in a mutual friend's home. They were lying on the floor, a small marijuana plant between them.

They spoke slowly and tried not to move their bodies for fear of sweating. Every ounce of energy was required to fight off the need for water. But the plant was also thirsty.

"We take turns sweating on the leaves to give it water." Johnny laughed through a tight and exhausted smile.

Still waiting for word from U2, I took a walk up to the IRC house. It was a modern home on top of a hill behind the Kosovo hospital. On my walk I passed a community of Gypsies who had found themselves trapped in the city. They wanted money and candy but I had nothing to give. I kept my eyes locked on my target, not wanting to make eye contact. I was sweating when I arrived and waited outside a few minutes hoping to cool down.

Inside there was a small crowd of locals and expats lounging in the living room, drinking Danish beer and eating chocolate. I'm not a zealot like Graeme. He would have chastised these people for having something while the people outside had nothing. He is stark in his moral and ethical decisions. I am more muddled. To me it's more fluid. I opened a beer, guilt-free, and drank until it was gone. Then I opened another.

"I think they are going to bomb one of these nights," said Fred Cuny, the Texan. I asked him why he thought that.

"Washington is getting tired of screwing around with these kooks Milosevic and Karadzic. They are yanking our chain and everyone knows it."

"But we've known it for years, why now?" I asked.

"A few more stupid mistakes on their part and that will be the end of it," he said. "Pretty soon someone is going to haul off and beat the holy shit out of them."

Fred went on to tell stories of other countries he'd worked in—Angola, Somalia, and Cambodia. His entire life had been spent bringing gas lines, water treatment plants, and infrastructure to countries in dire straits. I wasn't sure who he worked for or whom he reported to but his heart seemed large and generous. When he learned I was living in the UNIS towers he wouldn't let up.

"That is a dangerous place, son. Serbs use that heap for target practice," he said.

I told him I was fine. And I was. Besides, I didn't want his opinions on my housing.

When I left that night John gave me a box of food and told me to come by the office for anything I needed.

The last time I saw Fred was at Ciba's studio. By that time Ciba had begun a small cottage industry painting portraits of UN officers who wanted a picture of themselves from their time in Sarajevo. Fred had wanted Ciba not to paint him but to paint his favorite inanimate object, fighter jets. Ciba had produced several canvases of jet fighters in action over the city. Even then, in the studio weeks later, Fred was still telling us, "They are going to bomb soon. They just have to." His voice was strong and hopeful, but I could tell he felt helpless in his efforts to get the ear of anyone in Washington.

That last day in the studio he handed me a shirt with his company name on the front. On the back was some bizarre lettering that looked like Arabic. "That's Sudanese for 'Don't shoot'," he said.

As I write this I can't help but wonder if that was his good-luck shirt. I later heard that Big Fred from Texas went off to Chechnya and got killed. It seemed he was kidnaped. John Fawcett said they never found the body, just documents and some clothing that were linked to Fred. The story made all the newspapers. They were even going to make a movie starring Harrison Ford. Well, RIP Fred, and thanks for the shirt. It has worked for me. So far.

"Heard from Graeme?" asked Wally, the man from Senegal with the beautiful eyes. It had been a week since I'd faxed U2 in Dublin. Wanting not to burden IRC's phone, I had come to ask if I could use Equilibre's powerful maritime radio. They were usually very strict about it but I gambled that Wally, who like me, was alone here, would want some company. He agreed and went about setting up the call.

"Did you ever smell his teeth?" I asked, speaking of Graeme.

"No," said Wally.

"Horrible," I said.

Wally appeared genuinely disturbed by that thought.

"You seem thinner," he said.

"Yeah, well."

"Maybe you should take a break. Go to Split."

"I will. I will. But I need to know what's going on with this."

I was agitated. I'd felt myself losing patience lately and had spent more time in my room or just walking the streets for no reason other than to walk them.

Wally set the radio to call Lyon, where the operator was based. Equilibre had special permission from the French government to use this ocean radio from Sarajevo as if they were a boat. I thought it was an ingenious idea.

From Lyon the operator hooked up the radio to a phone and you could call anywhere in the world. It was a time-consuming process. We tried for more than an hour but heard only static.

"I am tired of the Chicago Bulls," Wally said.

"Yeah, I hear that," I replied.

The radio crackled to life.

"Hello," said a voice. It was an Irish voice. It wasn't the same one as the time before, but I wasn't picky.

"Hello," I said.

"You have to talk very loud," said Wally.

"Hello. This is Bill Carter calling from Sarajevo. Did you receive our fax?"

"Yes, we did." She sounded startled.

"Is there an answer?" I yelled.

"I wouldn't know that," she said.

"OK. Well, I can't talk very long. When will you have an answer?"

"It has been sent by fax to the band on tour. We will get back to you as soon as we know."

"You understand how difficult it is to get a phone line out?"

"I understand."

"OK. Well, please tell them to hurry up."

"I'll do my best."

"OK. Thank you," I said.

"Goodbye."

Wally hung up. "You still think it's going to work?" he asked.

"Absolutely. How can they ignore a fax from here?"

"OK, but come on . . . it's from you."

"Yeah, but they don't know that."

46

The most common occurrence in war—more than scenes of blood and guts, for they usually happened elsewhere to other people—was the daily reminder that life is made up of random events that seem to repeat themselves.

You see, I had come full circle and was back in Split, sitting across the desk from the same sergeant who had issued me that press pass a few months back. It was toward the end of June and I had left Sarajevo a few days earlier. And in that time I had lost my press pass. To be honest, I wasn't sure I would ever need it again. I told all my Sarajevo friends I would be back, but since I hadn't heard anything from Ireland regarding the interview, I had left thinking perhaps I wouldn't return. Besides, leaving Sarajevo that morning was so hassle-free. I went to the airport, showed my UN-accredited press pass, and in forty-five minutes landed in Split, where by sunset I had joined a handful of other beach-goers swimming in the warm waters of the Adriatic.

Maybe Graeme was right. The U2 interview idea was doomed not because it was a bad one, but because they were a bunch of "posh punters."

During this idle time waiting for the phone to ring I began to ask myself about what I had done. Up to this point everything had worked because I'd never questioned my motivation. Thus far my mind had no sense of need, want, desire, or personal gain. In Sarajevo I was surrounded by what it took to live life fully in the present moment. People had an intimate relationship with death. They weren't friends with death. That would be too simple, morbid, and fatalistic. It was more like they were resigned to the fact that death might come at any moment and they didn't want to be caught flat-footed worrying about it.

The concert was in three days. Sitting in the airport I made a decision. If they didn't call I would take a break from Sarajevo. I told myself I would take a job with Mooner, a Scot who had come to the Balkans with his suitcase and tennis shoes at the beginning of the previous year. He'd come with no money or contacts and within nine months had been awarded a large European Union contract that allowed him to begin a $5 million housing operation in Tuzla, rebuilding homes destroyed in the war. He was a well-known success story in the shoestring aid business and over beers he told me he had a job for me. Convoy leader. I would drive a Land Rover with a large radio and lead convoys of supplies from Split to Tuzla, through hostile Croatian territory.

I agreed, but first I had to replace my lost press pass.

I wanted the press pass because with it I could fly for free on a military cargo plane to either Greece or Italy. Either one would suffice. I needed a break from the land of the Balkans. I wanted my feet not to be touching this place, whose war seemed to be dragging me down by my toes. I'd have to borrow some money but figured I could get a loan from Jason or an advance from Mooner.

The sergeant? It took only a few seconds to spot the lazy motion of his hands and lips and realize nothing fundamental had changed in his life. He woke every day to ham and eggs in the mess hall and then remained in this office, unaware of the war to which the planes departed from outside his window. In relative terms, I had traveled a lifetime since I saw him last. Yet it seemed I had been here just yesterday conning him for my first press pass. While he, for all intents and purposes, could be sitting in a desk somewhere in London selling insurance.

He remembered me right away, but that didn't stop him from breaking into his dreadful mantra detailing the rules of how to obtain a press pass. The same rules and the same lecture we had gone over last time. This felt wrong, as if I was going upstream just for the sake of running out of breath. I imagined sticking his head into the laminator machine. I told him I would make him a deal: if he gave me a pass he would never hear from me again.

Again, he repeated the rules as if he had a tape recorder jammed down his throat.

Then the phone in the office rang. It was Ivana from Jason's office, which was only twenty minutes away, in downtown Split. I had told them I would be at the airport, at the press office, if they needed to get in touch with me.

"They sent a fax," she yelled in my ear so loud even the sergeant paused. "It says Bono would like to do an interview with you in Verona."

She faxed a copy over to the press office and, even though my situation was no different from a few moments before, the sergeant didn't hesitate to issue me a press pass. He wished me good luck. I had no idea at the time, but this was my first look at what fame or, more precisely, the association with fame does to people. They become giddy and stupid with vivid hopes that by being accommodating they will somehow be a part of some larger, more public narrative. "Shit, I gave that bloke the pass that allowed him to interview those fuckers in the first place." Something like that.

But the other side of the story, the more interesting and hopeful side, was this: rules, in fact, *were* made to be broken.

47

3 July 1993.

Italy in June is full of sweet possibilities. The flowers are in bloom, the women are in short pastel skirts, red wine comes in green jugs with no corks, and the food is—well, Italian. We had taken the overnight ferry from Split to Ancona and drove to Verona on the day of the concert. For Jason and Ivana this was the first time they had been away from their desks in almost a year. For Ivana's sister, a teenager, this was her first big concert. She was glad just to be out of school.

And the fact that it was Jason I was traveling with was not lost on me.

Jason was the only friend from my past and present who had actually met Corrina. He visited our flat in San Francisco one afternoon. That day she had been wearing a summer dress that breezed across the top of her thighs. Her hair was down. She'd laughed loudly and called me a dreamer as Jason quietly sized up my choice of mate. I have never asked Jason what he remembers of that visit, or even if he does. Regardless, there is a part of his brain that has a snapshot of her voice, her smile, and her laughter. The fact that he holds that small grainy film in his skull is enough for me to make sure I will know him the rest of my life.

As for the interview with Bono, Jason was excited, in a reserved sort of way, but there was no way in hell he believed it would happen.

We checked into a cheap hotel on the edge of town with small kitchens in the rooms. The red ball in the sky was beginning its mythical journey downward when we started for the stadium. Restless, I urged Jason to drive faster. My insides were all knotted up. We were late, and it was then that I began to worry about how we were going to get inside. All I had was a fax from them and I realized that might not be enough for the security. I reminded Jason that I hadn't had the best of luck with passes.

"Bill. Listen, we have to take it easy," he said.

At the stadium, as if to add to my sense of doom, Pearl Jam, the opening band, was already playing and we couldn't find the ticket booth for the comps. At this point Jason, Ivana and her sister wanted to forget the interview and use their tickets, bought months before, to get inside. I convinced them to stick with me a little longer. I thought I was fine about going it alone but I needed Jason to run the camera, and I suspected I really needed him to help me keep my balance.

We went round to the gates leading into the back of the stadium. There, like humpbacked gargoyles watching over the sacred temple, stood two Italian security guards with a multitude of passes round their big fat necks. One was wearing mirror sunglasses and had a silver crucifix dangling down by his sternum. They smelled of cologne and were engaging in small talk with some young fans, who were begging to be let in the backstage area. Lazy smiles smeared across their faces, they clearly enjoyed this role of bouncer. With great hope that the shadow dancers of my secret world would guide me through this, I showed them the fax. Jason and Ivana shook their heads as if I was crazy.

"Do you think I am stupid?" asked one guard.

"This is a real fax, from U2. We're from Bosnia and supposed to be in there doing an interview," I said.

"You don't have a pass, you don't go in," he said.

"I think I need to get in to get the pass."

Jason was my back-up. He was a black belt in karate and had spent his time in Japanese dojos getting the holy hell beaten out of him. I was sure he could deal with one of these clowns.

"Listen. We are from Sarajevo and have traveled a long way," I explained. I could see my reflection in his glasses. With my long hair and sallow cheeks I looked something between a hippie and a street person. However, I did feel I had the upper hand because I felt invisible.

"If you could just ask someone on the radio to alert the U2 management I'm sure this would all be—" I started.

"I don't care about that stupid war. They are all crazy fucking bandits over there."

What happened next is unclear, but I suspect it was my fault. I do remember my body being pushed up against a fence as the guard held me still. Before it got out of hand an American dressed in black with combat boots broke it up. He had even more passes round his neck and looked like he worked for the band roadshow, not the stadium. The Italian said I was a gate-crasher, a loafer trying to get a free ride. Jason, the diplomat, interrupted and explained the situation. He handed the man in black the fax.

"Oh yes, we've been waiting for you. Let's get you some passes," he said. I looked back at the guard and was surprized that I felt a certain kinship with him. He was no different from the guy burning clothes in Metkavitch or the English sergeant handing out press passes. Everyone had to etch out his or her notch in this life. I found myself feeling somehow connected to the guard and everyone else I'd met on this journey, as if we were all in this massive relay team together. I just happened to be in the front because I had the deepest belief that we could win. Win what? That I wasn't sure of, but I did feel I had the support of many people, whether they knew it or not.

I suddenly had a very tired feeling wash over me, the same one I get when a plane takes off; as if my need to be alert and in control of the situation was now over. All I was supposed to do was take the ride. I was extremely relaxed as we descended into the underbelly of the stadium. So relaxed that if I hadn't had an immediate task at hand, I would quite easily have fallen asleep.

First things first. The sisters were given passes and cold beers and taken into the stadium for the show.

"I don't believe this. This is going to actually happen," Jason said.

We sat on the concrete floor where we'd been told to wait.

"Just don't start asking why," I said. I felt bad for Jason. He had come here to forget the war for one measly day and I was sucking him right back in, but by the look on his face he was enjoying the slippery uncertainty of this very moment. We had no idea what would happen, if anything. But there was a giant wind at our backs and all we had to do was steer the rudder. Nature would do the rest.

A woman dressed in slacks, with short black hair and a slight furrow in her brow, sat down on the floor next to us. Her name was Regine, the press officer for U2.

"In all the years I've worked with this band Bono has never done an interview before the show. They go on stage in forty-five minutes and usually they are alone, getting their thoughts together to go in front of 50,000 people," she said. "But he knows you are here and he wants to do the interview now."

"Sounds good," I said.

"Can I ask what it is you want to talk about?" She asked me as if I knew what I was doing, like I was some journalist sent here by *Rolling Stone*.

"I'm not sure," I answered. I knew I was inside the twisted in-testines of this bluff and had no idea where to take it. I wasn't a journalist and was deeply curious why this wasn't visible to the naked eye. Maybe Shibe was right and I was now using surreal-ist tricks to penetrate the unreal world. Maybe they couldn't quite see me. In truth I had no idea what to talk about with a rock star. I wanted to be talking to the NATO commander, giving him coordinates for the hills of Sarajevo. Or to President Clinton and asking why he was wavering on this issue.

"Something about Europe, the war, art and that sort of thing," I said.

"Well," she said, "he's in a very strange place right now so he may be a bit out there." There was a sense of trepidation and yet importance in her voice.

"I wouldn't worry about the state of mind thing. I'm in a pretty strange place myself so it should be just fine," I said. Jason laughed loudly at that. She glanced at him as if he might be slightly deranged. That made me laugh.

She told us to wait and then she walked down the hallway as if storming the West Wing on the way to the Oval Office.

When she returned she led us to the VIP room and a few famous supermodels were asked to leave. We were told to set up the camera there. We would have fifteen minutes alone with Bono. I scanned the room. There was a table full of wine and a refrigerator stocked with cold beers. There were plenty of cold cuts and plates of small sandwiches.

"Jason," I whispered. "Make sure to grab some of the food."

"OK, OK." He laughed. "I'm pretty sure they won't mind."

I was nervous; yes, that would be accurate. I was not nervous about meeting a pop icon, I was nervous the camera wouldn't work, the sound wouldn't work, or the interview wouldn't hit on anything of importance. Or that I would not be able to convey what was happening in Sarajevo without sounding gloomy.

That was what real journalists did.

The world was already watching twenty-four-hour news shows dedicated to showing blood and guts in wide screen and split screen, and deaf viewers were even accommodated with subtitles: *This man was shot in the head as he walked toward the center of town.* There would be books, photographs, films, speeches, plays, and college courses all dealing with death in the Balkans.

I wanted to talk about the music in the disco, Don Guido and the Missionaries, Ciba the painter, the soccer games. I wanted to talk about Shibe and the surrealists and the beautiful women who still wore high heels and fancy bras. Straight talk of death without humor invites only pity, or in the worst of cases utter confusion. It's my experience that people want to do something, but become confused by an overwhelming sense of hopelessness, not knowing *what* to do, and in the end do the only thing they believe they possibly can: nothing.

As I saw it, my job this one evening was to be a catalyst between the outside cultural world and Sarajevo, a culturally forgotten world.

The interview lasted around twenty minutes. Bono sat in a dark green chair wearing black leather. I was dressed in the same soiled clothes I'd been wearing for four months. I held the microphone wrapped in a diaper and Jason, who wasn't used to operating a video camera, zoomed in and out and did a few funky fade and cuts along the way.

After a bit of small talk I said, "I find it a bit depressing that we have heroes, wars, and history but we don't seem to learn. Every so many years we have to have this killing. Do you ever think about that?"

"It's the subject of a lot of our songs," Bono said, shaking his head. "See, I come from Ireland and Ireland is also divided. Again they say it's religion, but you know it's not religion. The human heart is very greedy and seeks many excuses for that. Religion is one," he continued, "and what does this word 'peace' mean? Bullshit, flowers-in-the-hair hippie talk . . . I don't understand what's going on and people deserve the right to defend themselves against evil. But if there's any other alternative you got to seek it. I know that's what they have been trying to do but haven't been allowed. I just hope in the middle of that . . . they do not become like the animals."

He went on to say, "Dignity, self-respect. These are things people can't take away. And humor. Humor is the evidence of freedom."

I interrupted. "Sarajevo is the heart of black humor. You're talking about someone who sees their mother die and the next day they try and find a way to laugh."

"That's when you are winning in one respect. If they can't take a person's humor away."

"I think you would like Sarajevo."

"I think I would. I'd like to play there."

"We could arrange that."

We talked briefly about getting him there to play some music and then the interview ended. Bono offered me a tape of the show to play on Bosnian television.

And when he left the room I thought for just a moment about what it would be like to command the minds and twisting bodies of 50,000 people. But really nothing changed. It felt no different from how it had felt a half-hour ago. Except that we had the interview on tape and I was very thirsty.

"I think that went well." I poured a glass of wine for Jason and one for myself.

We touched glasses.

Jason was shaking his head. "I can't believe this just happened. We did it. You really fucking did it."

48

The concert was a huge fantasia of lights, images, and music. Like a traveling minstrel show, the extravaganza dazzled the local crowds with exotic accounts of the world beyond.

Remote-controlled ninety-foot televisions, connected by satellite to the rest of the world, would flicker with changing images. In one moment 50,000 people were all watching sumo wrestling in Japan or camel-racing in India. Hit the button and there would be a shot of war in Africa or race conflict on the streets in America, or a swastika and then a cross.

And at one point Bono stopped the show to talk about Bosnia. He said that he didn't know what was happening over there, but that there were innocent people who needed our prayers and thoughts. What seemed like 50,000 lighters lit up the stadium for a moment of silence. Jason and Ivana hugged and I hugged them both. We couldn't help but laugh hysterically and uncontrollably at the impossibility of it all. At that confusing moment something was happening at a deep level within my body, in the intricate synapses of my mind. I was overcome with the disorientation you feel when you have the definite sense that you are living inside your own realized dreams.

I felt slightly outside my body as I watched a culmination of my hopes. What more can I say? Either you believe in the power of thousands of people meditating on one subject and what that can accomplish or you don't. At that moment a breeze swept through the stadium. I imagined it continued over the sea until it hit the Dalmatian coast. From there it rode over the hills of Bosnia and then down into the valley across Sarajevo. To most there it would just be a cool breeze, a short relief from a typical hot summer night. Then again, maybe a few people would feel a chill down their spine. Or maybe not. I just knew something was happening and I was in the epicenter.

Then someone put their arm around my shoulder and whispered in my ear. His syntax was crisp and exact. "Would you care to join us at the villa after the show?" It was Paul McGuinness, the manager of the band. He had a jovial smile that stretched wide on his cheeks, a balding head and clear blue or maybe green eyes. I told him I was with Jason and Ivana and her sister.

"We were thinking just yourself and Jason."

"That is impossible. We all came together."

"Then all of you would be just fine."

49

At the villa. Nobody was humping in the shallow end of the pool. Nobody smoked crack from the asses of Italian divas. It was a quiet but elegant affair. Long-legged models in slinky evening gowns strutted around the cabana like gazelles in the Serengeti. The opening band, Pearl Jam, splashed around in the shallow end while U2 did press interviews. A team of crew and support personnel ate a fine dinner while I lurked in the bushes replaying the tape in the camera to make sure it had actually recorded. Jason and Ivana and her sister had some dinner and tried their best to make themselves comfortable. All in all it was pretty low-key.

That is, except my brain. I wanted to take the steaks from their laughing mouths and shove them in a box and take them with me. The money here was staggering. I didn't find it offensive like some liberal bleeding heart. I never blamed money itself, just what people did with it. Or, more to the point, what they didn't do with it.

I asked one woman, one of the management types, if I could get a box of T-shirts and CDs to give away in Sarajevo.

"Well," she said with a perfectly straight face, "we would like to make sure they go to the right people."

I waited a beat, to see if she was kidding. She wasn't.

"I could drop them off a building and the right people would get them," I declared with a hearty laugh.

"Yes. I see." She took a few steps backward, screwing up her eyebrows.

It was 3 a.m. when we said our goodbyes. Jason and the sisters were tired and the buzz of hanging out with superstars generally loses its edge when there's no one to talk to but the people you came with. Besides, we planned on getting an early start back to Croatia.

We were told to get in the black limousine waiting in the driveway. It would take us back to our four-door Yugo, which we hoped was still sitting alone at the stadium car park.

"Hey, where you going?" yelled a voice from the dark. It was Bono coming out from the shadows of the villa.

"Back to Sarajevo," I answered. "Wanna come with us?"

"OK," he said.

Stop.

Surely, when looking back, our lives can, for the most part, be accounted for in our interactions with others. That is where memories are stored, in one another. And yet each person is unique enough in his or her own thoughts that no two people are going to remember the same experience in the same way. So I have no idea how Jason remembers this story, or Vlado or Johnny, or Ivana or Lejla or Selma or Ciba or Bono or my brother or Graeme or anyone else mentioned in these pages. All I know is how it came together in my mind's eye.

"We are in Italy for ten more days," said Bono. "If you can think of a way to get us in there I will go." There was clarity in his eyes; the kind that aches to know more, to see more, to do more. It was compassion mixed with curiosity. A person who would do what he could.

Soon an inner circle and an outer circle had gathered on the lawn under the Italian stars. On the inside stood Jason, myself, Bono, and Edge, U2's guitarist. The light coming from the villa partially blocked the faces of those in the outer circle, but I counted eight or nine bodies.

"You can't bring this whole roadshow in there. Just a few guys and you play in the disco. That is real rock 'n' roll, the heart of punk."

I distinctly remember hearing the sound of feet shuffling in the outer circle, followed by a few coughs.

"You're making a film, right?" asked Edge in a soft-spoken Irish accent. He also had wide, curious eyes. Unlike Bono with his more kinetic energy, Edge radiated a calmness that felt reserved yet also well informed. His comment also had the feel of a well-placed volley to my aggressive serve.

"Yes, I'm in the process of filming at the moment."

"Well, Bono, maybe that's the way to really get the word out. Get those tapes made into something we can put on the air," he said.

"OK. When you are done filming you let us know," said Bono. "You come to Dublin and take two weeks or whatever in our studio to make the film."

Shuffle, shuffle, shuffle. The outer circle were shifting their weight from side to side.

Before I could allow that invitation to sink in we were on to the next thing.

"So is there a bad guy?" Bono asked. I had just met the man, but he had already asked more questions about the details in Bosnia than anyone I had met outside Sarajevo. And even better, he was thinking in big terms. If there was a bad guy we could appeal to the people because, like it or not, we, the huddled masses, want our public figures to be good or bad but rarely allow them to mix the two. Not good *and* bad. We place people in these categories, which then creates a smooth storyline but also a dichotomy. It's why we like our male movie stars to be either bad boys or heroes, our leading ladies sluts or soccer moms. We like our politicians to be tough guys or saints. What we don't like are any signs of actual humanity, a mixture of the two. So we are left with the question: who is the bad guy? And is the bad guy in control of all that is bad?

All that said, the reason many journalists called the Bosnian war their generation's Spanish Civil War was because the bad guys in charge of this massacre were clearly worse than bad. They didn't have any good in them.

I explained who Karadzic and Milosevic were. War criminals. Milosevic was based in Belgrade and his puppet Karadzic, leader of the Bosnian Serbs, ruled from Pale, twelve kilometers outside Sarajevo. I explained how Karadzic had been a psychology professor at Sarajevo University before the war. He was also a professed Serbian nationalist, which was most likely a cover-up for his aspirations to power. Also, since he was a failed poet, it was even possible that he was exacting revenge on Sarajevo, a city known for its artistic tendencies but one that had failed to accept him into its intellectual circles. As for Milosevic? He was strictly a power player, more interested in personal wealth and power than a Serbian empire. He was using nationalism as the most convenient tool to mobilize his people for war. The result of these two men's ambition was the creation of a war machine targeting a civilian population. The mystery was not their actions—that is the stuff of history books—but instead the complete inaction on the part of the Western leaders who might have done something about it.

"So can you get us in?" Bono asked again. "I would love to play there."

"Jason?"

"I can most likely arrange for blue cards that can get you a flight," said Jason. "A C130 French military transport jet."

I stared at Jason, willing him not to go into a lecture about safety. Still, I had to appease him.

"But you should be warned," I said, "once you get in, the airport can close down due to fighting. Sometimes it's a day, sometimes it's ten days. And this is a war zone so it's beyond anything you or the United Nations can control. And truthfully, dying is a real possibility."

Jason nodded in agreement.

Again the outer circle shuffled in the wet grass. I would find out later that these people were the band managers, tour managers, publicists, assistants, and other members of the corporate entity known as U2.

"But I promise you it would change the very way you think about music. It would change your life," I said, and I meant it.

"I don't know if we need to take it that far," said Edge. "But it's clear we need to think of something radical and do it."

"OK. You think of something in the next ten days and we will do it," said Bono. With that we all shook hands and headed our separate ways. "God bless and thanks for coming."

Paul McGuinness caught up with me and shook my hand.

"We are glad you could make it," he said.

"Thank you very much for having us," I said. "This tape will mean a lot to people in the city."

Earlier McGuinness had given me a tape, as Bono had promised, of some of that night's concert to play on Bosnian TV.

"Tell me . . . really . . . just how dangerous is Sarajevo?" he asked.

"People are dying miserable deaths as we speak."

"Well," he said with a slightly nervous contortion of the face, "thanks for coming and take care now."

Regine, the woman who had prepped us for the interview,

ran up as I reached the car. Strangely, the early part of the evening, the reasons that had brought me here in the first place, already seemed very far away. Like another life. This new one was full of possibility.

She looked animated and genuinely excited. "Bill, you have the ear of the most powerful rock band in the world. Do something great with that," she said and gave me a long hug. I didn't want to let go.

The chauffeur-driven car headed down the hill like an H. G. Wells time machine bending around resistance, a black magic carpet with electric windows and a sunroof that wrapped around the corners like liquid. The four of us wiped our brows.

"He wants to know what the hell is happening," I said, nodding my head.

"Does he mean it though?" asked Jason.

"I think so."

"I don't believe that just happened," said Ivana, stunned.

"Bono is shorter than I thought he would be," said the younger sister.

This made us all laugh. My stomach cramped in pain and, just like the vehicle, we seemed to have no brakes to stop our insides from coming out. Finally, wiping my eyes, I noticed a bottle of white wine on ice. I leaned toward the front seat and asked the chauffeur if it would be all right if we opened the bottle.

"What's that, sir?" he asked.

"I was just wondering if we could open this bottle of wine."

And then the driver looked in his rear-view mirror and smiled. Suddenly he looked like he had been part of the plot— what plot, I don't know—for the last four months.

He nodded his head and said calmly, "Sir, you can do anything you want."

50

Back at the hotel, I had just one thing on my mind: "Think of something and we will do it." That was what Bono had said. But what? I downed the end of the wine and walked circles around the room, touching every object and talking quite wildly to myself. I was flying high on the wine and adrenaline. With each step I replayed the night's success until eventually I found myself exhausted by the present and lost in images from the past.

I remembered that confusing afternoon when Father had sat my brother and me on the sofa and pointed his finger and told us not to move a single hair on our heads.

Father went into the bedroom, but left the door open. There was Mother, on her knees, her head resting on the desk. Her breath was short and measured. Her black hair was messed up and dried tears crusted her pale cheeks. I remember her looking tired, the kind of tired I saw later in hospitals when patients woke up after traumatic surgery. Tired of working so hard trying to live, but refusing to give up.

Father hit her with electrical cords, belts, wire hangers, whatever he could find. Eventually he threw her on the bed and strangled her just enough to make her cough. The light through the bedroom window cast a pale yellow tint on their bodies. It was golden. I stared out of the window and noticed that the swing on the oak tree was moving slowly from side to side.

And then, for no apparent reason except for the random nature of memory, I was in the southwest, in a lightning storm.

Corrina had been dead two weeks when I drove at 100 m.p.h. into a storm in Arizona on my motorcycle with no headlights. I was on a stretch of road between Prescott and Jerome. "Just a sign," I yelled, "one sign that I am not alone here." I didn't care if it was God talking or Corrina or both, I just needed a little sign.

I made camp under a juniper tree as the clouds cleared. Hoarse from yelling, I kept on mumbling at the sky, delirious with exhaustion. A sign, a sign, a sign. My eyes were blurry. From anger or tears? My face was puffy from drinking wine and not sleeping. Then it happened. A meteor blazed across the night sky like a thin rip in the skin of the universe, almost as if negotiations had finally been completed to let this one piece of magic happen, just this once. After some smaller pieces had broken off, the largest chunk from the cosmos fell to earth in the field just beyond where I lay.

And then, like a time traveler in my own universe, I skipped across time and landed back in Sarajevo.

Less than a hundred hours before, I had been sitting on the eighth floor of the UNIS building talking to Vlado about my chances of succeeding in Verona. He had been smoking a Winston cigarette and drinking coffee.

"Do you think it will work, this U2 thing?" I'd asked nervously.

"Of course it will. Everything has worked so far, right? Besides, what matters is that you come back."

Finally, lying down with my feet pointed toward Africa, I stretched out my legs and put my hands to my sides. I closed my eyes and concentrated on breathing slowly and deeply, inviting sleep to overcome me. And then I waited.

For what?

For whatever was going to happen next.

We were leaving Trieste, on the border between Italy and Croatia, when Jason and I agreed that the band could not come to Sarajevo. People would gather to see them play and the Serbs would launch shells at them. That was a certainty. We had to think of something else.

As we drove east into Croatia I remembered that Joyce had once lived here, when he was researching *Ulysses*. Joyce also once wrote: "History is a nightmare we are trying to wake up from."

The same could be said of this land. In World War Two Marshal Tito had made his stand against the axis powers at Trieste. Thousands had died in the fields defending a hill, a trench, a line. But, like most soldiers in most wars, they'd defended themselves while someone they didn't even know tried to stab them in the eye with a knife. It was Tito's victories in battle that would establish him as the supreme leader of Yugoslavia, still revered by all ethnic groups to this day. Although Tito's rule over Yugoslavia lasted forty peaceful years, it would be his death that would trigger the country's undoing. Under Tito's rule the ethnic groups in the Balkans agreed to ignore their unresolved nationalistic problems. His success was largely due to the fact that he was a Croat who had fought on the side of the Serbian partisans in World War Two. By blood and battle victories he symbolized the perfect marriage of twin brothers who actually hated each other.

So how did this particular war start?

More than likely, some ambitious drunks from the city drove to the countryside and told the peasants that the other guys, the ones with a different religion, were calling them names. Religion didn't matter to the city drunks but they knew it mattered to the village people. What the city people wanted was land. Power. But because that all sounds rather greedy and a bit crass, they made it religious and ethnic. And what mattered more than religion was how a person's last name was spelled. It would be their ethnic background that would define this war, even though most had lost any pure ethnic lines in the past wars through raping, killing, and migration. The city drunks gave the villagers a bottle, some fuel, a car, and a few guns and told them they were the front line in a war for the survival of their grandfathers' graveyards. Go make your heritage proud!

OK, sure, war is always more complex. Economics, history, religion all have a role, but not for the ones dodging the bullets. They just get blown around like seeds in the wind until the city folk with calculators and Swiss bank accounts stop talking rot from a bunker under a mountain.

We drove through the fields of northern Croatia under a scorching sun. The land undulated like a drying tanned hide, its back spotted with wheat and cows. We passed a scene out of a page in an old book: a man on a hay cart being pulled by an ox. To think this fertile land was once a theater of war gave one great hope that all things, however daunting at the time, do pass.

And then the car sputtered and choked and came to a stop on a desolate stretch of road, somewhere between then and now.

51

After we had broken down, a local villager took us into his home. While we sat there in the late afternoon sun the man raised the hood and cleaned out the fuel filter. We were on our way before sundown.

When we returned to Jason's office there were already a few messages from U2. They wanted to know if I had thought of something.

I had. Jason and I had, together, as we drove down the coast. The idea was simple. Instead of bringing U2 to Bosnia, we would bring Bosnia to U2.

Bono and Regine,   3 July

I want to thank you for the interview and evening on Saturday. The interview along with the concert footage will be very special to the people in Sarajevo. This is the first direct message they have had that hasn't been politicians talking bullshit. It is a very cultured, sophisticated city that has excellent rock 'n' roll roots.

I've been thinking a lot about our conversation on Saturday night. Here's a couple thoughts.

Yesterday hundreds of shells hit Sarajevo, which I can assure you is enough to either lose your life or worse, lose your mind. I think coming to Sarajevo as a group would be very dangerous. There are serious problems with the concept. First, getting the proper passes from the United Nations to take a plane could take anywhere from days to weeks.

Second, Sarajevo is very likely the most dangerous city in modern history. The attacks are random. Thus moving around is difficult. As individuals I would say yes, let's make it happen, but as U2 the danger would be very high for the people of Sarajevo. They would gather to see U2 and there's a real possibility that people would be killed. Example: four weeks ago there was a big football match in a district of Sarajevo. The Serbs shelled it and killed 30 people and injured 125.

Third, if you make it into Sarajevo the airport could be shelled, as it is quite often, and then the airport could shut down. That can last anywhere from between 3 to 7 or 8 days. Personally I think U2 could be more powerful making the audience it speaks to every night aware of the situation.

I'm not sure you or I or anybody can stop the war. My original idea of doing the interview was to give some mental humanitarian help. That I think we can do. Peace here will have to come from the people, when they are tired of killing people they have lived with all their lives. El Salvador went on for 10 years. China has been silently killing Tibet for more than 20 years and Ireland rages on. The outside pressure must continue on the leaders of this massacre, but I think the power of U2 may lie in the images and messages it can make night in and night out.

Idea: Get the appropriate technology in here. Satellite receiver etc. with a couple technical wizards (most likely already here and available for hire) and get a jam session happening between ZOO TV and Sarajevo. Perhaps in the disco. Outside the disco door is the reality and inside are people continuing to survive with rock 'n' roll. The audience would realize, Jesus, lucky I'm here enjoying this concert and not in Sarajevo. Maybe they will think about not letting it happen in their country, their city, their house. Something along the lines of "I thought I had problems." I think this relates to what Bono and Edge said the other night about doing something artistically ballsy.

Potential problems:

1) Power source.
2) Military shuts us down.
3) The risk of shelling.

4) I will become a wanted man for the Serbs. I'm willing for all sorts of reasons, but I want you to know so you can make your own choices. Again, I think this answers the call for radical action. I can't wait for the world to decide something is very wrong here, and I get the feeling that U2 can't wait either.

We realized it might be a good idea to make a fact sheet of who's who in this situation. I know you as a group are informed, but with the news the way it is, it can be very confusing. And knowledge can intensify the action tenfold.

Leader of Croatia	Tudjman
Leader of Serbs	Milosevic
Leader of Bosnian Serbs	Karadzic
Leader of Bosnian Croats	Boban
Leader of Bosnian Muslims	Izetbegovic

Sarajevo: it represents the only place in Bosnia where people are joined together from all three Bosnian fronts—Serbs, Croats, and Muslims. In Sarajevo they don't call themselves these various labeling titles. Instead they are Bosnians. This is critical. There are 70,000 Serbs in the 275,000 people of Sarajevo and many are fighting against the nationalistic Serbs on the hills. Also this is the only place in the world where Muslims have been declared a race of people and not a religion. Thus your last name makes you Muslim and not your beliefs. This is a convenience for the ethnic cleansing that is going on.

So why is Sarajevo under siege? Sarajevo represents the soul of Bosnia. If the Bosnian Serbs can destroy the spirit and nerves of Sarajevo they can easily start to carve up what remains of Bosnia (not much—70% is occupied now). The Croats have started their own territorial claims and now the Bosnians face the crunch between two evil twin brothers. Sarajevo is Bosnia's future. It is a town being held hostage for political gains.

Let me know if the idea of the satellite link is in the right direction. Even though it could be frustrating it will be worth the effort.

Bill Carter

52

The other piece of news we received on our return to Split was that some members of The Serious Road Trip were being held in a Serb jail at the S4 checkpoint. The latest news was that they were to be executed within seventy-two hours. It seemed they had already made a delivery to Sarajevo and were on their way back when they were stopped in Ilidza, a Serbian-controlled town just outside the city. To make matters worse, it was my fault, or at least indirectly my fault. Meni, the British Iraqi Jew, the Road Trip driver who was a bit slow but big in the heart, had been caught with the expired blue card in Jason's name that I'd been given for an emergency. Before leaving Sarajevo I had hidden it under my bed, but for some reason Meni had taken it and put it in his pocket. When the Serbs searched him they found it.

I sat in Jason's office as he worked all day with UN officials and Serb liaisons to explain how his card had been found on a dark-looking man coming out of Sarajevo. The Serbs were sure Meni, who was darker than a stereotypical British subject, was a Muslim imported from Iran or somewhere to fight for the Bosnians. The detention and threat of execution were not uncommon for the Serbs, who were sometimes able to blackmail an aid group or government for the release of their nationals. A month before this incident a group of drivers from Première Urgence had been put in jail, also at S4, and given an imminent date of execution. Their crime? Supposedly running weapons for the Bosnians. The news reports, obviously doctored and fraudulent, showed Serb soldiers lifting up the driving seat to reveal a handgun. Another camera angle displayed a gun in a toolbox. But after negotiations—there was talk of money being exchanged—the allegations went away and the French drivers were allowed to carry on.

As for The Serious Road Trip's fate, it was tense for a day, but the execution was called off when they found out that Meni was Jewish and that Jason worked for IRC, a big player in the Bosnian humanitarian world, and thus an indirect source of black market goods.

War, Plato said 3,000 years ago, is always about greed.

The sky was cloudy and the air humid when I walked off the rear of the C130 French cargo jet back into Sarajevo. On the flight I kept looking out the window, sure I was flying over the Road Trip trucks as they began their journey to the Croatian border. Also there was a rumor Graeme was back from England, but I couldn't get any solid information on that.

During the war the only official UN transport between the airport and the city was by armored personnel carrier, usually with a 50 mm gun strapped to the top. A squad of Egyptians was on duty that day. Inside the APC the soldiers smoked hand-rolled cigarettes and played cards. A couple of them sang along to the Arabic chants on the stereo. For each of them, being here meant making more money than if they stayed at home. I remember deeply wishing at that moment that I could speak Arabic so I could ask the soldiers what they thought happened to the ancient Egyptians, the ones who wrote their stories on papyrus.

Back at the UNIS office I fed the cat and gave her some canned milk and a few bites of the dried salami from my pocket. Everything else was the same as before. It still smelled like rotting cabbage and week-old dog piss. Home, sweet home. I peeked into the ping-pong room. I returned the camera to the cupboard near my bed and put a few books I'd bought in Italy on the shelf. I replaced the burned-down candles with new ones and swept the floor. The Road Trip crew had left a new tank of propane for the stove. The cat brushed up against my leg and followed me to the window. Outside, the street, the snipers, the random shelling were all exactly as before, but at the same time it *felt* different, as if I had walked into a parallel universe where everything was the same except my perception of it.

But something was different.

U2 had given their answer almost immediately. They wanted to link up by satellite, not just at one or two concerts but at every concert for the rest of the European tour. The first one was in five days. All I had to do was figure out how to do a satellite link-up in a place where so far I'd had a hard time charging a video camera battery.

I arrived at Ciba's house an hour before two o'clock, their

lunchtime. The chicken I had bought in Split just before boarding the plane was melting but still fresh. I unloaded the carrots,
onions, garlic, and potatoes. I handed Amra a bottle of red
wine and a few cubes of fresh cheese. She shook her head and
made small clicking noises, *tsk, tsk, tsk*. She couldn't stop talking about it. "Imagine. Onions, carrots, bread, cheese, wine,
chicken. This will be a lunch we never forget," she said and
kissed me on the cheek.

Ciba set the table and I cut the carrots for a salad.

Over the course of the war we would have several of these
meals at their house. Without a doubt they were the holiest
meals I have ever experienced. Each cut of the cooked meat or
stab at a fresh steaming vegetable laced with butter tasted good
enough for it to be my last meal. That seemed the logical test:
was it worthy of being your last meal? Most aren't. We eat too
fast, talk through the meal or eat on the run. The food isn't
cooked long enough or in the correct way. But at this meal, the
chicken seemed to be steaming life out of its tender belly. The
wine demanded to be drunk one single drop at a time. It was always like this. Every sound was decipherable. Forks scraping
the plates, knives clinking against bone, and people swallow-
ing. Amra kept raising her eyebrows and saying, "You, you,
you."

I asked Ciba if he enjoyed the meal. He smiled and said
nothing. Why, I thought, do I need to confirm my feelings with
their words? Isn't it enough that they ate the first fresh meal in
their living room in seventeen months? Or that their daughter's
stomach is full this night? I knew he loved me like a brother
but I wondered if he ever hated me like a brother when I asked
inane questions like that.

53

The door on the fourth floor of the Bosnian television station was marked EBU, the European Broadcast Union. The term "satellite link" gave me the feeling that I had been subcontracted by NASA to work on the next Mars mission. Whoever I asked about "linking up" told me to go to the EBU office.

Inside, the room was long and rectangular. One wall was lined with telephones occupied by journalists talking loudly in different languages. They were calling in their daily reports on phones hooked up to the same satellite switchboard, the one that went through Pittsburgh.

Most of the journalists wore a slightly different version of the same thing. It looked like a Gap clothing advertisement, with everyone in tan trousers and tan photo jackets. The French stood out, as always, by wearing the French national attire, the scarf around the neck. One Frenchwoman, a blue scarf flung over her shoulder, was shouting into the phone. She looked straight at me as if her report was written on my chest and I was helping her remember her lines: "Today . . . in Sarajevo . . . there . . . remains skepticism . . . toward . . . the latest . . . round . . . of peace talks . . . in Geneva."

Like the others she had a press pass dangling from her neck. Ashamed to wear mine, I kept it hidden in my wallet.

In truth I was uncomfortable and insecure at the concentration of so many professional foreign journalists in one place. I was certain I had stumbled into a secret room that had answers hidden within. In all my time in Sarajevo, apart from an occasional stringer—someone freelancing for news agencies and hoping to land a more permanent gig—I had never met reporters. In this room the energy was fierce, frenzied and had all the buzz of a candidate's hotel room on election night.

The technology was something I'd seen only on television when they gave a behind-the-scenes look at how programs are made. A row of wires led into a large black high-tech apparatus with dozens of blinking lights. It looked like a stack of futuristic VCRs ten feet high. There was a man working the wires and watching the lights on a round green screen, the kind you see on submarines or in air-traffic-control towers.

"Yes?" snapped a woman in glasses with shoulder-length black hair and a pointy nose. Sitting with her was a big Asian-American man wearing shorts. He had his big-ass sandals resting on the table. They were both relaxed—too relaxed, it seemed—eating a large pizza lunch and drinking Cokes. Feeling out of place I walked closer to the woman in the hope of finding a kindred soul.

"I was told you are the ones to talk to if I want to do a satellite link from Sarajevo to Europe."

"To anywhere in the world," she barked. "Who are you with?" She was either Canadian or American; I'd guess East Coast, maybe Toronto or New York.

"Well, actually no one."

"Well," she said, "we don't work with no one. And this office is off limits to anyone who doesn't have an account with us in Geneva. Bye-bye."

She turned and resumed her conversation with the big man in the sandals. I stood there as if I had just delivered their pizza and was waiting for a tip. I hated this in me, the ability to feel as if I didn't belong anywhere I was standing. These weren't my people. I would never know them outside this room. I felt my heart pumping so hard I reached down to make sure it wasn't showing through my shirt. Dejected, I walked toward the phones in the front of the room.

"You don't understand," yelled a reporter into the phone. "I've got the guy dying in his wife's fucking arms. I mean it's beautiful. He just croaks in her arms. Jesus, you're gonna kiss my ass when you see this."

Feeling a surge of confidence that I was doing righteous work I walked back over to the lunch table. All I needed was the perfect moment. When it came I had to be ready to stick my hand through the fire to grab the golden urn. It would be the moment that would set actions in motion and make the whole process irreversible.

"What does it take to set up an account in Geneva?" I asked, interrupting their lunch again.

"About $100,000," said the man.

"You got $100,000?" the woman asked, pronouncing each word like I was a mentally challenged child: "You . . . got . . . a . . . 100,000 dollars?" Like that.

"And press credentials," said the man, loudly burping the last word. It smelled like Coca-Cola gas. I saw both of them dead. If I'd had a knife and an ability to disconnect from reality for two minutes I would have killed them both where they sat and stolen their food. Then I would have walked to the sisters' house for a sit-down pizza lunch.

Instead I went downstairs to the *Rat Art* office. They were already busy subtitling the interview with Bono. A wide-grinned Senad kept slapping my back and telling me that I had done a very big thing for Sarajevo.

"Very very big thing," he screamed with joy. "Now what? What now can you think of?"

When I told the *Rat Art* head honchos about the satellite idea they cowered like crabs crawling under rocks, afraid of the light. You see, any international transmissions would have to be done under the auspices of the national television station and thus out of their hands. They suggested maybe it was a bad idea, not because they thought it was a bad idea but because they would not be able to control the benefits.

"It is a fantastic idea," one man said, "but, Billy, it is so complicated and we have no cameras or anything."

"Don't pull that shit on me. Not now," I yelled.

"Billy, Billy. Please. We will see what we can do."

I told them I would do my best to involve everyone and exclude no one. I was learning that when Bosnians, like most people anywhere, feel themselves trapped in a corner, they smile, pat you on the back, and say something about how difficult things are.

"Very hard now. Very hot. Do you understand how difficult it is here?"

"I hadn't noticed," I said and moved on.

Back to the EBU people. I told them what I was trying to do: set up a link from here to U2 during an upcoming concert. And if that went well we might even try to do it several times. The woman almost choked on her Coke. She wiped the sides of her mouth.

"We don't do entertainment. We do news. And what the hell does U2 want to do? Beam a show into town?" They seemed to find this very funny.

"No. The transmission is going the other way, from here to their show. They have all the down-link equipment. We just need the up-link from here."

"This isn't MTV. This takes lots of money. Do you have money?" she asked. She looked at me from head to toe as if I might be hiding $100,000 in my clothes.

"No, but I think U2 does," I said.

"Oh, they got *bucku* bucks," said the man, grinning.

"Are you a journalist?" the woman asked.

"No."

"So you work for U2?"

"No."

Darcy was her name. She rose from her chair and walked round me to her desk. I thought how she must spend most of her life sitting on her ass, which would explain her apparent lack of connectedness to the events outside. She sat down in front of her computer and began typing.

ABC, CBS, NBC, CNN, CBC, SKY, BBC, ITN, WTN, the news of the world. It was all beamed direct from here, from behind the front lines to living rooms, and it all seemed so easy, so much less than it should be. As far as I could tell, most foreign journalists sat in this building or in the Holiday Inn eating cold sandwiches and drinking soft drinks, waiting for their local contacts to radio them with news of a disaster. Then they would run downstairs with the steely focus of a fire crew and race to the scene in time to get a few pictures of the blood before it dried. On slow days they covered press briefings by the UN high command or by local politicians eager to deliver their daily stroke to this painting we called war.

Clearly I had lost round one. I walked the four kilometers to town and into John Fawcett's office. I dialed the number for U2 management on the road. The man on the phone introduced himself as Ned O'Hanlon. He was to be my contact for the satellites. I told him about EBU and that we needed an account at their headquarters in Geneva. He said it would have to be a band decision, but if he got the OK he would try to arrange things with EBU in the next twenty-four hours. He gave me a telephone number in Ireland to use as a back-up. Our phone call was short and direct. His voice was calm and almost immediately I felt a sense of kinship with this stranger, which gave me great confidence that everything would work out after all.

The next day I walked back to the television station pumped full of adrenaline and nerves. The walk took almost two hours as I stopped occasionally to rest or say hello to someone. It was good to walk, mostly because people were out more than usual. There was no shelling and the snipers had been relatively quiet for almost five days. These lulls in the war were common, but they rarely lasted. Sarajevans used these times to gather water, wood, and food and to check on friends and relatives. They scampered about town like a people who knew some secret, like they knew the sun was going to fall out of the sky and they had to hurry. And in a sense they were right. The Serbs in the hills, like any experienced torturer, knew it wasn't the actual physical pain but the *anticipation* of pain to come that tore a person to pieces.

Inside EBU, Darcy was at her desk.

I shut my eyes and concentrated on one thought. Give her all the power. Give her ego all it would need to make this happen. My own ego didn't matter here because she controlled all the buttons that would allow me to do this work. I imagined seeing Vlado on ninety-foot television screens talking about music to 50,000 people in Budapest. It was too surreal not to try. I had only one choice—relax and find a way to get her on my side by making her believe it was a good idea.

Carefully, I leaned my hands on the edge of her desk.

"Don't take this the wrong way but I think you are missing an opportunity to be part of something extraordinary here," I said. "Something that could be very special for Sarajevo."

She stood up and walked toward the door, indicating that I should follow her. In the hallway I recognized a few Bosnians from the disco and other parties. We said hello to each other. No one knew Darcy. And she didn't look at them.

"Listen very closely to me," she said. "You . . . are . . . a . . . loser." Her words were slow and deliberate. "Do you understand me? A loser. I've seen your kind in here before. So get your big ideas of self-importance and self-righteousness the hell out of my office."

The whole time her finger had been pointing straight into my forehead, inches from my skin. I wanted to break each one of her fingers very slowly. I had been polite. Now I was tempted to unleash my real feelings. I wanted to hang her by her feet out the window. Once again I reminded myself that she controlled the computer.

"OK. OK," I said, slowly and calmly. It was time to use my last card. "Do me a favor. Call this number. If it doesn't work then I won't come back again." It was the number given to me by Ned, the number of the Dublin studio handling the U2 productions.

Darcy grabbed the piece of paper and walked toward the EBU door. She turned round. "One call and then I don't see you again."

I nodded and followed her into the office.

I sat across from her while she dialed the number. It had never occurred to me, until that moment, that these people were here only for the money, that they didn't actually care about the fate of Sarajevo. It seemed an impossible notion and it left me light-headed.

At some point in the next five minutes Darcy swiveled her chair so that the back of it faced me. She talked like this on the phone for a few minutes before hanging up. Then for ten more minutes she typed and talked with journalists, but she never looked over at me.

Then, like before, with the finger, she motioned for me to meet her in the hallway. "OK, it seems someone from U2 is in contact with Geneva and they are planning on doing satellites. *But* the person on the phone didn't know who you were." Her voice was still shrill and slightly pious, but it had a slightly different tone to it, and it seemed to me that we were suddenly on the same side and she was now very pissed off that things weren't working out as *we* had originally planned.

"I told you I don't know them. I just met them. I don't work for them and that's why the guy in Ireland doesn't know me. But I think this could be a great thing for the city."

She adjusted her glasses, pushing them up the bridge of her nose. "I'm only going to do this for one reason. One reason only," she said with quiet conviction.

"OK," I said. Maybe I had been too harsh. I was pretty sure I was crazy but that didn't mean everyone was. Maybe this was the jagged edge we always hear about—the survival shield journalists need in order to live and work in places like Bosnia. Maybe she couldn't afford to let her guard down. It would hurt too much, so much she couldn't do her job. Besides, I thought, who was I? Maybe she was right all along. In this room, full of professionals, I was a nobody. She had every reason to doubt me. I felt like an ass for misunderstanding her. A smile crept up from the corners of my mouth. I owed her an apology.

"I will only do this as a personal favour to Bono," she announced.

And with that she carefully placed a piece of hair behind her ear and strutted back into the EBU office.

54

Someone is waking me up. It feels as if a hand is pressing against the small of my back. I am lying with one side of my face on the pillow. All five fingers push down on my skin. I can feel my own thinness against the pads of their fingers. There is a breathing in my ear, like the roar of an ocean caught in a seashell. I open my eyes, slowly, to see a long strand of brown hair in my face. The room smells like rosewater and lilacs. The hair moves across my lips, tickling my nose.

It is dawn, the blue light of morning is poking its head out from under the dark blanket of night. My heart is racing, blood pounding through the vein in my neck. I've experienced these events before. Half a dozen and they are each memorable and encouraging and yet utterly frightening. They are not dreams and they are not of this dimension. They are somewhere in between.

I attempt to roll over, but I am held down. Not by the fingertips any more. Now the person is lying on my back, as if we were one body attached, back to stomach. I try to talk but my mouth is locked shut. The hair brushes across my face once again.

It's Her hair. She is here.

I say Corrina's name but there is no answer. Her weight holds me down so hard it feels like I am on the verge of falling through the earth. I put my fingertips into the floor and push with all my might, trying to turn us over. It's no use. The harder I push, the heavier the weight on my back.

I finally turn over and land on my back staring straight up at the ceiling. I sit up and look around the room. No one is here but me, naked in an abandoned office on the eighth floor of a shattered building. My heart is still racing and I look everywhere for her. I stand and look out of the window. Nothing. Nothing but the same old view, which is beginning to resemble a David Lean film set. Sure, the movie would be historical and entertaining but what mattered was that after they finished shooting it the locals would tear the place apart, piece by piece, hoping to find some slivers of wood they could use for kindling.

Remember, I told myself, what Joyce said. *History is a nightmare we are trying to wake up from.* In Bosnia people were twisting and turning in their own collective nightmare, unable to shake off a history riddled with the blood of revenge. As for me, I was living with the taste of Corrina's saliva in my mouth. I lay back down, closed my eyes and brushed her hair until we both fell asleep, her head nestled in the dip of my shoulder.

It was the knocking at the door that finally freed me from this state. It took the better part of two minutes to shake off the hangover of the other world, but eventually I opened the front door. It was Selma.

"Father was hit by a grenade," she said. "Getting water by the beer factory. He's at the hospital now."

I put a few cans of food in my pocket and locked the door behind me. I stopped. Selma asked what was wrong.

"Do you smell that?" I asked.

"Garbage?"

Yes, there was garbage, but there was something else as well. Yes. Roses. There was a distinct smell of roses in the room.

At Selma's house the mother brought in some spring onions from the window box and mixed them with rice and some carrots I had brought. We drank tea and divided a bar of chocolate into five pieces, one for the absent father. They said he would be fine, but they were still shaken.

Selma excused herself to go to her bedroom. I noticed her thinness. Every time I visited, both Lejla and Selma were skinnier than the last. Selma's arms were now the size of small plumbing pipes, the copper kind. Lejla's thighs had disappeared to the point where they held no shape in her jeans. And Mother. Her hair was grayer and her face more gaunt than before. I couldn't bring enough food and there was no end to this war in sight.

We drank chamomile tea while I told them about the trip to Italy.

"We're going to do satellite link-ups from the city to their concerts all over Europe. I think you two freakazoids should do one," I said. Lejla liked it when I called them crazy names.

She preened her hair and struck a royal pose. "I will only speak to the world if U2 promises to play here one day."

"Ask them," I said.

"Really?" Now she spoke in the hurried voice of a teenage fan.

"Sure. Why not? When you do a satellite, look into the camera and ask them to play here."

After our visit I descended the stairs into the tunnels, which

I had come to know well enough to walk like a blind man. I stood at the edge of Snipers' Alley and saw the rusted train that had once saved Graeme and me by blocking the forward thrust of shrapnel from a shell. It was one of those moments in life when you have a few seconds to realize it was almost over. We heard the sound of the mortar and ran for the train. Once there we waited until we heard the tiny pieces of metal stick into the side of the beast.

Lucky.

It was a warm evening. It was also very quiet. A breeze rushed up the avenue. I still didn't think I would get shot, but I'd be lying if I said I hadn't started to think I might die here. Something had begun to feel slightly different. I no longer felt psychotic, meaning unaware of my actions. Now I was involved in something. I had friends. I had a sense of home, however temporary, and this must be one of the motivations of traveling, to find a home. I had videotapes of people living large and defying the inevitable that now had a real promise of being made into a documentary. And now I had a chance to link people from Sarajevo live to the rest of Europe. I felt certain Corrina and I were working side by side. We were a team and one of us had to stay alive to make it all happen.

I ran into the street, ducking around cars, trying to shove my head deep inside my shoulder blades.

55

It doesn't seem like much, 5,000 German marks, roughly $3400, but it was enough to change my life in Sarajevo quite radically. U2 sent it via a German account to Jason's account in IRC Croatia. He then had the Croatian money changed back into Deutschmarks, the standard currency in Bosnia during the war. The envelope of DMs was sent to John Fawcett via one of the regular supply convoys, escorted through central Bosnia by

British Warrior tanks. John handed me the envelope; the edges were frayed and coming apart but the money was all there. He told me he was busy trying to bring Fred Cuny's pipes into the city while at the same time getting Radio Wall enough money to buy some equipment. He was also looking into getting money to buy water purifiers. The already scarce sources of drinking water had become more polluted during the heat of summer.

It seemed Mr. Soros, the man buying the privileged phones, now wanted to airdrop enough water filters for everyone in Sarajevo. The idea was to find a way to utilize the river water, thereby reducing reliance on the water pipelines, which, because they passed through Serb territory on their way to the city, were often cut off. It was brilliant.

John said the UN had turned the idea down. They said they were dealing with it.

I thanked John for his help.

"Hey," he said, shaking my hand. "Rock 'n' roll changed the world once. Why not one more time?"

I awoke the following morning and made a batch of popcorn that Jason had sent with the money. I have a thing for popcorn. Always have had. No matter where I travel in the world I look for the person in that city, village or hut who makes the popcorn. The Nepalese love popcorn. So do the Thais and the Indonesians. The Egyptians dig it. I had a hard time in Germany because they put sugar on it. And in Sarajevo it was almost impossible to find. That was why, when Jason or the Road Trip sent a gift package from Split, it always contained popcorn.

I had a twitch under my left eye that seemed to come and go with no regard for my attempts at deep breathing or other pitiful forms of relaxation. Like talking to myself. I talked to myself about the schedule for the day. Getting water, soccer, eating, having a vodka, all the rituals that had become staples of normality during my stay. But it just kept on twitching, eventually infecting my entire cheek. I took a candle into the bathroom to look in the mirror, but for some reason twitches always seem to know they are being looked at and stop. The circles under my eyes were now quite pronounced and turning a pale shade of gray. I guessed I had lost more than fifteen pounds and half a tooth. Onward, I said to myself; the sun was up and the sky a rich shade of blue.

For DM 800 a month, about $500, Ciba arranged to rent his own car back from his nephew, to whom he had sold it at the beginning of the war. I figured that even if the satellite link-ups didn't work we could at least spend the month driving around the city getting water for everyone we knew.

The car was the easy part; there were many hidden in garages all over the city waiting for the war to end. The problem was fuel. We went to visit Ciba's friend Branko who owned the café we sat in every day. His connections with the black market were strong, and he was in the special police, naturally. We loaded the car and drove across the river.

The last couple of hundred yards we whispered even though the windows were up and the diesel engine idled louder than our voices combined. There, by a crumbling building, near the front lines, was a man in a leather jacket with a gun resting in his belt. Above him was a window that faced directly into a similar window across the way. For almost two years men had been shooting at each other through these windows.

Another man, also armed, opened our door. Branko and the man hugged and talked a bit while motioning in my direction. Everyone shook hands and smiled. The deal was quickly made. DM 40 a gallon, roughly $25. At the time it seemed ludicrous to pay that much money, but by the end of summer the price would rise to $50 a gallon. Branko told the man of my plans to do the satellite link-ups. He shook my hand again and broke into song. He sang a few lyrics from U2's "Sunday Bloody Sunday."

He slapped me on the back. "You are welcome any time, my friend. You make big thing for Bosnia."

I filled the tank as well as a jerrycan to keep hidden in the bathroom upstairs.

"Friend," the man said, "if you wish to fire a bazooka I can arrange this."

"No. Thanks. The fuel will be enough right now," I answered.

"I live where the streets have no name," the man said as we drove away. "Get it?"

"Got it," I said, believing he was referring to a U2 song, but perhaps he was just declaring a truth about the state of his city.

Ciba drove that first day, showing me the short cuts around the city. He also drove straight down Snipers' Alley, bursting into fifth gear at almost 100 mph. I would soon find out that driving in Sarajevo during the war was, at times, more dangerous than running across Snipers' Alley. Official Bosnian statistics estimate that in the first year of the siege the number of vehicles in the city fell from over 100,000 to 5,000. But there were many accidents, most fatal because of the high speed at which people drove to avoid the snipers. It was a common joke among Sarajevans to say when you got in a car: "Drive safe, you would hate to die in vain."

Anyhow, Ciba kept shaking his head without saying a word. We often drove around like this, fast and laughing and not talking. He turned up the music and just drove. Being back on the road, even if it was confined to a seven-by-one-mile circle, made me feel the way the road has always done: free. It made me feel as if anything was possible at that moment. I suspect the same was true for Ciba.

A few days later, when I dropped Ciba off at his flat he put his hand on my forearm.

"Bill. I must tell you something. When you were in Italy I went to UNIS and stole a box of food from the warehouse," he said.

"Oh Jesus, Ciba. Don't worry about it. What is ours is yours too."

"But I have never stolen. This makes me a thief."

"Ciba. Don't worry about it. We'll call it a loan if that helps you."

The image of Ciba crawling in the dark over boxes of German clothes to get to the boxes of food was somehow worse than seeing people rummage through burning garbage to lick the last oil from a can of tuna.

This was a man I'd once found on a back street in the old

town wearing sunglasses and sitting in a recessed driveway, safe from snipers, painting landscapes of Sarajevo. As people scurried by with water containers, hunched over, with the eyes of wounded dogs, he painted and whistled and bid them good day. He once told me why it was so important to keep painting every day. He had a deep contempt for his fellow countrymen who'd lost their pride during the war and ended up begging, stealing, or cheating for food. Many times he would shake his head when talking of Bosnians.

"War should not change who we are," he would say, "but it does have a way of showing who people really are."

Ciba painted because his pride would not let him allow something as temporary and inconvenient as a war to alter his very essence, that of being an artist.

With Graeme still gone, in either London or Split, I was spending more and more time at Ciba's house. Finally they insisted I move in. Amra said I needed a family. However, either because of pride or because I needed my space in which to be crazy, I couldn't move in altogether. I needed to be alone so I could talk to myself, read a book in silence, talk with the dead, and eat popcorn one piece at a time. I agreed to sleep in their living room. Sometimes.

Regardless of the sleeping arrangements, each afternoon we met at their house for lunch. It didn't matter how small the meal was, the important thing was that we were together, sharing time and conversation. Sometimes if I had extra batteries we put the radio on. And each day I would stare out of that window and hear the echoes of a war. It never escaped me that I was living in some parallel universe that mirrored my childhood. Where the outside was war and the inside was calm.

Parallels in one's life with a broader context aren't always easy to see. And a person—take this writer—could be accused of overstepping the boundaries in relating the single story of an individual to a broader situation, especially a war zone. That said, I'm going to try.

Years after the war, when thinking of why I had felt so comfortable there, I thought there must have been a good reason for it. At first I thought it was the silent yet common experience of grief. After all, Sarajevo seemed to be shrouded in a constant fog of grief that hovered over the city. There was enough dense coverage in that fog for any one person's tragedy to just slip away.

But then I got to thinking about it some more. And I thought, strangely enough, about a feeling that I associated with my father.

For instance, once before dawn my brother and I had sat at the kitchen table playing chess. We often played at this hour. It was a time of peace in the house. My brother always won but I enjoyed the challenge. That morning Dad came out. He seemed very pleased we were playing what he termed a "mind game," something he encouraged. He watched and even nodded with approval at Cliff's moves. The sun was beginning to peek through the window on another country morning. Then, after twenty minutes of quiet, and without warning—it was always without warning—he grabbed us both and, tearing off our boxers, leaned us over the table, our asses sticking up in the air.

He grabbed one of his carefully shaved floorboards and drew it back. His face was convulsing with rage and his arms bursting with anger. He brought the board down with a mighty blow but stopped just short of our collective asses. Both my brother and I stayed sprawled across the table, our faces red with a surge of blood. We winced in anticipation of pain and then there was nothing. Dad put the board down and disappeared, going back into his bedroom, leaving us there in our bent-over state.

That was how it was. And that was how Sarajevo was. It is not a huge stretch of the imagination to make a connection between battered children and the people of Sarajevo. Sarajevans were a people unsure of themselves. Unsure of why this relative on the hill was angry with them. Unsure what they had done wrong. Even worse, they never even saw these relatives who were trying to kill them. Just a sound, a pop and then another one dead. I don't believe anger was the Sarajevans' main emotion, more confusion and a quiet sense of shame. As if they had done something wrong and were trying to figure it out, perhaps in the futile hope of stopping the violence.

56

The first satellite broadcast could best be described as a trial run. It was just Bono and me talking about war. I was beamed into Bologna, via satellite, on a ninety-foot screen. Truthfully I don't remember it well enough to write it down. All I remember was realizing that something was missing that night, namely a Sarajevan person. It is the second transmission that stands out as the first successful link.

The details of the link were agreed. We would beam from the television station in Sarajevo to the second concert in Bologna. My biggest problem was no longer technical. No, my biggest problem for this satellite and for the ones that would follow was this: finding Sarajevans willing to talk to 50,000 Europeans. Live. And unedited.

Vlado was my first choice but he was outside town, manning a mortar position on the front lines. Johnny was hesitant because of what he called his Indian English. Alan, the bass player in Vlado's band, was almost completely crazy by now and his English was no good. The sisters insisted they shouldn't be the first ones, just in case it didn't work. They were concerned with not having enough make-up and all that. Finally, on the afternoon of the first link-up, Johnny suggested two men in their early thirties who lived downtown. He told me one, named Vlado, a different Vlado, had a wife who had escaped in the first weeks of the war and he thought she was living in Bologna.

It took four hours sitting in the sweltering heat of their flat to convince Vlado and Darko, both Serbs with family on the other side, to be the first ones to try this satellite connection.

At first they refused on the grounds that they didn't have anything to say. I told them fine, say nothing and stare at the camera for ten minutes. Hell, maybe that was what was needed. Ten minutes of a crowd staring in silence at ninety-foot images of two men reduced to shadows, their faces marked by that irrefutable look of loss. That's it. Give them nothing. Up theirs.

In the end they agreed to do it just in case Vlado's wife was in the crowd. No matter how scared he was of looking like a fool, he didn't want to miss the chance to show her he was still alive. They went to the kitchen and, using water poured from a coffee can, washed their faces. They each took ten minutes to dress, helping each other straighten out their collar or buttons. Vlado, wearing a clean polo shirt and Levi's, wetted his hair and brushed it with his palm. He tightened his belt a few notches and looked in the mirror.

"This isn't a beauty contest, you know," I said.

They laughed like teenagers going on their first dates. It dawned on me that this was the first time in fifteen months they had even had a reason to look in the mirror.

It was dark by the time we drove the four kilometers to the station. I cruised at just over sixty with our headlights off, making it harder for the snipers to find their target. We arrived an hour before the satellite connection, just before nine o'clock. The mood in town was tense. The EBU staff told us that snipers had taken a few pot-shots at the windows and that all the link-ups for the day had been moved from near the window to the hallway.

I briefed Vlado and Darko on how the satellites worked. Darko's forehead was sweating heavily and I was sure I was losing him to a case of nerves. The atmosphere in the station didn't help. The hallway was buzzing with journalists getting ready to do live news reports that would be beamed out all over the world. Vlado and Darko hadn't been to this part of town since the war began and certainly hadn't seen the news business up close. It was enough to depress a person.

Vlado and Darko watched technicians drinking Coke while half-eaten sandwiches were left to rot on the table. On the monitors the expat news teams viewed clip after clip of dead bodies, their eyes scanning every angle for a glimpse of a story. The day's spoils. On one monitor a European diplomat in Geneva smiled as he shook the hand of the Bosnian Serb representative. Looking at the camera, he said something along the lines of "There is great hope for the future in Bosnia."

I took Vlado and Darko round the corner away from the lights and frenzy and I passed around a flask of Jack Daniel's.

"Take the edge off," I said.

Setting up the camera was Mirza, a local cameraman for Bosnian television. With him was Denis, the soundman. They were both quiet men, professional but nervous and heavy with worries of how to feed their families. As a team they would film and do the sound for all thirteen satellites, even though each time they had to navigate their way home through the curfew checkpoints.

"Tell me, how does the world see us? As savages?" asked Darko. Just then a man yelling "Coming through" ran a thick black cord under our feet.

"No," I said, "I actually think the problem is that the world doesn't see you at all. They see all these thirty-second news reports and fuckwit politicians in Geneva but they don't see people like you. Just people. Tonight you and your ugly-ass mug will be the face of Sarajevo."

"OK." He laughed. "But I do not wish to speak of the war. It is bullshit."

"Be a professional human being. That's all. Talk about how hot it is. Talk about how much beer costs on the black market. These satellites are for you, for this city. Just remember you will have the attention of 50,000 people, so don't go to sleep or something. And most important, don't be mad. Think of the people at the show as your potential allies. They are mostly young and in the dark on this as well."

A technician placed a small earpiece in my left ear and quickly retreated down the hallway.

"Live feed," he yelled from the other room, "5,4,3,2,1 . . ."

As with the previous transmission, the transformation was immediate. When the earpiece came alive I was transported to another world. It was like the roar of a fire ripping through a forest of pine trees or a thunderous wave smacking the shore during a monsoon. I have never hit the needle but I felt as if I was mainlining. My head buzzed with the raw energy of 50,000 people screaming into my ear and the band playing the

Lou Reed song "Satellite of Love." Hell, Lou Reed was singing it with them.

All I had was a small piece of technology in my ear, yet I suddenly felt displaced, as if I was staring into a foreign world. When I looked around the room it now seemed dingy and smelly. In a flash everything I was doing in this room made no sense. I quickly took out the earpiece and the screaming crowd went away. Cameramen were chatting to each other, busy cleaning their lenses. Over there a soundman quietly checked the microphones. Technicians were running cable down the hallway into CNN or ABC or whoever else was broadcasting to the numb world this evening.

I put the piece back in my ear. Now the whole world was united in a blissful song. I had an overwhelming sensation of not wanting to be here. It was like there was a hand reaching out and pulling me away. All I had to do was grab it. My cortex tingled with joy as the music ripped through my nervous system.

It wasn't the first time I'd experienced it, but it might have been the most overwhelming demonstration of the primal power of music. That it *can* cross any border, whether it be physical, political, linguistic, or emotional. Apart from the bizarre and mystical power of smell, which can transport a person across decades with a single whiff of freshly cut grass, this was the most powerful sense of displacement I had ever felt.

Vlado and Darko, both growing quieter and more nervous, sat in the dark, recessed in their own thoughts.

"They are getting ready. Speed in one minute," yelled the technician, the large Asian-American I had met that first day I walked into EBU. "Here we go."

Standing between Darko and Vlado, I placed the earpiece in Vlado's ear. His head, one moment vapid and leaning over as he stared at the floor, rose up. He turned to me smiling and his face glowed as if he'd just seen the light. He shook his head and passed the earpiece to Darko, whose expression was the same—astonishment. For the first time I saw the outlines of what these men must have looked like long ago, when they still believed it was possible to believe in something.

"Do I look like a peasant?" Vlado asked.

"You look great. Like a freaking playboy," I said.

Snap, crackle and then silence.

"I suppose the thing is with TV," said Bono, speaking in my ear, "you don't know if what you're seeing is real. You can't tell the difference any more between the adverts and what's happening on CNN or what's coming in on satellite. You can't ask the television tough questions. We sent a satellite dish to the city of Sarajevo. We've got a friend there, a cool guy named Bill Carter, a rock and roll fan. Let's see if we can get him on the line. Are you there, Bill?"

"Yeah, I hear you, Bono."

I spoke about the city, about the 15,000 refugees being attacked by artillery. I talked about how the city was becoming more desperate for water and food. I spoke about a friend who had died when a grenade got him.

Darko used his satellite time to talk about needing satellite equipment to speak to his parents, who lived four kilometers from Sarajevo. And how hard it was to be separated from his wife and kids. He was perfect.

Vlado then took the microphone. "I have a small message for my wife. Mia cara Mirita. My darling Mirita. I love you and I miss you. I am still alive and I feel good. Thank you. Thank you, Billy. Thank you, U2. And grazie, Bologna."

And then some music began playing and the line went dead. That would be it until the next city.

After the satellite link I sat in silence for a moment. Vlado and Darko were talking about what had just happened. We all felt it—the buzz of reaching out into the world of the living.

Later, after dropping off Vlado and Darko, I drove quietly around two police checkpoints and into the underground garage at the UNIS towers. The guard, the same toothless codger who was always there, cradled his old carbine and waited until I gave him two cigarettes to open the gate.

After I turned the headlights off there was not one trace of light. Sometimes it was as if light had not yet been invented. And apart from the soft dying hiss of the engine there was no sound. Nothing. I was blind and didn't have a flashlight, but of course by now I didn't need one. Straight ahead, reach out to grab the first door to the stairs. Watch the first step and then climb twenty stairs to the first floor. Open the second door and walk up those steps to the lobby. Down by the main door at the other end of the lobby was an armed guard but he would be asleep. He was there mostly to protect the building from the locals looking for loot or food or scraps of wood. Go down the hall, stop by the missing lift and use the moonlight coming through the broken glass to see the way to the staircase. During this stretch, with full exposure to the snipers, it was important not to light a lighter or flick on a flashlight. Once at the other end, grab the railing and walk up the steps until there is a bend in the staircase. Turn right at the bend and then up again. Each flight of stairs had exactly twelve steps and each landing spot between the flights lasted three medium steps and a half turn to the right. Eight floors up and at the open lift shaft turn left. Go down the hall ten steps and put the key in the door.

On this night the solitude of the empty building, which I had found comforting for so long, was suddenly completely overwhelming. I walked to the window and looked out over Sarajevo. The dark city spotted with flickering candlelight had a medieval quality. I thought of Darko and Vlado in their flat not far from here. How were they adjusting to the contrast between the absolute silence and the screaming in their ears of all those people in Bologna?

And, hell, yes, I wondered if by reaching into the cosmos we had woken God from his slumber.

"So, God," I said, sitting on my bed, "you have wars to weed out people? I see. Well, that seems a bit sadistic. To teach us a lesson? To teach suffering? Or are you not involved at all? Is this the handiwork of men alone and your hands are tied? I mean are you just sitting there, helpless as the rest of us, watching it all take place? And if we are part of your overall plan of things we seem to be a ruthless bunch, we humans. Like to dismember each other, piss in the other guy's eye, rape his wife and daughters . . . any thoughts on all this?"

But there was no answer, only the continuance of a disturbing silence. Finally, someone fired a shot. The ratatatatatatat of the gun vibrated off the wall and against my cranium like conversations in the far-off distance. It sounded like grown-ups talking about things in another room. Or a television speaking softly about nothing in my ear. It felt like blue noise. Finally, I could sleep.

57

A few mornings later I met up with Ciba for soccer. The sun was out. Some birds were flying from window ledges to trees. People seemed a bit happier. It was days like this, and there were many, when it was easy to imagine Sarajevo as an idyllic European city with parks, rivers, art galleries, cafés, and easy access to the surrounding mountains. I felt a lightness come over me that reminded me the autumn would come. Followed by winter and spring. It always does and yet somehow it's easy to forget.

I teamed up with Merke and Branko—friends from the café who played soccer with us—but, as always, we lost against Paja and Ciba. Afterward, Ciba and I ran through the alley for beers at Branko's café, near the UNIS towers. Hidden in a small causeway nearby Branko had a car up on blocks with wires that ran from the car battery to the café's stereo. He would send one of the waiters out to start the car every once in a while to make sure the battery didn't die. This was the reason Branko's café was so popular. He had music.

"Celo invited us to dinner," said Ciba.

"Could be interesting," I said.

As we talked, our waitress served us tea. It was always the same waitress. Thankfully. Her name was Elma and she was a gorgeous redhead. She was tall and had thin calves. Her breasts were full and firm. And her shy smile was seductive at the same time. I sat there many afternoons just to order tea and watch her smile.

"Do you know her story?" I asked Ciba.

"She's from Srebrenica," said Branko.

"No!" said Ciba, with great surprise. To urban Sarajevans Srebrenica was a hick town.

"Yes."

"She looks so Sarajevan. So beautiful," he said.

We all looked at her as she took a few empty cups inside the bar.

Branko talked and Ciba translated the story for me. It went something like this.

She and her father were taken by Serbs. They raped her many times while her father was tied up. Watching. After she got pregnant they kept her prisoner for eight months. Then they told her to leave, go back to her people. But before she left they killed her father in front of her. Somehow, after being on the run for some time, she ended up in Sarajevo.

After retelling the story to me Ciba nervously ran his hands through his hair and made a few grunting sounds.

"You see. You see. This place. These people are barbarians," he said under his breath.

We sat in silence for a moment.

"So when is Graeme coming back?" he asked with a sudden surge of enthusiasm.

"I don't know," I said.

"I love how he played football. Very English. Aggressive."

For a while we talked of soccer and it worked to fight off the images of the story he had just told.

Then Elma came back to our table. She brought hot water. I swore she smiled a little longer this time.

"More tea?" she asked.

"No, thank you," I said.

I couldn't place her fragrance. She walked away. I didn't want to, but I couldn't help but notice her calves flexing slightly with each step.

"Branko," I said.

"Yeah?"

"What happened to the kid?"

"No one knows for sure, but probably she left it somewhere in the forest."

Meanwhile, like I said, it was a startlingly beautiful day.

58

It was raining shells the night we went to dinner. We met near the back of the UNIS towers and ran under the cover of darkness to the restaurant. Ciba had his studio in the front of Celo's new restaurant, Bohemia. It was freshly painted and the windows allowed for a long glow of afternoon light. And since Celo was the owner of the building the lights worked.

At dinner there were a few dozen people gathered around the table. We all recognized each other from parties, soccer, or the street. Lots of talk. *You are from where? You have been here how long? Oh, that U2 satellite thing? That is great.*

Large platters of freshly cooked beef were passed from table to table. There was wine and shot glasses of twelve-year-old Scotch. A bowl of potatoes came my way. Then some bread. Up near the potted plants a man played the piano while a woman in a red dress lay across the back of it singing 1930s jazz songs.

"Celo has young energy," said Ciba.

"Yeah, but he's a little off," I replied.

"But I like it that he is a real Sarajevan. He doesn't care what ethnic group you are as long as you are not from the villages."

This was an old conversation with Ciba. Many Sarajevans—meaning those who were born in the city—had long ago turned this war into a battle between rural and urban mentalities. To the hipster urban crowd of Sarajevo, the Bosnian Serb hillbillies on the hill were turning their city into a refugee center for hick Bosnians fleeing the massacres in the countryside. To these city dwellers it was like having white trash as your neighbor. Coming from a rural background myself, I thought the whole thing seemed a bit snobbish.

"Billy. How long will you stay? Maybe you should marry a girl and stay here forever," said Mirko, another of Ciba's soccer buddies.

"Who knows?"

"He is already here for so long. He must be crazy," said someone else.

This made me pause. Had I been here too long? There were scores of foreigners living here. Journalists, aid workers, and empathizers who had come during the war. And some had married and moved in for life. Graeme and I used to say they had fallen into the black hole. I thought of swimming the current of the Sacramento river. Many times I've swum straight out, glad at first to feel the vastness of the water. Then, as always, I come to a moment when I stop, tread water, and start to wonder when going any further will become too dangerous. How long is too long in a place like Sarajevo? To this day I'm still not sure, but perhaps the moment you ask yourself the question is the moment you reach that point.

Anyhow, it was a feast to remember, but I was worried about one thing. Had Celo found the old man on the hill? The one with the secret cow, feeding the village babies.

"Ciba, what's up with the meat?"

"You like it?"

"Yeah, it's great. But where did he get it?"

"He traded a Serbian sniper for it."

"What?"

"His men caught a Chetnik. He told the Serbs he wouldn't kill him if they gave him a cow."

Someone poured me another glass of wine. Celo was at the head of the table making toasts and singing along with the singer.

"Bill, the satellites are very good for our city," said Mirko. "Very good. How long do you think they will do it?"

"I don't know."

A waiter came by with another platter of meat.

"Sir, would you care for some more?" the waiter asked in Bosnian.

"Sure, thanks," I said. I held out my plate and he slapped down another piece. I ate it. It was delicious. Not too rare but not too cooked.

The wine. The food. The music. The bombs. I felt like a Roman seizing the day. It was exhilarating, except for one thing. I was still trying to figure out how many steaks one man was worth.

One day I stopped by Ciba's studio. In it sat a Belgian UN officer in his pressed uniform with a few medals on his chest. He had a large bushy moustache and was overweight, with the kind of puffiness that comes from too much red wine. He smoked a pipe and spoke in broken English to Ciba about how he would get him out of the city.

"I will arrange for this. For you are an artist and should not be here," he said, as he waved his hand around the room, as if it were full of pests we couldn't see. Ciba thanked him, smiled, and moved him back into place. Arm here, chin there. That's it.

"Yes, you and your family will be in Brussels soon."

Ciba tipped the painting in my direction and shrugged his shoulders. At first I didn't recognize the portrait, but then I took a closer look. The painting was indeed the same man but the portrait showed a thinner, more handsome and younger version of the bloated UN officer sitting before us.

At the café I asked Ciba about this difference between reality and the painting.

"They want to look young and brave during their time in war."

"Do they ever notice the difference between the painting and themselves?" I asked.

"Of course not. People see themselves how they want to," he said.

"Why not give them the truth? Fat and stupid."

"I would not get paid." I found his attention to the true reality of the world immensely reassuring.

The following week the man came for a final sitting. Again

the conversation was the same. Again the pipe, the wave of the hand and promises of freedom. He turned his attention to me and asked if I was an artist in training.

"No, just a friend."

"Oh, an American?"

"Yes," I responded.

He looked slightly worried, as if someone who spoke English had been listening to his speeches of promised freedom and would have realized they were the drunken lies of men who have titles of power but no authority to exercise it.

"And you are a friend of Ciba?"

"Yes."

"He is a very good artist."

"Yes, he is."

"He shouldn't be here," he said with conviction. He smiled at Ciba.

"No. He shouldn't, but then again there's a lot of people who shouldn't be here."

"Ah yes, the problem of politics." He took a deep puff of his pipe.

The man paid Ciba DM 200, or about $140, and walked out of the studio carrying a large painting of someone who probably resembled him ten years ago. He climbed into his waiting UN vehicle and the local driver handed him a radio.

"Ciba, see you in Brussels. I will return with the blue cards soon."

On our way to soccer Ciba was laughing and rubbing his hands together like he had just got away with robbing a bank. "Ah, 200 Marks. I can buy good food, good bottle of wine maybe," he said. "Tonight, Bill, we celebrate."

"Do you think he will come through with the blue cards?"

"Oh, that does not matter. I have money. Let's go to Branko's and have beers. Heineken."

"What about soccer?"

"Yes. Soccer first, then beer."

"What if he doesn't come through?"

"I cannot worry about that. Come on, we celebrate."

I read somewhere once that the irrepressible joy of an artist is addictive: when they are able to eat from income raised by the work itself all else pales.

After soccer we drank Heinekens at the Holiday Inn bar, but it was too depressing. Even Ciba's jubilation at selling a portrait and having cash in his pocket couldn't bring us to enjoy being served six-dollar drinks by waiters with long gray faces and thin undertaker-pink lips dressed in cheap 1970s tuxedos. From the outside, the hotel was mustard yellow. Built by a quasi-communist trying to fit a capitalist venture into a socialist society, it was square with windows set back in deeply recessed portals. There was a large amount of glass, which proved to be a problem once the war broke out. On the inside, the atrium was like an alien pod sucking the life out of anybody who entered it. We paid the bill and went to the black market to buy vegetables and chocolate.

We strolled down the street like old buddies going to the pub. We dodged the exposed alleys and talked only of hitting the road, traveling to the American southwest to hike the canyons and fish the rivers. Ciba wanted to fish in Lake Tahoe and eat crabs in San Francisco. The shells were falling somewhere in town, but I kept telling stories of travel, and Ciba kept asking for more journeys. By the time we got home we had driven all the way to Baja to see the whales give birth in the lagoons.

59

Later that night I filled a one-liter plastic Pepsi bottle with warm water and was in the process of taking a sponge bath in the office bathroom when I heard a noise in the hallway. I wrapped a towel around myself and tiptoed to the office.

There, busy trying to start the stove, was a man wearing a green flak jacket two sizes too large, making it almost impossible for him to turn his head. He fumbled with the levers and made small animal noises. *Humph . . . tsk, tsk . . .* that sort of thing. On his head he wore an oversized army helmet that made him look like a tortoise peeking out of its shell in a hostile environment.

"Looking for something?" I said. The man made a shrieking sound.

"Oh. Right. Bloody hell. I was trying to figure out how to make this stove work. Maybe have a touch of tea."

"Yeah, OK, but who the hell are you?"

"Oh, I'm sorry. Ethan," he said. "The Road Trip sent me. I left a note earlier today."

"Who in the Road Trip?"

"Tony and Graeme."

"Where are they now?"

"In Split. Said to tell you they are coming soon."

"So Graeme is back from London?"

"Yes. I met him at the office in London but we met up again in Split."

"How's his teeth?"

"I don't know anything about his teeth."

When he spoke it was as if he were watching a polo match in his white chinos and talking with men named Jeremy and Smythe-Jones about summering in Tuscany.

I asked why he was here.

"Freelancer actually. Radio." He smiled as he pointed to a large microphone on the sofa. Headphones rested on the chair alongside a sophisticated recording device. "I was hoping to do some spots on the Road Trip and their idea of an alternative humanitarian aid convoy. I rather think what they do is bloody brilliant."

"Ever been in a war?"

"Afraid not," he replied.

"How long you staying?"

"Don't know offhand, but I was also hoping you would direct me to the local radio station. I believe it's called Radio Wall. I'm hoping to do some shows with them as well."

"Sure," I said, "they aren't far from here."

He took off his helmet, revealing a high forehead with a

rapidly receding hairline. The remainder of his brown hair was curly and slightly elevated, like Larry of the Three Stooges. His eyes were pale blue and bulged out of their sockets. His body was thin and his skin pale, most likely from the London rain.

"The Road Trip said it would be OK if I crashed here."

"Well, it's their castle, I just live here," I said, throwing my arm around the room.

I showed him how to light the gas on the stove and where the water was. "Don't just take food off the shelf. We keep track of how much we have. We're getting down to baby food at the moment."

I told him if he stayed here he would be responsible for getting our water every other day.

"Absolutely. I will do my part."

I grabbed the key to the bathroom and led him down the hallway toward the burned-out elevator shaft. I opened the door.

"This," I said, shining the flashlight at the two toilets, "is the most important thing we got going up here. Clean bathrooms. My toilet is the one on the right. You can use the one on the left. If you piss, let it be. If you shit you have to use the water from the jerrycan to wash down your load. Keeping this area clean is key. Don't let the crapper become an issue."

"Got it." He smiled again, as if he thought I was being funny.

"I'm not fucking around here. This toilet stays clean."

His smile turned into a nervous tugging at his nose and then a nod. "Loud and clear."

"OK." We went back to the office. "Snipers are behind us so don't shine a light in those rooms. Play ping-pong at your own risk. You are exposed in that room but we've done a pretty good job of barricading it. I would not recommend walking around town unless you find a local to go with you. Cool?"

"Cheers. Yes, I think I have it all," he said with that smile.

Splurging for my guest, that night I allowed each of us a can of German vegetables. Ethan commented on how good the food was, as if he was on a one-day camping trip, the kind where the novelty of outdoor hardships is quaintly attractive. I knew exactly where we stood when he whispered, "Are we in danger? I mean right now?"

Later, because I could, I stepped up on the ledge and peed out the window, eight stories up. When I'd finished I opened the other bedroom door. There was Ethan on the floor, snoring. His flak jacket was over his chest like a blanket, and another one covered his crotch. His head was tucked under his helmet.

I felt sorry for him, which is different from liking him. I gave him two weeks, tops, before he either got shot or went mad. Not because he was scared—that was normal—but because he was apprehensive. To survive here you had to have the gut-tugging fear that keeps you on your toes and can make a person go gray. But I sensed that he was afraid of death itself, as a concept, and that had nothing to do with Sarajevo. That kind of fear creates hesitation and that will get you killed.

Take Vlado's neighbor, a young man in his twenties who was so scared of dying he hadn't left his flat for several months, not even to step outside. His sisters, parents, friends had all pitched in to make up for his reluctance to get water, food, and firewood. Then one day, a few weeks ago, the sun was out and the Serbs hadn't fired a shell for almost a week. The snipers were quiet and people, being people, began walking the street with a lighter bounce in their step. Vlado's neighbor decided it was time to go outside. At first he just sat on his stoop. Then, after a while, feeling more confident, he jogged across the courtyard to the laundry-room basement of his neighbor's building. It was a concrete room with a concrete sink and a few rectangular windows of thick glass. I wonder if he felt safe at that moment. A shell came through the tiny window of the basement into the laundry room. No one else died or was injured, just the man who was afraid to die.

In the morning I forgot I wasn't alone. The pencils, poised like darts, still stared down at me from above. I continued my conversations with myself. I lay in bed an extra hour enjoying the voices of children going to school down below. Their collective chatter, an incomprehensible smatter of foreign voices, sounded that morning like a holy echo of life.

The day after the most recent satellite link I had talked to Ned, the U2 television producer, in France by satellite phone. He said the transmission in Bologna had gone well. "Powerful stuff," he said. The next stop was Budapest. I thought of having Vlado do that one. Ned said they had received a phone call from the Serbian ministry of information in Belgrade requesting a meeting when the band arrived in Budapest. He asked me what they should do.

"Beef up security," I said, "take the meeting, and don't listen to anything they say. They are going to try and tell you about the complexities of this war. How it is rooted in history and how you should stay out of it. Tell them thank you very much and then ignore them. Listen, I'm not saying the Bosnians are all saints or even capable of running a sane country. That's not the issue. What I'm saying is that nothing they say will explain why grown men in the hills are shooting four-year-olds in the head in Sarajevo."

After getting water with Ciba, I carried a five-gallon container in each hand up the eight flights of stairs. Sweating and feeling slightly nauseated, I took ten minutes to climb the stairs. The water would normally last me three days, but because of Ethan it would last only two days, if we were lucky. I opened the office door and slid the canisters across the tile floor like a bowler intent on hitting the pins. They slammed hard into the far wall, which made me laugh.

Ethan was on the sofa reading my book, wearing his flak jacket, and eating a can of lentil soup.

"Anything I can do to help?" he asked.

"Get the next round of water."

"I understand," he said. "Well, I don't know what you are doing today but I'd love to tag along, to get a feel for the place."

I felt it was my obligation to assist any friend of Graeme and Tony's. Besides, there was always the chance he might tell a great story that would get the Road Trip donations in London. Who was I to say no?

With Ethan a few feet behind me, I walked out of the building and headed straight for the back route, through backyards and empty alleys. We ducked into an abandoned cinema and crossed the road where it was narrowest. I hugged the buildings and walked quickly from doorway to doorway. As we walked Ethan kept his microphone very close to my face. His headphones barely fitted over his helmet. They didn't even touch his ears. He moved like some animal that hadn't figured out its own skin yet. He was nervous and slightly out of breath.

"Do we really have to run all this way?" he asked.

"No, absolutely not. You can walk and get your head blown off."

"Right."

I walked up a hill and came to an intersection. Two men, dressed in polyester slacks and vinyl shoes, stood with machine guns resting on their thighs. I nodded and they nodded back and I went round them. Ethan jogged to catch up with me, whispering into his microphone.

"We just passed two men in an alley carrying what seemed like automatic weapons. I'm not sure if the guns were Russian, Chinese, or quite possibly American. Tell us, Bill Carter, American humanitarian worker who has spent time on the ground in the war zone, who are those men?" he asked, sticking the microphone further in my face.

"I don't know."

"They had machine guns. Is that legal?" he asked.

"Legal?"

"In Britain the police do not carry weapons. And in the rare moments when they do, it's certainly not machine guns of that calibre," he said.

"Ethan." I stopped near the edge of a building. It was the one where I'd almost caught a bullet when I shook hands with a doctor one afternoon. That day the bullet passed between the other man and me, clipping my jacket and going straight through a car window. We never could figure out where the sniper's bullet had come from.

"You do know there's a war going on here, don't you?"

"Of course. But they were not dressed as soldiers."

"Everyone in town is a soldier. You are standing 400 meters from the front line."

"Right," he said and took a look around, for what was quite possibly the first time.

That night, Ethan and I sat in the office drinking lemonade and vodka. I didn't expect any of the locals to show up. Vlado wasn't due to return from the front line for another few days and the rest of the band were hiding from the conscription vans busy cruising the city. That was how the Bosnian army recruited new soldiers. Once, as I looked out my window, a van stopped and the back doors swung open. Four soldiers jumped out and grabbed all the young men in sight, and threw them into the back of the van. This made up a certain percentage of the volunteer Bosnian army. I spoke with young men who took those rides in the van and they said they usually had to spend a few weeks making sandbags and digging trenches for the regular army. After their two weeks they were released back into the city until more bodies were needed. This was what Johnny and Dutzo were avoiding, at least this month.

I hadn't seen the sisters since the weather had turned hot and moving around had become a liability. As for Ciba and Amra, they were home, in bed, with their daughter snuggled in between them.

"So what are you doing here?" asked Ethan.

"What did Tony and Graeme tell you I was doing here?"

"Graeme said you and he were working on a documentary. Tony said you were doing something with U2."

"Both are true." I took another slug of my drink.

"But what brought you all the way from California to Bosnia?" he asked.

"I really didn't have a plan, it's just working out like this."

"And the satellite link-ups?"

"What about them?"

"Well, what's the point of them?"

"Maybe to just give some people here a voice."

"I suspect U2 are feeling rather full of themselves at the moment."

"I have no idea. I'm in here."

"And you?"

"What about me?"

"A little self-promotion, eh? Don't get me wrong, I think it's a great way to make a name for yourself. I wish I had thought of it." Again he smiled, as if by some clever design he was going to pull the dirty truth out of me.

"Ethan," I said, "changing the topic is probably the best idea at the moment." I stood up and walked into the ping-pong room. I thought of throwing him out the window. It would be easy. I would say he'd lost his sanity and thrown himself out. Who would care? Then I remembered Graeme and Tony had sent him.

It was still early but the riptide pulled again and I was now violently tired of talking. I went into my room and lay down. I arched my head back and stared upside down into the sky. The night was warm and outside the stars blinked on and off, like some giant switchboard of Morse code signals. From outside a few conversations floated up and right past me, ghostly voices bouncing up and down with no particular inflection. A breeze swept over my sweaty brow and time, that bastard, slipped on by. And like a tick of a grandfather clock one of Graeme's pencils fell from the ceiling, striking my forehead, eraser end first.

60

The day of the Budapest satellite, just after lunch with Ciba and Amra, I walked home hoping to take a quick nap. Johnny, the drummer for Don Guido and the Missionaries, was standing in the hallway next to the elevator shaft smoking a cigarette.

A hard light slammed in from behind him like a blast of radiation, silhouetting his body form.

"Bill, hey, man, where have you been?"

"With Ciba. *Dobra dan?*"

"Good, good, well, not bad. I just missed being picked up today," Johnny said. "Vlado is in the office. It's not good. Maybe you can talk to him."

Johnny looked anxious, even a little frightened. This was worrisome as he was our gang's backstop. Whenever someone was feeling a bit sorry for themselves, Johnny made sure to lighten up the mood. He hated it when people took themselves too seriously. Thank God someone was looking out for us. The smoke drifted up past his 25-year-old face and suddenly made him look old.

In the office Dutzo rubbed his fingers in the hot wax of a candle. It was dark, but no darker than usual for the office. He smiled but it was only a polite gesture. "Hello," he said. The whole scene felt like a drug deal gone bad, or at least what I thought that would feel like.

Vlado, sitting on the sofa, didn't look up. His skin was gray and his complexion waxen. When he took a drag on his cigarette his inner cheeks touched. His eyes were fixed and cold.

"Coffee, anyone?" I asked. No one responded so I made a fresh batch, Turkish style.

Vlado's hair, usually in a ponytail, hung down loosely over his shoulders. He looked a little meaner that way. He looked less like Frank Zappa and more like a Balkan Jesus.

Alan, the bass player, walked in and said something to Dutzo. They talked and talked and then suddenly Alan started yelling. Dutzo yelled back. The only thing I understood was Vlado's name. I could tell they weren't angry, they were just trying to figure something out. Vlado didn't move, except for the constant stroking of his goatee with his long bony fingers.

I wanted everyone to stop talking in Bosnian and speak in English, but they knew that.

After another few minutes Alan started yelling again. He

couldn't take the silence. He yelled and yelled but no one answered him. He got up and walked out of the door. We could hear the echo of his yelling as he descended the stairs.

"I told you, before the war," Vlado said, "I was a tour guide in Medjugorje. People from all over the world came there hoping to see the vision of Mother Mary. It was a good job. I learned English and made, well, good money. I remember part of me thinking it was stupid, you know, looking for Mary in a church just because some kid saw tears come out of the picture's eyes. But after a while part of me also started to believe she was there because so many people wanted her to be there."

I poured the coffee and silence returned for another few minutes.

"Do you know how many people can fit into a garbage bag?" Vlado asked suddenly.

"What happened, Vlado?" I asked.

"They were good guys. Really good."

"Who?"

"Do you have any more Jack Daniel's?"

I poured everyone in the room a shot. I suddenly remembered I had a satellite link-up in four hours. I assured myself that if I couldn't find anyone I would just get some Bosnian in the television station who worked for an international news organization to read the day's news, as if someone was actually listening.

Vlado cleared his throat. "We were up on the line just like most times. I ducked into the bunker to recalibrate the mortar. Not a big bunker, just a sandbag bunker in a trench. A shell hit. I came out into the trench and they were gone."

He took a sip of coffee.

"Brains everywhere. In my hair. Their stomachs were falling out of their bodies. I mean, I don't know! I went to our safe house and it was hit also. More body parts. A few of us put what we could in garbage bags and walked down."

I poured Vlado another shot of bourbon. A breeze drifted through the room, and a few pieces of paper suddenly caught updrafts and floated around like leaves falling from a tree.

Johnny lit a cigarette and drew it near his eye. "This is unbeliev-
able. This cigarette paper is from my maths class in high
school." He read the equations on the cigarette paper. The Bosnians had long ago run out of cigarette paper and had resorted to
using pages from the textbooks of bombed-out schools to roll
their tobacco.

"I still don't know the answer to this question. I will smoke
it instead."

We talked about the satellite link-up to Budapest. I told
Vlado I would find someone else.

"I will do the satellite," said Vlado.

"You sure?"

He looked as if he might vomit at any moment. His teeth
were rotting, the blood was still red in his eyes, but I knew he
would cast a long shadow on Hungary.

"Hey, the show must go on, right?"

For the next few hours we all listened to Vlado talk and then
not talk. When it got dark we huddled around the candle and
drank vodka. Johnny started singing and Vlado joined in from
time to time. This was as close to family as I remembered in
my life and I told myself there wasn't anything I wouldn't do
to protect the people in this room. I wanted us all to stay together the rest of our lives.

Toward dark Ethan came in with a microphone in one hand
and his arm wrapped around a local girl named Inela, whom
we all knew to be slightly crazy. He reached out and shook
everyone's hand, including Vlado's.

"Vlado. Oh, I've heard so much about you," said Ethan. "We
will have to arrange to do an interview." Vlado looked at me
for an explanation.

"Graeme and Tony sent him. He's doing a story on the Road
Trip."

Vlado nodded.

"I have a show on Radio Wall," announced Ethan. "I am to
do a theatrical reading of a novel."

"What novel?" asked Johnny.

"I will read *Charlie and the Chocolate Factory*," he said
with a flourish.

This made us all laugh and somehow I found myself feeling grateful to Ethan for being here.

Later, down at the television station, Vlado stood in the dark hallway pulling at his beard and mumbling to himself. A breakdown was imminent, it was just a question of when. Like a drug dealer eager to soothe his lover with junk, I put the earpiece in Vlado's ear.

His face went blank as if mainlining into oblivion. Then a smile. His jagged and rotten teeth looked like a dwarfed mountain range capped with black granite. His eyes closed and he moved his body while he held the small earpiece against his head. He began singing along with the words of the concert several hundred miles to the north. I noticed some of the EBU staff glance at the monitors as the camera lined up on Vlado. His face, although lost in the music vibrating in his mind, bore witness to what he'd seen.

He was nervous of telling his story, but when the time came he spoke loud and clear. He told the concert-goers he was a Serbian fighting on the side of the Bosnian army against Serb nationalists, and that there were many who chose to do so. While he tugged at his small beard I could only imagine what he looked like ninety feet tall. He said he had lost six friends in less than ten seconds. He ended by telling the crowd to have a good time and peace and love to all.

After the transmission, both of us high on adrenaline, we drove through the curfew checkpoints to the disco.

We parked near the club and Vlado took another swig of whiskey. "My old friend Jack. Oh! How I have missed you," he said.

He seemed to want to sit for a while, so I gave him a cigarette and tried to ease my body off the adrenaline high and back to normal, whatever that was. The twitch in my left eye had become more pronounced. I wondered if anyone else saw it.

"I turn thirty-three in a few months," Vlado said.

"Seems like a good age."

"Jesus died when he was thirty-three."

"Well then, you got a long life ahead of you," I said.

"Yes." He laughed. "I think that's what worries me."

At the entrance to the disco he stopped and quickly looked up at the stars, as if seeing them for the first time in a while. "I just talked live to 30,000 people in Hungary. What a trip," he said. "A trip, man, a fucking trip."

Downstairs Vlado walked on stage and the crowd clamored for Don Guido to begin his set. He put the guitar round his neck and plucked a few chords. Johnny, Dutzo, and Allen waved and nodded toward Vlado. I gave them the thumbs-up. Vlado said something about speaking live at a U2 concert, about how he had talked to 30,000 people. But he could have been speaking about the price of jumping beans in Mexico. No one knew what he was talking about. How could they? With no electricity it was doubtful the city would see these transmissions until after the war, if ever.

"Are you ready?" he screamed in English.

The crowd jumped up and down and yelled out, "Don Guido!" He opened with a version of Jimi Hendrix's "Hey Joe." Tonight Vlado was the rock star. Tonight he *was* rock 'n' roll.

61

In 1992, not long after Corrina's death, and after drifting around the southwest for some time, I lived in Trinidad for nine months. My flat had a view that looked toward Venezuela, seven miles away. Every night promised another Caribbean sunset. I shared a small one-bedroom unit with Mike Fagen, a fellow English teacher in Asia and the friend I rented an apartment with in San Francisco. He took the bedroom and I slept in the front room on a mattress on the floor. The only other furniture in the room was a small table, which I had turned into a shrine. It was layered with tarot cards, feathers from eagles, shells from the ocean, and items of Corrina's. The whole tableau was covered in a layer of wax dripping continuously from several candles I kept lit around the clock for months. The wax slowly crept across the floor toward my bed.

You see, the problem was this. I understood she was gone, but just because the object of your love is gone doesn't mean you stop being in love with that person. Does it? If heaven on earth is finding love in another, someone who accepts you for who you are, then hell is being in love with no one there to love.

Here is my point. In Trinidad I meditated for nine months on how to make sense of this separation. All I could come up with was to pray for the universe to use this love for something good. That became my mantra, my salvation. Don't waste our love. Use it. Connect us across the cosmos by allowing our love to bridge the distance. Then I went to Colombia.

I climbed into the Colombian Andes with no coat and an old pair of running shoes. I walked to a glacier lake at 16,000 feet. The lake was inside what looked like a giant volcano and the surface was like wet black sand. I decided this was a good place to build my signal. I spent one day assembling rocks into a giant sign that stared straight up into the sky: *Corrina I love you*.

What is it about love, or the grief of losing love, that makes a person want to swallow the wide world whole? At what point does the everlasting love for one convert into love for many? When the perfect circle made by two becomes so expansive that it includes many others, whether intentionally or not.

Since Corrina's death she had become like a distant star, and I some kind of cosmic astronaut trying with all my might to reach that star or at least send a signal that I was on my way. What happened in the process of grasping for the star was of no concern. Life and my presence in it had become a side-effect of reaching into the heavens in hopes of catching a glimpse of Her.

Were the satellites a manifestation of this prayer? Was this a means of communication between us? During the war I didn't have time to ponder this question. I was too busy living, but still there were moments when I found myself giggling in the darkness on the eighth floor, like some cracked-up mental patient. But wasn't it possible? Maybe it was all in my head. Or maybe I was so self-obsessed I couldn't see how selfish I had become. Perhaps, but when I think of ways to repeat the feat today I come up blank. Any self-doubt, hesitation or fear would have crumbled the journey like a proverbial house of cards.

Besides, the notion that Corrina and I were secretly communicating through the cosmos, using man's highest form of technology, makes believing in Love seem a hell of a lot more sensible than doubting it.

62

The satellite link-ups continued. Ciba spoke to 50,000 in Copenhagen about being a painter during the war. He was also the first one directly to invite U2 to Sarajevo to play. For the Swedish concert I recruited Enis, a young fireman who I'd heard had a girlfriend living as a refugee in Stockholm. U2 found the girlfriend and brought her to the show, where she watched the young fireman talk about being young and in a war. At the end of his transmission he gave the girl in Stockholm a ninety-foot hello. A few days later, Amra spoke to Oslo about being a mother during a war. She was eloquent and charming, and explained that as a mother she sometimes prayed that if her daughter was one day hit by a grenade she would die quickly instead of being left without an arm or a leg in a town where there was no medicine. After the broadcast ended she turned to me and said, "I wonder how I sounded? Like an Indian?"

For weeks I had been alternating my choice of beds between the office and the floor at Ciba's. I can no longer remember how long I was at one place or the other, but I am sure it depended on whether I felt I needed to be alone, or if I needed to feel like I was part of a family.

Or if I was drunk. Then I went to the office to pass out.

Ever since the satellite link-ups had begun I had been sleeping long into the morning, sometimes for a solid ten hours. Sometimes I didn't get out of bed at all, I just let the sun rake across the room and back out again. It was what Graeme had been doing before he decided to leave. Sometimes the only time I got vertical was to light a candle and go to the bathroom.

It was around this time that clumps of my hair started showing up on my pillow. As best I could tell, I had fallen into a wave of depression because of a lack of food and sleep and an overwhelming sense of going faster than I had the juice to sustain. As well as all that, I missed Graeme.

If a person asked me what I was doing in Sarajevo, I would reply by asking them why they were still here. I stopped participating in conversations about the war with foreigners who saw it, like I had for a while, as a scorecard where there were winners and losers. I finally saw it for what it was—an infinite series of draws.

I had stopped filming since my return from Italy. Either I was too tired or I was too fragmented to keep taping other people's stories.

One morning, in late July, I put on some tea and ate a can of baby food and stared around the office. Dim, dank, and cold. I wondered how long I had lived here. Then I noticed Ethan was not in his room and the office door was wide open. He hadn't locked the door. He still hadn't retrieved any water. I made a mental note to beat the holy hell out of him when he got back.

On returning from the town with two canisters of water I noticed the back end of one of the Road Trip trucks coming out of the underground garage at the UNIS building. I hurried up the stairs and into the office.

"Skidder," yelled Graeme. "Having a laugh, are you?"

I gave him a hug, but he quickly threw me off and looked over at Tony. In the room were Tony and Dougie and a few of the Australian drivers.

Tony threw me a bag of popcorn, which I immediately tucked into my front pocket, like a squirrel hiding something away for the harsh months ahead. Tony kicked the propane tank. It was almost empty.

"Brought two more of those," he said.

"Great."

He took a quick look around the office, like I had earlier that day. The shelves were thinly stocked and the bedroom where Ethan was sleeping was a wreck.

"Still in the office, I see," said Tony.

"Where else would I be?"

"I thought maybe you might have moved over to the Holiday Inn by now."

"What the fuck does that mean?"

"Doesn't U2 put out the dosh to pay for your arrangements?"

"No, it's not like that."

"Yeah, Tony," said Graeme, "they're Irish, almost as cheap as the Scots." Tony, being Irish, laughed, but then stopped short.

"Well, we wouldn't know about your arrangements, would we?" he said.

"Should I have sent a pigeon?"

"All right then, ladies, let's get the trucks unloaded." This from Graeme.

After the unloading, Graeme and I headed for Vlado's new hangout, Obala, a bar by the river.

"How are the teeth?" I asked.

"Fixed 'em all up, the dentist did," he said.

"So . . ."

"So what?"

"So what's Tony all about?"

"Ah, he's just sore he isn't here doing what you're doing."

"And you?" I asked.

"Fuck off. I don't want to deal with those wankers anyhow. Besides, we're leaving soon. Got a convoy going Split to Zenica every other week with loads of food."

"Who's buying the gas?"

"The Jews," he said.

"The same ones you told to fuck off a couple months back?"

"The same ones." He laughed. "Can't seem to leave us alone."

It was easy to imagine that no time had passed since Graeme had left for London. That we could just slip into the Sarajevo time warp and stop whatever was happening out in the world. We walked in step past the sniper barricades and through the park. A few shots cracked somewhere else in town.

"Why don't you stay? We could keep filming and you could help me do the satellites."

"What would I do?" he asked. "Wipe your fucking arse?"

"Fuck off. I don't know what I'm doing. I just find people to talk and then they talk. That's it. But I think it's working."

"The Serbs asked for you at the checkpoint," he said.

"Seriously?"

"Wanted to know where you were staying. Said you had been with us so we should know."

"Holy shit."

"Big shit. They asked Première Urgence too."

"Shit."

"Wouldn't be surprised if that lot told them," joked Graeme. "I'd say you are causing a bit of trouble."

"Oh well," I said, "that's a good thing."

"It's causing a bit of news in Europe," he said.

"Really?"

"Calm down, superstar. No one's pumping sunshine up your bumhole. No one knows who you are, but the press seems pretty fucked off that there's news in a rock 'n' roll show. Say it's out of place, that sort of thing. Very fucking British, saying you are taking advantage of the situation."

"Do you think that?"

"I didn't say that."

"I'm asking."

He stopped walking. "Some of the others do. I say I saw you under the gun in here. I remember our conversations and I know what's in your heart . . ."

"But?"

"But I just hope I'm right."

Later that night at the party we put new batteries in the boombox and everyone danced. The place was packed with the French, some locals and even the building guards. Tony was polite, but wouldn't look me in the eye. Neither did the others. I felt pressure building in my head, like a muggy hot night with no rain in sight.

Time, so easily forgotten here, was suddenly rushing by and I was standing still. The Road Trip had come from the outside world where things change and decisions are made. A couple of the drivers had taken off back to London. New drivers had shown up. Josh, the American, had driven one of the trucks into a car near Prozor. Peter, the mad Australian, had driven another truck off the road and over a cliff in Split. They said the only thing that had saved him was that he was drunk.

Tony was considering ending the Sarajevo operation and focusing on central Bosnia. To date the Road Trip had delivered almost a thousand tons of food and supplies, and Tony seemed to be obsessed with his new project: a mobile bakery to serve the villages.

The only words Tony and I spoke were about the future of the office.

"Should I move out?" I asked.

"Whatever you want," he answered.

"Listen, about the satellites . . ."

"No worries. Good on you. I just hope you remember how you got here."

"You know the Trip is part of all this."

"Are you sure about that?"

"I consider myself part of the Trip," I said. He ignored that statement, which was half-question, half-declaration.

"I'm just saying when the time comes, don't forget."

"Do you want to stand in front of the camera? You do it."

"That's not my thing."

"You think there's money to be made? Don't you?" I was pissed off now.

"Well, is there?" he asked.

"I haven't asked for anything from them. But I promise if I can I will hook the Trip up somehow."

"Fair play," he said.

For the next two days we delivered the five tons of supplies they had brought. We gave half to an orphanage and the rest to the Islamic Women's Centre. We saved a few boxes for friends and their families and restocked the shelves with cans of vegetable soup.

On the last night of their stay the mood was tense between the drivers, Tony and me. I told Graeme I was going to sleep at Ciba's and would come over in the morning.

As I crossed the basketball courts I could hear the laughter from the eighth floor; the music was loud and the candlelight flickered on the ceiling. A dog growled over by the rubbish bins. As I climbed the stairs to Ciba's I could still hear the noise coming from the UNIS towers.

It seemed things changed after that.

For some reason Tony began telling people I was "selling out" and taking the money and leaving the Road Trip behind. This got back to me via the humanitarian grapevine. And some Bosnians, not my close friends but people who had heard the rumors, began attacking me for not sharing the "wealth." I told everyone who would listen that there was no damn wealth. The $3,400 had been going fast: buying fuel, paying people off, giving money to friends for food, buying booze on the black market, buying fax and phone time—I hadn't spent anything on myself. As for my own money, I was down to under $100 in my shoe.

When in doubt, refer to the words of the wise ones. "Resist much, obey little," said Walt Whitman. I had been following that creed for as long as I could remember and it had served me well, but there was one thing Mr. Whitman should have also mentioned: it can make people around you a bit angry.

Some time in August, while arranging for an upcoming satellite link, I was hitchhiking to the television station. I was out of fuel and couldn't arrange to purchase any for a few days. A car pulled over. It was a young man who went by the name of Buffalo Head. He was part of the surrealists' troupe. Shibe described him as being "soft-headed." He had long brown hair and big bulging eyes and a crazy laugh. The Volkswagen Golf had two passengers in the back and one in the front. Even though

I didn't know them well, I recognized them from the disco scene and other parties around town. I sat in the front on the man's lap. We all said hello and the car lunged ahead, toward the south of town.

I felt accepted here when things like this happened. When people picked me up on the side of the road as they would their neighbor or friend.

Buffalo Head asked me about the U2 satellite transmissions. I told him they were going well. I told him Vlado did one.

"They are very rich, no?" he asked.

"Who?" I asked.

"U2."

"I guess so."

"How much money do they make at each concert?"

"I have no idea."

He asked how much I was being paid. I told him I wasn't being paid.

"This ride will cost you eight hundred marks," he said. The people in the back laughed. Knowing Buffalo Head was part of Shibe's comedian group I laughed along.

"How about I pick you up the next time I see you walking?" I said.

"No. This ride will cost you eight hundred marks," he repeated, but this time with a straight face and a shrug of his shoulders.

"I will owe you," I said, hoping to outfox the Bosnian black sense of humor.

He brought the car to a stop. The car idled as we sat there, pressed against one another in silence.

"Get out then," he said.

"You sure about this, Buffalo Head? Are you saying either I give you five hundred dollars or you won't give me a ride to the television station?"

"That's right. Everyone has to pay to ride."

"And these folks here have paid eight hundred marks?"

"Of course not. They are Bosnians. You are not."

I stood on the pavement, in Snipers' Alley, still a few miles from the television station. Buffalo Head shut the door and waved goodbye. In the back a young man shook his head and raised his hand as if to say "What to do?"

It was the first time in a while that I had been so blatantly reminded that I was just a visitor here. I suddenly felt a need to protect myself from all the Sarajevans I knew. As if everything I thought to be true was a lie. Maybe Ayn Rand was right, and everyone was just using everyone else for their own selfish ends.

Later that day, on my way back from the TV station a car stopped. It was Shibe. He opened the door and yelled for me to get in. I told him about Buffalo Head.

"Don't listen to such bullshit. He's an idiot."

It felt good to have an ally like Shibe but the damage was done. Years later when I told Vlado this story he shrugged his shoulders in disappointment. At the time I was just thinking that if I kept this up it was going to be a very lonely trip.

63

Ethan was busy doing whatever he was doing, and he still hadn't brought any water. Whenever I mentioned it he explained how it was difficult to carry the water from so far away.

Then one afternoon Brigitte showed up in the office and introduced herself as the new Sarajevo station officer for Equilibre. Wally, the Senegalese, had left for Paris. We were alone in the building. Me and my dirty hair and mad eyes, and her with her swelling bosom and half-drunk smile.

Graeme had said she had ditched Tony and was back to David, the head man at Première Urgence, who had influence with Equilibre. Hence the job. She stood in the office wearing a tight T-shirt, which showed her lovely nipples pressing against the fabric. Her trousers were slung fashionably low on the hips and her large blue eyes, as always, set off her red hair.

"Maybe it is possible that I stay up here this evening. I am afraid to be downstairs alone," she said in a serious tone. She had that serious tone when she looked at you. Or I should say up at you.

"Brigitte," I said, "no."

"Just for twenty-four hours. I have not got used to the place yet."

"You have been here plenty of times. Besides, we don't like each other, remember?"

"Oh Bill, that was a long time ago."

"It was a few months ago."

"Just this first night."

"You can stay until ten o'clock. Curfew, and then you are sleeping downstairs."

"You are not serious?"

"Dead serious."

A man, even a desperate man, has got to draw the line somewhere. As she turned to walk out, I, with great internal resistance, turned away from her fleeing backside. I poured myself a glass of water and when I had finished that one I poured myself another.

But the episode did get under my skin, which only agitated me more. I went to take a dump. I picked up the jerrycan of water, lit my candle and grabbed my book, and sat on my throne, the right-hand one. It was all going pretty much as planned until I smelled a serious stink. I am not the kind who thinks my shit doesn't stink. I know it does. But not like this. It was suffocating. I wiped and flushed the goods down the drain. Gotta take care of business.

I held the candle up and looked in all the corners of the room. Maybe someone had gone mad and crapped all over the room in a fit. It was possible, even understandable. Nothing. I checked my own toilet again. It was clean.

Then it hit me.

I opened up the other stall, to Ethan's toilet. I held the candle close. It was full almost to the brim with shit. The only thing keeping it from overflowing was the upward curve on the seat.

It wasn't until just after six o'clock that Ethan returned. He was quite happy and telling me about recording somebody saying something about the war.

"Ethan," I said and stopped.

"Bill," he said and smiled.

I smiled back.

"Ethan."

"Bill."

"Ethan, follow me for a second." He jumped up, like a jack-in-the-box eager to have his buttons pushed.

I walked down the hall and stopped in front of the bathroom. I opened the door. The stink flooded into the hallway.

"What are you doing?" I asked.

"Oh, that," he mumbled. "I can explain."

"OK?"

"I was having a hard time getting water and . . ."

"YOU STUPID FUCK. IF YOU DON'T FLUSH THAT SHIT DOWN THE TOILET IN THE NEXT HOUR I AM GOING TO STICK YOUR FACE IN IT."

He was against the wall, his eyes on the verge of bugging out of his head.

"DO YOU UNDERSTAND ME?"

"Yes."

"I AM NOT FUCKING AROUND HERE. I WILL DROWN YOU IN YOUR OWN SHIT."

After I had finished yelling I went back to the office and grabbed my pants, well aware that I was losing it.

I was late for dinner at Ciba's. Ciba was also late. I sat by the window while Amra prepared the bag of pasta I'd brought.

"Tell me, Bill, why are you here?"

"Dinner," I said, even though I knew where she was going.

"No," she said. "Why did you come here, to such a barbaric place?" Her smile was so soft and genuine it had a way of making me feel like I was sitting in my own living room. This was the house I'd always wanted to grow up in, where laughter and understanding were assumed as part of the daily rituals, like eating or breathing or kissing a child on the forehead before bed. Sometimes, as I sat there, I imagined Amra was my wife and

Anja was my daughter. I didn't imagine Ciba was not there, just that I was somehow an extra husband and father.

"Do you believe things happen for a reason?" I asked.

She sliced some spring onions from the window box. "Yes, of course, but a person has the chance to go in one direction or another. I mean you are here and may die here."

"Sometimes I think I was supposed to come here."

"I find it so strange. You are not a rich man. You are not a professional journalist. You live terribly at that UNIS tower and yet deliver food to people and give so much to us and now with these satellites you are doing so much for the city."

Ciba came and dinner went on as usual. We talked of traveling, soccer, and fishing, but I knew it now. Amra and I were approaching something I had avoided here.

The truth.

64

U2 faxed me at EBU. They had a request.

In need of information, I was told to see Mustafa, the proprietor of the SOS café. I knew Mustafa from our daily soccer games. He played once or twice a week. The things I remembered about him were his deep baritone voice and his smoking. He kept a cigarette lit on the sidelines while he played soccer.

The café was on a hill near the Olympic stadium, which had been host to the 1984 Games. During the war it was a landing site for UN helicopters bringing in wounded people from places like Goražde. The café was well protected from snipers. Mustafa recognized me right away and offered me a drink. Excited, he grabbed me by the arm and led me downstairs into his basement. There, in the middle of the room, was a car engine up on cinderblocks. Electrical wires were attached to the battery, which then ran up the stairs into his café's stereo and lights. He spoke loudly over the sound of the engine, telling me he had taken it apart last year and had rebuilt it in the basement. I told him it was very impressive.

Back upstairs we sipped tea.

"What can I do for you, Mr. Bill who has done so much for us?"

"I need to find a person."

Besides owning the café, Mustafa, like so many others, was also part of the secret police, which as far as I could tell meant he didn't have to wear a uniform but could carry a handgun. But at least Mustafa acted like he was in the secret police. I told him I had received a fax from U2 with the name of a woman. She was the mother of a young man named Goran, who was now living as a refugee in Glasgow, the location of tonight's satellite feed. From what I could piece together, Goran had been in a popular rock band in Yugoslavia before the fighting broke out. After a short stint in the army he'd escaped from Bosnia during the early months of the war. U2 was looking to connect the two for tonight's satellite transmission. I asked Mustafa if he knew the name of the street Goran's mother lived on. He laughed and told his barmaid something in Bosnian.

"Billy, Billy, Billy. This is my city. Goran is my friend. Of course I know where she lives."

The street in question was in a quiet, spooky part of town. There were no animals, not even the odd dog searching the rubble for scraps. I rarely saw a cat and assumed they had died long ago, eaten by the dogs. There were no sounds of human life, not even the cries of a child playing. It was silent except for our footsteps as we trod on glass and pieces of broken buildings. Those still standing were riddled with bullet scars and artillery pockmarks.

"Here," Mustafa whispered and took me by the arm into a doorway. Then he leaned back and loudly shouted the woman's name up the side of the building. Down the street a window cracked open but there was no face. Just a slit of blackness. Mustafa ducked back into the doorway and lit another cigarette. We waited for a few minutes but there was no answer. Mustafa let the smoke drift up his mustache into his nose.

"I was in the merchant marine, you know," he said.

Mustafa. The man was a traveler at heart. He told me he'd spent several years sailing the world's oceans, docking at harbors from New York to Singapore to Durban. He told me they were the best years of his life, but that Sarajevo was his only true home.

"Maybe she's dead," I said quietly.

"I don't think so," he said. "I would know."

Truthfully, part of me didn't want her to be home. Besides feeling like we were standing in the cross hairs of a sniper, I was nervous about reuniting a mother with a son she probably thought was dead. And all this on a live satellite link in front of 70,000 people. Too many things could go wrong. I wasn't sure if anyone would be better off emotionally witnessing that display.

Mustafa called out her name again, this time even louder.

"Goran was a hero in the army. But he escaped and now if he were to return the army would arrest him. Bullshit, really bullshit."

The doorknob moved. There was a small creak and Mustafa leaned in and whispered to someone on the other side. I could see the person's wrinkled face. It was an older woman; her eyes shifted between Mustafa and me. Finally she let us in.

We followed her up the stairs and into her flat. Mustafa and the woman talked in Bosnian. I went into the kitchen, which had more of the amenities of modern life than most homes in Sarajevo. Stove, oven, refrigerator, microwave, toaster, juicer, and rice cooker. They were almost all new, but covered in a white dust, like they had been living under a spewing volcano, idle for two years.

In the living room were two sofas, a few chairs, a rocking chair, some lamps, and a large television set. The windows had lace curtains and the rugs were all in good shape. I felt a breeze; there was no glass in the windows. I felt faint. The woman must have noticed because she opened her palm and motioned toward a sofa. She moved with the humble grace that starving people seem to acquire, as if everything was going to be OK as long as it was not loud, urgent, or disruptive to the steady rhythm they have established to make it through one more day. Their very body movements seem to be saying "sshhh, not so loud."

Mustafa said he was waiting for me to give him the OK to inform her of her son's situation.

"Yes, all right. Let's pray someone didn't screw up. Go ahead, tell her."

He talked slowly and directly, as if speaking to a trauma victim, which I suppose he was. He bobbed his head left and right to emphasize certain words. He looked at me and then she looked at me. She brought her hands up to her face and began to cry.

"For a year and a half she thought her son was dead," said Mustafa.

Oh shit, I thought. He better not be.

We agreed to pick her up at eight o'clock and take her to the television station. As we walked away she was smiling and crying and talking non-stop, like a delusional person wandering the minefield of their own mind. My legs were shaking as we walked back toward Mustafa's café.

I asked Mustafa what would happen if something went wrong. If the satellite phones didn't work, or the transmission, or her son didn't show or, worse yet, if it wasn't her son.

"Billy, Billy, don't worry, be happy," he said as he lit another cigarette. He told me she would do fine. "When she was younger she sang in the nightclubs of Sarajevo. She was a great performer."

There was a point, if you were driving from the old town to the television station, that could best be described as a last exit. It was near the front of the UNIS towers. After this turnoff, if you didn't take the right-hand turn, which led to the back route, you were trapped in a sort of turkey shoot on Snipers' Alley, with no way out. All the side streets were blocked by trains, buses, large slabs of concrete, or hunks of rusting metal, all to inhibit the view of the snipers. Most days, especially if I had passengers, I took the back road, ambling along behind aid trucks, water trucks, UN Land Rovers, and Bosnian army soldiers racing around in Volkswagen Golfs.

But sometimes I just wanted to get where I was going as fast as I could.

As I approached the cut-off point I slowed down. Mustafa was in the front seat and the elderly woman was seated in the back. I asked Mustafa which way he wanted to go.

"Hey, we all gotta go some time, right?"

I hit the gas and topped eighty miles an hour just as I passed the section of street where the sisters lived. I couldn't tell if the gunfire was meant for us or if it was just an echo. Mustafa was smiling and looking straight ahead.

"I have children," he yelled above the roar of the engine, "so be careful."

"Where are they?"

"Prague."

I looked in the rear-view mirror and caught a glimpse of the woman. She was crying, but she didn't look scared, just sad. I nudged Mustafa and he spoke to her in their language while I raced to the end of the danger zone. I pulled into the car park of the television station and only then could I actually hear the sobs of the woman in the back seat.

Feeling bad for driving down Snipers' Alley, I asked Mustafa if she had been scared.

"No, no. That was the first time she had left her neighborhood since the beginning of the war. She had no idea how destroyed the city was."

I was trying to figure out what to do when the woman stepped out of the car. She straightened her graying hair and ran her hand over her skirt, ironing out any wrinkles. I did the only thing I could. I checked my shirt for any stains or grease marks and followed her into the TV station.

In the EBU room, as always, there was a buzz about the day's news. Daily news, for the most part, has the life of a common gnat. It lives only until the masses fall asleep with blue light dancing on their eyelids. Occasionally the news enters our dreams as some ludicrous monster that is trying to shove us off a cliff or drown us in the river. Dream or not, the next day is just another day and the only news that matters to most of us is when it affects you and your loved ones.

Then there are impact moments, when history begins to form a pattern, when the news takes an actual shape. A circle, like Vietnam, with a center no one could find. Or a square, like US–Russian Cold War politics, neither foe able to think outside the box. In Bosnia, the shape had begun to resemble a triangle, with the Europeans and the US on one slanted side, the Serbs on the other slanted side, and the Bosnians underneath trying to hold up the two sides while the whole thing was sinking.

Meanwhile over there in the corner, a mother was speaking hysterically into the phone, screaming her son's name over and over. Yes. I felt as if I had done something important in making this link in a person's life, and at the same time I felt ridiculous, knowing it would not make the slightest difference to this city's fate.

Darcy, the EBU woman, walked over and asked me what all the noise was about. Smiling with joy, I pointed to the old woman and explained everything. She listened carefully and when I had finished she told me the room was off limits to anyone who wasn't a paying client.

"That means him." She was pointing her finger at Mustafa.

Back in the hallway. Like every other transmission, there was chaos and confusion in the moments before the link-up. The only difference was that when I put the earpiece in the mother's ear she didn't look like the others. From a different generation, she looked bewildered, as if she was listening to the television and radio at the same time and couldn't hear either clearly.

To Glasgow she spoke in Bosnian while Mustafa bellowed out the translation in his low baritone. She spoke slowly and deliberately about her city, about her people. She wished all the people in Glasgow a good time and told them to enjoy the music. At the end she took a brief moment to tell her son she missed him. I tried to imagine myself as the son seeing his mother ninety feet tall when he had thought for a year and a half that she was dead.

After the show the mother and son spoke once again on the satellite phone system. Then we were told that our rented time in EBU was up for the evening.

I thought back to my original meeting with the EBU staff.

"We only do the news here, not entertainment," they'd said. I wasn't sure what we were doing constituted news. I suspected not, at least not in a traditional sense. There was no information, no solutions in these satellite link-ups. Just people talking to other people. Written down, it sounds almost mundane: people talking to other people. In a world where politicians, religious figures, celebrities, and the occasional montage of sad images dominate the media, perhaps it was so simple it was revolutionary. I can't say for sure. All I knew was that on *this* night *this* mother talking to her son *felt* more important than anything I had seen on the news in a long time.

I pointed the flashlight down the dark corridor as we headed for the stairs. As we descended the older woman put her arm on mine, as if asking for assistance. She said something in a high but soothing voice. I asked Mustafa what she had said.

"She said that now she has spoken to her son she can die. She says thank you."

65

One day, not long after the woman talked to her son, I wandered down to the television station. I waited for a break in the action to use the satellite phone.

"Hi, Mom, it's me. How you doing?" I asked.

"Oh Willy, where are you?"

"I'm calling from Sarajevo."

"Are the phones working?"

"Not really. I'm using a satellite phone, so I don't have long. How's Chico?" I asked, speaking of my home town.

"Everything here is the same. The letter you sent was published in the town newspaper." She was talking of a seven-page letter I had written to friends and family the first time I left Sarajevo back in April. It spoke of the Road Trip, their mission, our journey, and the situation inside the city. An edited version of it showed up in the local newspaper. I didn't think about it until years later, but that letter was my first published piece of journalism.

"Great. I wanted to tell you and John that I'm doing these satellite link-ups between Sarajevo and U2 concerts all over Europe."

"OK."

"U2 are a huge rock band."

"Oh, U2, I know who they are. Where are you sleeping?"

"That's a bit complicated to explain, but it's OK. Yeah, well, what happens is each night there is a concert—Paris, Amsterdam, wherever—a Bosnian gets to talk live to 50,000 or 60,000 people. It's pretty amazing."

"That's fantastic. When are you going to leave?"

"I don't know. I'm pretty busy with everything at the moment."

"I have accepted that whatever you are doing, you are doing for a reason."

"I hope so."

"I know so."

"OK, well listen, there is a line of people here waiting for the phone so I better go."

"Will you please be careful?"

"I will. Tell everyone hello and I'll talk to you soon."

"I love you."

"I love you too, Mom."

66

I had been in the Holiday Inn only a few times before, mostly to get my camera batteries charged or have an occasional beer with Ciba in the lobby. I'd never been in the cafeteria. Maybe it was the call home, but suddenly I felt hungry. Very hungry. Like I'd forgotten to eat for a week and was just now realizing it.

As I ran across the field to the back door of the hotel I could hear Graeme's voice in my head. "Parasites, all of them. I wouldn't eat there if it was the last place on the burning planet."

Still hearing Graeme's words, I told the Bosnians in the lobby that I was looking for someone upstairs. Something to do with the satellites. They all smiled and patted me on the back. Word of the transmissions was by now beginning to get around and occasionally people just smiled at me, thanked me, and wished me luck.

The first thing I noticed in the cafeteria was the murmur, like bees in a hive. Dozens of journalists were seated at long tables with white tablecloths, hammering away in conversation. I recognized a few from the EBU room. They were dressed in khaki trousers, vests, and soft- soled shoes. I was dressed in the same soiled shirt I'd been wearing for weeks. And on my feet were the same damn smelly boots and my crusted socks.

The waiters carefully placed salad forks and soup spoons in front of us. They didn't smile as they served the evening's meal. Beef, rice, and cooked vegetables. The man sitting directly across from me had a bushy mustache and a flabby gut. He was slightly older than most in the room. I guessed he was the chief of a news organization, used to giving orders from a chair. He shook his fork at me.

"Aren't you the one doing those satellite link-ups with U2?" He sounded American.

I told him I was.

"I think it's great."

An English voice chimed in, "Bollocks if you ask me."

"Oh," said the American, "do you think the masses listen to nightly news more than they listen to rock stars? No. That's why it's ingenious."

"Bono's a fucking prat," the Englishman said.

The American laughed with great vigor and cut into his steak. "Well, I didn't say anything about that. I was talking about the concept."

"The wanker is always on his goddamn high horse. And what about you?" he said, pointing at me. "Paid by them to come in here and make them look like bloody heroes?"

"No," I said. "I'm not paid by anyone."

"John Lennon said it," the American continued. "Rock 'n' roll will change the world."

They talked a bit more about the concept, but I quickly lost interest. My lust for food had developed a primal intensity. My energy levels were running low. I had stopped masturbating quite some time ago, which worried me. It shouldn't take that much effort to make oneself happy, if only for a fleeting moment, I thought. My eyes were becoming slightly paler and my patience was running thin. But the sight of a hot meal brought it all back, like I had just slain a caribou for a village in the Arctic and we were now eating it raw while wearing coats made from polar bear and wolverine.

I took a bite and let the warm cooked meat slide down my throat. All I could hear was the steady gnashing of my own jawbone. The chomping of teeth, the slow dissolving of tissue by enzymes. I followed it up by heaping spoonfuls of rice into my mouth. The sensation of eating warm food erased, at least momentarily, the thought of everyone I knew in Sarajevo sitting at home eating whatever scrap of food they had managed to acquire for that day. I thought of the sisters and of Vlado's nephew. I thought of all of them and then shoved another slab of meat into my mouth. In the ongoing and never-ending conversation in my mind I told myself I had to stay healthy to keep doing my work. That I had to eat, even if my friends didn't.

But in Sarajevo there was no escaping the mirror of guilt. Over the next few weeks I would return several times. Of course Ciba knew I was sneaking off to the Holiday Inn for food but he never said anything about it. Whenever I told him I was going there to meet some journalists interested in the satellite transmissions he would smile and tell me to bring some chocolate for Anja. The silent guilt is the worst. No one has to say a thing and you still feel the rot.

One August afternoon I went to EBU and Darcy, the woman who ran the show, was gone. Before she left she had become quite pleasant to me. No longer did she ignore me or treat me like a fool. Then, just before leaving, she dropped a hint that she would be passing through London the following week, about the same time U2 was to play Wembley. As much as I wanted to stick her head in a vat of boiling pig fat, I also wanted her to experience a satellite link-up from the other side. I spoke with Ned and a pass was arranged. My thinking was that if this seemingly cold-hearted woman was moved by seeing a link-up then there was a good chance we had reached a lot of people in the past month. She was my secret litmus test.

The new person behind the desk was Swiss. We'll call him Philippe. I introduced myself. He said he was from Geneva, the head office of EBU, and that was all he said.

The following day I was talking to a reporter from the Canadian Broadcast Company when the phone rang at Philippe's desk. He answered it and said in a thick French accent, "Who? Who? I do not know," and hung up. For some reason I felt an urge to investigate.

"Who was that for?"

"You," he said. "You were busy talking so I said you were not here."

I walked to the edge of his desk. The Canadian woman looked stunned and followed.

The phone rang again. Again he picked it up. And again he paused, listened to what the voice on the other end was saying and then said, "I do not know," and hung up.

Again I asked who the phone call was for.

"You," he said and returned to writing something on a piece of paper.

"Hey, fucknut, what are you doing?"

"You are not news. I do not have time for this bullshit entertainment."

I felt the slow burn of violence growing inside me. "OK, here's the deal. Don't hang up that phone again on me."

"Oh shut up," he said and kept writing. I slammed my fist down on his desk, which got his attention.

"Hey. If this place is too much for you then call home and check out, but while you are here you work for us. You are the rental house and I am the client. And so is she and him and everyone in here. Got it?" I had learned a few things dealing with EBU. Like if I let them, they would walk all over me.

The Canadian woman pointed her finger at him.

"If you knowingly hang up again I will have my home office call Geneva and report the incident."

Other reporters in the room all stared at Philippe.

The Canadian woman and I walked to a corner of the room.

"He's an asshole," she said. "I think he's hung up on me a few times too. I think he hates French Canadians."

"Well, you can't blame him for that," I said, which made her laugh.

After a pause everything went back to normal. People returned to talking on the phones about numbers. It was always numbers. This many dead, this many injured. This many missing. What's with the numbers? Aren't obsessions with numbers one of the characteristics of crazy people?

Needing some air, I walked into the hallway. A cameraman from CNN came up and said if I had any problems with EBU, with anything, to let him know. He offered to loan me his camera or the use of their equipment. He said they would lean on EBU on my behalf. I thanked him and found myself feeling like a fool for lumping all journalists together. Why would they be all the same? As with any profession, any war, any city, there were bullies, lovers, conmen, the greedy, the caretakers, the strong, the weak, and the helpless.

The EBU secretary, a Bosnian girl with her black hair pulled back tight in a bun, stuck her head out the door.

"Excuse me, Mr. Carter. The phone is for you."

67

Wembley. The stadium ballbuster. The numbers were big: 100,000 people, 200,000 eyes, 400,000 legs and arms, minus a few limbs of the unlucky. Maybe counting is the salvation of the mad. Count to stay sane. Is that why the UN counted the dead and wounded every day in Bosnia? To keep an official record of their own sanity? It made sense. How else would the men driving around in armored cars with the words *UN monitor* on them be able to go home and sleep at night? The answer: they were busy counting. So busy they couldn't stop to think about it all.

Who knows? I only knew it was time to shove it down the gullet of John Major, the Prime Minister who'd sent Bosnia Lord Owen to work out a peaceable solution. When asked if there was any hope for Bosnia, Owen had said, "Don't dream dreams." A realist? Perhaps, but don't forget he was a politician. Then, during a ceasefire in 1994, Major sent Michael Rose to take charge of the military protection of Sarajevo and other safe zones. His first action? He removed the sniper barricades in Sarajevo. He said it was a gesture of good faith. The Serb snipers must have been dozing during the good faith lecture. After that it was like shooting ducks on a pond.

Don't get me wrong, London politicians were no different from any other country's politicians, including Bosnia's. They were all just pissing from the balcony onto the heads of the hunched-up masses below. The only difference was that Wembley would that night be hosting an Irish band, satellite-linked to an American speaking from Bosnia. We were confident 10 Downing Street would get the message of tonight's transmission loud and clear.

Vlado and the band wanted me to videotape them singing a version of "All You Need Is Love" and have the tape play at the concert. I thought it was too obvious. I told Vlado and he said let's do it anyway, use it for the documentary. We agreed to meet downtown. He knew a building where the light was good.

Inside, I was introduced to a man sitting on a bunk bed in the back of the room. Short and slightly round, the man had a thin mustache and greasy black hair. His smile was nervous and slightly deranged.

"Welcome, friend," he said. "Welcome to my country." He had a pistol in his waistband, which wasn't that strange; it was the trumpet under his arm that startled me. Vlado explained that this was the Bosnian army band's practice room and this man was the guardian. He was also the trumpet player for the band.

"Once a week we practice here," he said and slapped me on the back, "but you are welcome today."

Vlado was on temporary psychological leave from the army and had been since the day he had placed his friends in rubbish bags. He spent most of his time at home taking care of his sister and her new child or at the UNIS office smoking cigarettes and drinking Turkish coffee.

Johnny set up his drums near the window, where the light was best. Allen and Dutzo set up their instruments on either side of Johnny, and Vlado sat in the middle, one leg crossed over the other, with a guitar resting on his lap. There was an odd quietness to the scene, as if we needed to remember the reason for doing this.

As expected, things didn't go well. Vlado developed a series of twitches and couldn't stop fidgeting when he looked at the camera.

"Vlado, let's do this another day, what do you say?" I asked.

"No, no, I'm cool. Let me do it a few times. I'll be fine."

"You sure? 'Cause it's no big deal. This is all just bonus stuff."

"I'm sure."

A moment later we were back at it, them playing and me filming.

Then six explosions, one after another, hit somewhere outside the building. The window behind Johnny pushed in for a moment, as if it were buckling under some great pressure of water, and in the next it pulled itself back together again and shattered. Johnny took the blow and was covered in glass. The room exploded with debris. Everyone ran for the hallway, where we stood for some time before walking outside.

"I am beginning to think they don't like us," said Vlado. He lit a cigarette and stared at the deep blue sky. It was the golden hour, the best time for photography, when everyone holds a certain glow in their faces. A bird, it looked like some sort of jay, flew in from a tree and landed inside the shattered window.

"Yes. Don't they know we are just honest people trying to make an honest living?" said Johnny, with his usual witty sarcasm.

"You should put that explosion in the video. It will be the heavy metal version," said Dutzo.

"We can edit in the chicks with motorcycles and big boobs later," said Johnny. Then he changed the subject. "Bill, have you heard the difference between Sarajevo and Auschwitz?"

"Uh, let me guess. At least they always had gas? Freak, of course I've heard that one."

"I think I better get some new material. This is a tough town."

Feeling better, we walked up the stairs, behind the army trumpet player. Everyone was talking about something else. Small wisecracks offset by a mention of some gossip about a friend or agreeing on what time to meet later. We cleared away the glass and moved the instruments to a different part of the room, away from the window. The bird stayed put, twitching its feet under a few flakes of glass.

As they played, I focused the camera on Vlado's singing, which was always good and had a sense of immediacy to it.

At some point I realized the army trumpet player was standing next to me.

"Friend," he said, "I am the best trumpet player in all of Bosnia." He had the smile of a town drunk and was slurring his words. I told him I was sure he was a wonderful trumpet player, and that after we were done it would be great to hear him play. I returned to the filming.

Then, through my camera, I saw Vlado put down his guitar and raise his hands in the air, as if to ask a question, like Italians do when they pinch their fingers together.

I felt the cold bluntness of steel against my skin. The trumpet player had the mouth of his gun resting against my cheek.

"I be in the music video," he said and pushed the gun further into my cheek.

"You want to be in the music video?" I asked.

"Yes."

"And if you don't get in the music video are you going to shoot me?"

"Maybe." He shrugged his shoulders, as if he hadn't decided one way or the other.

Vlado walked over and said something in Bosnian, but it was too late. I was too far gone for him to save me.

"GO AHEAD, SHOOT ME. COME ON. DO IT. SHOOT ME. ALL THIS AND I GET SHOT BY A DRUNK OVER A VIDEO."

"Hey, all we need is love, right?" Vlado said.

The gun was still in my face. The man was breathing hard now, feeling the heat of his decision. I looked at Vlado.

"This city sucks," I said.

I suddenly felt very much like weeping. I felt the delicate fabric of my mind beginning to unravel and I was clueless as to how to stop the process. Vlado talked some more to the man with the gun and the weapon was slowly lowered. I shook my head violently to keep from weeping.

"Go ahead, get in there," I yelled. "Come on, Dizzy Gillespie, get in there and blow your fucking horn." I pushed the man hard in front of the camera. I handed him his trumpet.

He smiled. He was happy to be in front of the camera. His moment of fame was here. All for a video that would never be made, for a transmission he would never see. For the next few minutes he played loudly out of tune. It would have made dogs bark, if there were any still alive. The band sat in their chairs, not playing.

Finally, it was over. The man stopped playing. His breathing became labored and loud and he mumbled something to himself. The trumpet was in one hand and the gun in his waistband. He looked to be in pain, not physical but some deep trouble coming from the inside, like alien life was preparing to exit his chest cavity.

He arched his head back and screamed from what sounded like the bottom of his belly, and then threw his trumpet across the room, where it landed with a loud brass bang. He went into a rage, a fury bordering on insanity, such that it seemed he was going to kill the rest of us one by one, with his bare hands. He ran toward the instrument, stumbling over desks in the way. He kicked the mangled trumpet and screamed until spit drooled down his shirt. Then, as suddenly as he had started, he stopped, slumped to his knees, and began to cry.

At this point I felt as if we had no right to be there, as if the room had suddenly become a confession booth, or a shrine.

"Vlado?" I said.

"Let's go."

We gathered our equipment and walked out one by one. I glanced over at the twisted trumpet. It was beyond repair, like the man crying alone in a room with a broken window.

Outside we walked quietly up the alley. Finally Vlado spoke. "I think he is nervous. No one in the band has shown up for almost a month. He thinks they may be dead."

We separated and then gathered again later that day in the office. It was hot and there was a heavy feeling among us, like a wet cloth suffocating us. Johnny switched on the battery-operated radio and tuned in to Radio Wall.

"Hey, it's Ethan."

And it was. He and the crazy girl were reading *Charlie and the Chocolate Factory* line by line. His voice was like that of a grandfather speaking to a five-year-old. Slow and deliberate. The woman was translating the whole thing into Bosnian using the same patronizing voice.

"This is better than humanitarian food," said Vlado.

"Why?" I asked.

"Because it helps me understand that I am not totally crazy," said Vlado, running his fingers through his hair. "He comes here and reads us children's stories. *That* is crazy."

That's how it goes sometimes. Right when you think you've hit the bottom all you have to do is look around and someone else is already there.

One more thing from that afternoon stays with me. I couldn't help but wonder, when melted down, how many brass bullets they would get out of that trumpet.

68

By now, some time in August, I had lost some more hair and a little more than half a tooth. The fighting on the edges of town was fierce and constant. I was weak and tired and running out of room inside my mind. I couldn't always remember why I was here. I was beginning to have doubts, which led to hesitation. In short, I had become an easy target.

The following evening, while I was inside the radio station, the back window of the car was cut open and the camera was stolen. Most of my footage was already safe in Dublin, thanks to Jason, who had sent it to the U2 studio a few weeks before. Still, I didn't have another camera or the five thousand dollars to replace it. I sat in the car and cursed this city. I wanted to leave as soon as possible. Or maybe I just needed some sleep.

"I think we can take care of that for you," said Ned, a man I had never met but who was the invisible voice of U2.

I explained that losing the camera was the last straw. I briefly told him about the trumpet player and the gun. He said it sounded "tricky."

I borrowed one of Graeme's phrases and told him I'd "lost the plot." I asked again about replacing the camera.

"I really don't think that should be a problem," he said.

So many afternoons over the last several weeks I'd looked forward to my talks with Ned. It was an elixir of sorts, having a voice to reach out to that felt calm. The Irish lilt has a way of lulling one into a state of tranquility. I began to relax, especially knowing they would help me replace the camera, which, adding to my stress, I co-owned with my friend Bob in Berkeley.

"Good. Now, about Wembley," he continued. "I think you

should pull out all the stops on this one. It's the biggest show we do in Europe and it's in London, which tends to be difficult for U2 'cause they're Irish."

I told him I had something in mind.

"Remember, end by having the person ask a question. Leave them hanging."

I spent the day driving crazily from place to place with Ciba trying to find the three women who were to speak that night. They were friends of Ciba and Amra. The three women, all friends for twenty-five years, were of different ethnic backgrounds. One Muslim, one Croat, and one Serb. This was the Sarajevo everyone in the city loved to brag about, the city of multi-ethnic marriages and friendships. These women were to be the symbols of why Sarajevo was worth fighting for, and why, in my opinion, it was worth dropping bombs on the Serbian artillery positions in the hills.

Ciba was riding shotgun, wearing sunglasses and singing along to the music from the tape player. We were laughing about something. I drove the maze of streets as if I'd lived here all my life. While we drove, the car was enough to make us feel civilized, as if we were somehow above the chaos all around us, shielded by plastic and steel. Speeding by, we passed people slouched over and carrying loads of water they couldn't possibly manage. We couldn't help all of them. Instead we got water for the ones closest to us—Branko, Mirko, Seo, and others.

At Ciba's request, we stopped at Celo's flat. Ciba was determined to get my camera back and was confident that Celo would help us. The logic was simple. Celo controlled a portion of the black market, so if someone wanted to trade the camera he would most likely be the fence.

As he knocked on the door, I pointed out to Ciba that maybe it was Celo's guys who had stolen the camera in the first place.

"Yes, I thought of that."

The mobster answered the door while two pit bulls desperately tried to bite our legs off. It was just barking, gnashing, and more barking. I wanted to pull out their tongues. Celo had a strange way of playing with his dogs. In the middle of the conversation he would stand up and point a pistol in their faces. It made them go crazy, and they would spend the next few minutes trying to bite the end off the muzzle.

Eventually, after fifteen minutes of dog-barking and play-time, Ciba explained our problem. Celo didn't speak any English so I sat there staring at the dogs, which looked angry that they didn't have a gun in their faces.

Ciba asked Celo to keep an eye out for the camera. The mobster opened his arms, like a condor ready for flight. "Of course," he said, but he was also quick to add that he couldn't promise anything. "Of course," said Ciba back as he opened his hands, like all Bosnians, to indicate "I know this, you know this, we all know this. We can only be friends."

I had Ciba's 35-millimeter still camera round my neck. Celo asked me to take some pictures of his dogs. I snapped away while, dressed in a purple tracksuit, he shoved the gun down the throat of one of them. More barking. Then he picked one up by the scruff of its neck and swung it round in circles. Finally we all ran into the yard, where the most feared man in Sarajevo rolled in the grass with his dogs.

I remember one night smoking hash with a henchman of Celo's at the disco. The man went by the name Bulldog. I commented on how Celo seemed to be slightly mad.

"He has killed so many people I don't know how to count any more. But let me tell you, if you want to kill him you had better use a bazooka and hit him in the heart because he is a very hard man to kill." I remember that he smiled when he said this.

Nervous that Celo might turn the dogs on us, I laughed and kept pointing at Ciba while saying, "Great soccer player." Celo would respond by moving his foot in a kicking motion.

Back in the car I took a deep breath and looked over at Ciba.

"No wonder he's crazy. Those damn dogs," I said.

"I don't think he is going to get your camera back," said Ciba.

I could still hear the dogs barking as we sat in the car on the side of a hill laughing for quite some time.

. . .

A footnote on Celo. It wasn't long after this visit that he was shot in the heart. Some suspected it was one of the other warlords in town. Others suspected the government shot him to try to get a grip on the mafia, which had a large hand in running the town during the war. Curiously enough, no one I spoke to suspected a Serb sniper. But the story didn't end there. Celo was airlifted from Sarajevo to Italy by a UN plane and operated on. Another footnote: Bosnians were, by UN mandate, not to be airlifted out of Sarajevo for any reason. The UN argued it would make them accomplices in ethnic cleansing, the priority of the Serb forces.

Anyhow, according to the story, which was passed down second and third hand, Celo was saved by a team of top surgeons and eventually relocated to Germany, where he opened a restaurant. Soon after, the story goes, he was arrested for attempted murder, jailed, released, and then after the war he returned to Sarajevo.

Of course the three women dressed in their very best for Wembley. They ran round Ciba's house putting on make-up and dressing each other like three women triple-dating at their high school prom. Their energy made me remember my own dating days. The proms, the late night runs in the Ford LTD to the park where teenagers fumbled in the dark trying to get their respective panties off.

As soon as we reached the television station the women said nothing, except to whisper occasionally in one another's ear. The cameraman, Mirza, and the soundman, Denis, set up their equipment, as they had for the previous twelve satellite linkups. Mirza gave me the thumbs-up, meaning his camera was ready for transmission.

I reminded Dada, who spoke the best English, to end the link with a question.

"Live from Sarajevo in five . . . four . . . three . . . two . . . one."

Dada turned it on. She explained to the Wembley crowd that she had a Serbian mother and a Croatian father. She said if

Bosnians agreed to the peace plans made by Britain and other countries in Geneva then what should she do? Cut her house in half? Cut herself in half? It was almost a plea: this isn't a civil war. We are not separate but living next to each other. We are already in the blood of each other.

She went on to say something along the lines of "I am glad you are listening to wonderful music tonight. You should enjoy yourselves. But I want to ask one question. What are you going to do?"

I was in the EBU room watching Dada on the monitor and hearing the concert in London via a loudspeaker. Dada had the earpiece and could hear the pause in the audience. Like a pro she waited. For a second or two there was only silence coming from either side.

Then Bono began, "Well . . ." and, without knowing it, she cut him off.

"Excuse me but I think nothing."

After another short pause, in which it seemed Bono was trying to recover from the question, he started up again. "Well, it ain't much but it's all we can do right now. It's a rock 'n' roll song."

The phone rang in the EBU office, as it always did, from the stadium. It was Darcy, the previous EBU manager in Sarajevo. She was with Ned at the show.

"How was it seeing it live?" I asked. She was the great experiment, the only one who would ever see it both here and out there.

"Well, the greens and blues were a bit shaky around the edges and the sound could have been better. And . . ."

I hung up.

The phone rang again.

I picked it up. It was Ned. "Do me a favor," I said. "Don't let that woman back on the phone."

The next concert was in Cardiff and I had convinced Shibe to speak. It was time to unleash Shibe's surrealism on the masses. He was reluctant and agreed only when I said he didn't need to tell me what he was going to say. At the television station

Shibe, Vlado and I poked our heads into the EBU office a few hours before the scheduled time.

"You are done," said Philippe with a big happy smile. "Yes, your rock 'n' roll pals have pulled the plug. So sorry."

Over the phone Ned explained that the backlash from the previous night was overwhelming. "Those three women were a hard act to follow." He said the press was killing them. Politicians were angry. The British were livid. It sounded like U2 were being run out of town with an axe-wielding crowd at their heels.

And so that was that. As quickly as it had begun it was over. We had done thirteen satellite link-ups.

Leaving the station with Shibe and Vlado, I turned off the headlights and hit sixty down Snipers' Alley. I nearly ran into a UN tank.

"You are like a Bosnian driver. Drunk." Shibe was laughing in the passenger seat.

My mind was jolted, altered, as if I was falling quickly down through a hole to nowhere. As I fell I felt the rising of something resembling my ego. I felt that the EBU machine had bested me. I felt I'd let down my friends. And what about a little consultation before U2 decided to shut it all down? I thought back to when I'd first arrived in the television station. EBU'd asked if I worked for U2. Maybe I had been doing so the whole time and hadn't known it.

My face must have betrayed how I felt, which was, oddly enough, betrayed.

"Indiana," said Shibe, "you went too far. You woke the dragon and it stopped you. This is a great thing. You are now a true citizen of Sarajevo. A surrealist."

"I don't know," I said. "Hey, Shibe, what were you going to say tonight on the satellite?"

"Nothing. I was going to move my lips but say nothing at all. They would have been adjusting their controls and panicking about the technology, always about the technology, but before they could figure it out I would smile and wave goodnight."

Right then I slowed down. I had been flicking my headlights on and off to see the road. Up ahead there was a roadblock, but there were no guards in sight. Then suddenly there were five men dressed in black commando outfits with ski masks and holding machine guns. They waved us down. I stopped and they stuck the guns in the windows, in each of our faces. We could see only their eyes and mouths, and even that was just through small holes. I turned the key to off. They asked for my papers. I gave them my passport.

"Shibe," said the one looking at the papers.

"*Da*," said Shibe, "it's me. Shibe."

They pulled off their ski masks and each one took a moment to shake his hand. Vlado lit a cigarette and I took a few deep breaths and slid my hand into my groin to check that I was all still there.

"This is Bill Carter. A great man. A great friend of Sarajevo," said Shibe.

We continued into town while Shibe told a joke, as if nothing had happened.

"Momo is knocking at the door where his friend Uzeir lives. Uzeir opens the door and sees his old friend in very bad shape, very thin and pale, hardly able to stand on his own feet. He's obviously starving. 'What the hell's wrong with you?' asks Uzeir. Momo says, 'I haven't eaten a thing for three days.' Uzeir looks concerned. He puts his hands on his friend's shoulders and says to him, 'Listen, man, you have to eat something, *even if you don't feel like it*.' Then he closes the door and goes back to lying down."

We laughed.

"Shibe?" I asked.

"Indiana?"

"Who were those guys?"

"What guys?"

"The commando dudes with the guns."

"They are just friends. Let's drink. In celebration of irony."

I looked at Vlado in the mirror. He shook his head and smiled and exhaled some smoke. I already knew what he was going to say.

"With friends like that who needs enemies?"

69

By the time I had spread out the blanket on Ciba and Amra's floor that night my skin felt clammy and sensitive. I was aware that I was losing myself to an inner spiral of psychosis. It was as if I had been on a bicycle pedaling uphill for so long to reach the top, and now, with no brakes, I was flying downhill, headed for the crash.

A wave of exhaustion overcame me like no other since Corrina's death, an exhaustion that wasn't a sleepy tiredness, but an absence of corporeality. Like I was floating slightly above ground, unable to feel the weight of my own skin. The twitch under my left eye was now under both eyes.

"Corrina, Corrina, this is clever," I said in a fit of the mad giggles. "OK, I've been playing the game hard, now what? *Huh?* What now? Should I stay or should I go? I mean I will push it more if that's what we're talking about here. You aren't getting away that easy. Fuck, no."

Hearing the bedroom door open, I shut my eyes. That has always been my primal reaction—to run, hide, or just act like I don't exist.

With her nightgown buttoned to the top, Amra knelt down next to me and put her hand on my forehead.

"I think you are ill," she said.

"The satellites are over," I said, my breathing labored now.

"Yes. Ciba told me."

"I had no idea they were going to end so suddenly. Shibe would have been great."

"Now what?" asked Amra.

"U2 invited me to Ireland."

It was the last thing Ned had said on the phone earlier that night. "The band would like to invite you to Ireland for the last two concerts of the tour," he said. I told him, thank you, but I couldn't leave. He said the videotapes had been transferred to BETA tapes and were ready for me to edit into a documentary. I told him I would call him back.

"You should go," said Amra.

I looked up at Amra. "I don't want to leave."

"Maybe you should go home, to California." Nothing in her voice wanted to drive me away, only to be kind. For her, home, even in the cross hairs of a howitzer, was the most peaceful place she could imagine.

"I don't live anywhere any more," I said.

She went to the kitchen and poured me a glass of water from the canister. By the time she returned I couldn't lift my head. It was as if my body had given up on me. I couldn't make a fist. My eyes burned from lack of sleep.

"Amra. I feel strange."

"Like how?"

"Like I'm dying of some weird disease."

"You are tired. You really don't know how hard you push."

She spoke so softly and gently, it was like a gentle breeze in the forest of my mind. She put her hand behind my head and lifted my lips to the glass. The water slid down, cooling my innards.

"Tell me, Bill. You never told me. Have you ever been in love?"

"Why do you ask?"

"Because I think maybe you have."

The moonbeams were rippling across the window, making everything seem distorted but in a good way.

"Yes."

"What is the woman's name?" she asked.

"Her name was Corrina."

"What happened?"

I told her. About how Corrina loved stealing flowers from other people's gardens. About how I loved to watch her sleep, just watch her breathe as she drifted off into dreamland. And her smile. God, her smile. It was crooked and beautiful. Or how one time we stood on the edge of the Pacific Ocean, our feet in the wet sand. You know, just where the tide tears the water from the side of your feet. And if you stand in one place long enough you feel as if you are sinking right into the water. It was there that Corrina told me something. She said, "My mother used to bring me here when things were not so good. She would bring me here and we would put our toes up against the water's edge. She always put her arms around me and told me to look straight ahead, at the horizon. She said, 'Whatever is behind at this moment is done. It is past. Out there is where we are going.' "

And finally I told her how Corrina died. Alone in a hospital bed.

Amra and I sat in silence for almost twenty minutes, staring at the vanilla moonlight raining down on a blue night. A few mortars landed elsewhere.

"This love with your woman," she finally said, "it is the saddest story I have ever heard."

How could she say that? In this place? We sat silent for the longest time.

"You will find another," she said.

"I don't want another. I want what we were. How I felt."

"People are not supposed to be alone."

That's the last thing I remember her saying before I closed my eyes. I breathed deeply and tried hard to remember the vague rules of Buddhism. Life is suffering, things are permeable and we don't ever own anything. We are only caretakers, even of ourselves. Then I thought of Christ's teaching. Be good to one another, do unto others as you would do unto yourself. Don't judge. Give freely and expect nothing in return.

And then I thought, bollocks. What I really want is a woman to run her fingers over my eyelids until I fall asleep.

70

I woke up under a blind sky, dotted with clouds thin as paper. Time to go. The day before I was to fly I went down to the television station. I ran up the stairs and into the EBU office. Ciba told me to forget about it, not to go into that building again. I just couldn't let it go. I spent a few minutes telling people I was leaving for a while but would return, but by the look on their faces no one bought it. My smile must have given it away. It was too crazy, even for a crazy person.

Finally, Philippe arrived: my purpose of the visit. At six feet two he was much taller than I was and I noted this as he stood in the doorway with a crate of eggs in his arms. I walked up and pointed my finger at his throat.

"I just want you to know you are the biggest asshole I've met during my whole time here," I said.

He shoved me aside with the carton of eggs. Jesus, didn't he know they went for $6-7 an egg on the street? He spoke to someone in French while he put the eggs down and tore off his jacket. The reporters on the phones turned their heads to see what was going on. I saw one man chewing his fingernails, eyes intent upon seeing the war come from the outside to the inside.

Philippe came straight at me. I retreated and flipped him all the way over my body, landing on top of him in the hallway. There I beat him round the face. I punched him low in the stomach, wherever I could pound his flesh. He was fighting me because I offended him by my very presence. Because I didn't dress right or because I didn't do the "news" or who knows why. And that was why he could never win a fight with me. I was fighting him because he was the Serbs at the check-point. He was the trumpet player. He was Buffalo Head. He was Tony. He was the Grim Reaper who had taken Corrina away. Hell, maybe he was my father. I don't know. I'm not a good fighter and avoid fighting at all costs. But on that day, the poor bastard could have been King Kong and I still would have taken him on.

When the locals tried to pull me off, the big Texan techni-cian, who hadn't spoken much to me during these past months, told everyone, "Back off. Let them fight it out."

Then Philippe wrapped a leg around my head, throwing me backward. Now he was ready to get in his punches. The Texan stepped in and stopped it. "All right, that's probably enough."

So it was set. U2 had arranged for a flight from Croatia to Dublin. All I had to do was get on the next military jet leaving

Sarajevo. I had about DM 500 left over from the satellite fund and around $80 in the toe of my boot.

The next morning when I arrived at the UN headquarters to catch the morning flight from Sarajevo to Croatia, in time for the connecting flight to Dublin, Philippe was sitting on the steps. He had what looked like a shiner. I felt nervous and bad about the fight but decided to say nothing. The Texan was with him and when I said so long he walked over to me and said Philippe was going back to Switzerland.

It wasn't until almost a year later that I finally pieced together the story on why Philippe decided to leave. Some details are vague but it went something like this.

Shibe, who I had told about the fight on our final night of drinking in the office, went to the EBU office the next day. Even though, apart from secretaries and translators with accreditation, no Bosnians are allowed in EBU, Shibe walked in and asked for Philippe. He told Philippe that in this building the foreign press had power. And in this room Philippe was free to do whatever he wanted. Then he told him if he went outside, for any reason, any reason at all, to watch his back. He told him, "This is your room, but this is my city."

I suspect Philippe laughed when Shibe told him to watch his back. And why not? Shibe was just a local in a town of locals who all claimed to be in the secret police. Besides, Shibe was probably laughing when he said it. I'm sure Shibe even shook his hand and said, "Yes, yes, yes." And when he walked out Shibe probably said goodbye to the locals, kissed a few on the cheek and then, who knows? Maybe he leaned in the door one last time to repeat the words in a slightly high-pitched comical delivery, like Gene Wilder might say: "OK, so don't walk outside. OK?"

Philippe might have dismissed it as an idle threat, but for the Bosnian secretary, who told me this story some time later. When Philippe asked her who that man was she answered truthfully, "Oh, that is Shibe. His father is a general in the Bosnian army. Shibe is a very well-known man in this town."

Perhaps Philippe had a family emergency back home or

perhaps his contract was only for a few weeks or he wanted a few days in Split for R and R. Or perhaps he started seeing every Bosnian with a gun as his assassin. Whichever, he was on that plane.

71

I think it was the air conditioning that did me in. I shivered in my seat while a woman who smelled like jasmine served me a drink with a small swivel stick in it.

There was a first-class ticket with my name on it at the Split airport. The flight was just under three hours from Croatia to London and on to Dublin. Outside was nothing but gray.

I spilled the first glass of wine on my trousers. My hands were shaking; they had been shaking for a few months now. I assumed it was the cheap vodka, but maybe it was something else. I spilled the second glass of wine on my shirt. I was wet, stained, and now shivering in a flying icebox. The stewardess, God bless her, leaned in and in a calming voice asked, "Sir, is everything all right?"

I nodded.

"Scared of flying?"

"Maybe that's it."

Then the plane landed in a different country, a different world. And of course there was customs, which has always been an interesting and stressful moment of self-reflection. *What are you? And where do you live? And how do you make money?*

The form asks: what is your occupation? I wrote "farmer," which seemed to put them at ease.

In the past I have written "wolf trainer," "brain surgeon," "helicopter pilot." Without a flinch they punch me through and wish me a pleasant stay. Once, for fun, I wrote "writer." That brought out a suspicious grin from the agent, which was followed by "Sir, how much money do you have with you at this time?"

I woke up in a room on the fifth floor of the Conrad Hilton, in downtown Dublin. I was feeling lost, sleep-deprived, and dizzy. And as far as I could tell I was in a state of post-traumatic stress with a mild case of culture shock. Still, I was glad, and at the same time shamefully guilty, that the water in the bathroom worked. I locked the door and took a bath. When the water went cold I refilled the tub with more hot water. I found it very amusing and whenever I thought of my friends in Sarajevo I imagined them here, in my shoes. They would have already ordered room service and invited over the neighbors.

The phone rang. It was Ned. He told me that they, U2, wanted to give me some monetary compensation for my work on the link-ups. I told him I hadn't done it for the money.

"We know, but everyone needs to get paid," he said.

"I really didn't do this for money. That was a very important aspect of the relationship."

"I appreciate that. So what do you think is fair?"

"I really don't know what it was worth in dollars."

"We were thinking something like five thousand dollars."

"OK, sure." I hung up.

Five thousand dollars. That was a lot of money for something I'd had no intention of making money from. It was a backpacker's fortune.

Oh shit, I thought. Taking the money would cheapen what I had done. I walked round the room. I had multiple conversations with myself as I dug my toes into the carpet. The mirror in the room was much too big and I found myself standing in front of it, pinching my skin to feel my thinness. Take the money or not? It was useless. And then I remembered the man burning the clothes in Croatia. By now he was probably making $8,000 a month clearing inventory for next year's US military budget. Suddenly $5,000 wasn't enough. I had to be worth at least what he was making.

I called Ned. I told him about the man burning clothes and the US Congress and the senator from Mississippi who would be getting fat on pork-barrel waste. I told him UN aid drivers get paid extra for hazardous duty. He asked what I was driving at.

"Perhaps we should make the fee, if we are going to have one, eight thousand dollars."

"Oh, now money is starting to mean something, eh?" He laughed, but I didn't know why. Ever since I had arrived he'd acted like a lawyer, constantly wary of me trying to outmaneuver him. His recent conversations had taken the tone of cross-examinations and it felt like the walls of the hotel were closing in fast and I had no pole long enough to stop the inevitable crush.

Instead of worrying about it I called everyone I knew in the world and told them I was alive.

The concert in Dublin was exactly like the one I'd seen in Verona, except that people seemed to know me. Not the audience, but all the people backstage. Stage hands, holding a guitar in one hand, would come up to me and say, "I thought it was amazing," or "Very powerful stuff."

For the most part I walked around like I was lost in some country fair. Finally a woman, maybe the one I'd talked to from Sarajevo, ushered me into a tent where a very large man was standing guard. He shook my hand and said in a hushed voice, "Balls, man. Balls."

Inside were glasses of champagne and plenty of food. Ever since my arrival there had been plenty of food. I recognized some of the famous people in the tent talking among themselves, but I knew absolutely not one person. I wanted to go for a walk. I thought, wasn't the ocean nearby?

Instead I walked back and forth behind the stage, unsure of where to stand or, more to the point, why I was standing here, meaning in Ireland. A holiday? I didn't need a holiday, I needed to make a movie. Bearing witness had now overtaken me as if I was a farmer desperate to get his crop in before the rains. I had no time to sleep, drink, or talk.

Later that night, after the show, I found myself drinking in a bar with the same supermodels who had been in Verona. I recognized their faces from magazines and billboards. They must have been doing OK because they bought all the champagne. Occasionally I would wiggle my toes to feel my secret stash, which was now only $50. Also there was Bill Flanagan, a writer, who was in the process of finishing up a long biography of U2, called *At the End of the World*. I had met him too that night in Verona, where, when I finished my interview with Bono, he asked me what it had been like in Sarajevo. I told him it was "intense." At the bar with the supermodels he kept asking me how it felt to be here in Dublin when my friends were still in Sarajevo, under the gun. I told him, "I've taken several baths."

Around 4 a.m. I felt a tidal wave of exhaustion come over me, as if I had overdosed on my last shot of adrenaline and it was wearing off. I excused myself and started for the door. Everyone at the table seemed quite concerned that I would get lost on my way back to the hotel. That is until someone said, laughing, "If he can survive Sarajevo he can survive Dublin."

I managed the walk without any problems. As always, it was nice to be alone in the midst of a new foreign country. I walked through the lobby doors just as a woman got out of a cab. She was one of the beautiful women at the party. We walked side by side into the lift. I took a closer look at her. She was of Indian descent and had slick black hair. Her dress was golden and had a slit that ran up to the top of her thigh, revealing her golden brown skin.

"What floor?" I asked, gesturing to push the proper button.

"What floor are you on?" she asked.

"The fifth," I said.

"OK."

We walked down the hallway without saying a word. I stopped at my door and she walked a few steps beyond and then stopped. She turned on the heel of her tall shoes and slowly twirled round. She nodded her head toward the door. "Aren't you going to ask me in for a drink?"

I poured us each a vodka on ice.

"I fell in love with you during the satellites," she said. I felt sweat begin to drench my pits. A tightness in my trousers. She went on about how I was a true artist. I told her I was more tired than I had ever been in my life. She asked if I wanted anything.

"Sleep?"

She looked into my eyes with her own crazy eyes. What was needed here was a compromise.

"Perhaps a massage?" I queried.

She turned me over and took off my clothes, all of them. There I was ass-naked but more tired than I could explain to her. How could she know that sleeping had become my form of sexual intimacy? Falling asleep had become my way of showing true emotion toward a woman. If I fell asleep it was a sign she had found a way to make me comfortable. Sexual intercourse, at this point, felt like a fantasy. She hiked up her sari, revealing a pair of brown legs. She nestled herself on my rear end. She asked if there was anything else I wanted, "anything at all."

And then I fell fast asleep.

The next thing I knew, Corrina was standing next to me at the window, her mouth against the glass. She was blowing hard so her cheeks expanded and it gave her a goofy face. Next to her were Vlado and Johnny. We all laughed and ran down the alley.

I woke up to see sunlight coming in through the windows. I scanned the room. Where was I? What room was this? There were two vodka glasses and my clothes were on the ground. There was the distinct smell of a woman lingering in the air. Fuck, I yelled, and put on my trousers and pulled on my shoes.

God, I didn't want to betray Corrina, but upon waking I also realized I really wanted to feel a woman underneath me, or on top of me. I ran down to the front desk, shirtless and still loaded but beyond tiredness. I asked the front desk clerk if he had seen a beautiful Indian woman pass by lately.

"No, sir, I haven't seen anyone by that description. Perhaps the gentleman would care for the morning paper?"

Back in my room, paper in hand, I turned on the television to find all the channels devoted to sport or news. I settled on a cricket match. Grown men were drinking tea in the outfield while one man, dressed in white linens, swatted a bat at a small ball. It went on for hours, like a dream, and was enough to put me back to sleep for a while.

72

We had been at it for three days in Windmill Lane Studios, where U2 had made some of their earliest recordings and which they still used to edit their music videos. For the most part we were just watching raw footage, trying to figure out how to edit thirty hours of tape into a thirty-minute documentary for television. It was going to be hard work, especially since I had never done it before.

On the fourth day I arrived in the morning and, like most days, a woman knocked on the door to the edit bay and then brought in tea and biscuits.

The phone rang. Seated next to me, with his fingers on the AVID edit system, was editor Stephen O'Connell, a 24-year-old Dubliner, who had been assigned to work with me on my documentary.

Ned was on the phone.

"Bill," said Ned, "I don't have much time to talk." He was talking on a mobile and said he was boarding a plane. "Perhaps you should start thinking of your next port of call."

"What's that?"

"Where you want to go next."

He told me it had been a "good run" but that I was to be on a plane by Friday. In four days. I asked if he was serious and he said, "Listen, I gotta get on this plane. So I need to get off the phone. It's been great working with you. Give it some thought and just let the office know where you want to fly."

In shock, I told Stephen about the conversation and he shook his head a little. He had flushed red cheeks and an innocent smile that made him seem even younger than he was.

"I have a confession," he said.

"Bring it on."

"I've never worked on a documentary."

I took a sip of tea and asked what he was getting at.

"You were given the most inexperienced editor in this building. Maybe you were given me so the documentary would fail." He frowned and looked at the footage on the screen. It was Lejla and Selma frozen, smiling.

We had four days. Stephen and I worked until the sun came up and made a ten-minute rough-cut demo tape.

I had another idea.

73

Two days later there was a party at Bono's house celebrating the end of the tour. I spent the first ten minutes in the bathroom lecturing myself on how to behave in other people's homes. Relativity was the key. Be quiet and don't lecture people not to eat because other people are starving. Life is relative to where you are standing, at any given moment. These are the sorts of things I was telling myself. And I was wearing the same clothes I'd had in Sarajevo, since washed, but my shoes still stank.

At the buffet a man introduced himself as the head of a major magazine and said maybe we should work together. He'd heard I was a danger junkie and invited me back to New York on his private jet in the morning. I told him, "No thank you, but I think I am making a film."

It was hard not to notice that in the bushes, not far from the tables, were men in black suits with headsets. They carried what seemed to be automatic weapons, attached by a strap to their shoulders, under their jackets.

Inside the house, I caught the eye of the woman serving wine. She smiled and then quickly walked into another room. I followed her and introduced myself. She said looking at me had made her want to cry, because it made her think of all the people still in Sarajevo. She was a pretty woman with a soft smile and a gentle but confident voice. Her hair was jet black. She was what the Irish call "Black Irish," referring to the centuries of trade between Spain and Ireland, when the Spanish effectively spread their gene pool among the pale, freckle-faced Irish.

Vibrant and radiant, this woman's voice was full of emotion and her compassion was etched into her large black eyes and smile. She felt like a friend. I asked her name.

"Ali Hewson," she said. "I'm Bono's wife."

I thanked her for inviting me into her home, and she told me I was welcome and to enjoy myself.

Later, I was standing on the patio by myself when a man walked up and leaned on the railing. We introduced ourselves. He was Salman Rushdie. He was the reason for the men in the bushes with guns. The Fatwa, the death contract from Iran, was still in place. He was worth a cool million if I were to stab him in the jugular with my ballpoint pen and report my deeds to the supreme leader of Iran. Instead I told Mr. Rushdie that I'd enjoyed his books, especially *Midnight's Children*. He answered by telling me about another book of his that I had never heard of. Then he talked about the satellite link-ups with an eloquence I had never attached to them myself. He created a web of metaphors that made the transmissions of war into a rock show seem almost grotesque and yet powerful because they were so upsetting. He said all the criticisms had been from people who couldn't think outside the box. That a rock and roll arena was the perfect setting for live feeds from Sarajevo. It was perfect because it was so wrong. That no matter how surreal it was, it was better than the alternative, doing nothing. And wasn't that the problem? That the world had done nothing. We shook hands and I walked out to the railing feeling a squirt of pride shimmy its way up my spine.

Still, the problem remained. I was supposed to leave town in three days. I checked my trousers for the video and decided it was time to take a chance.

Edge, the U2 guitarist, ambled past with a piece of dessert in one hand and a cup of tea in the other.

"Edge," I said, "I'm using 'Numb' as a centerpiece for the film. I've got a short demo with me. If you got some time maybe you would want to check it out."

He didn't hesitate. "Absolutely."

"Numb" was a song he'd written for their latest album, *Zooropa*. As far as I could tell it was a comment on mass apathy and indifference.

We walked away from the main house toward a guesthouse. People were still coming to the party. One man had on a pinstripe suit with what looked like bowling shoes and a very beautiful woman on his arm. The house was a perfect backdrop. It was enormous but not garish. It was old and beautiful, something I told myself I would choose if I had lots of money.

With us was a Frenchman who had made a documentary on the Zapatista revolution in Chiapas. I didn't know the connection to U2 but he was in the guesthouse with his documentary. We watched it and when it was over we had a small discussion on the situation in southern Mexico.

Then it was my turn.

Edge sat on the floor cross-legged, like a Buddha in training. He asked a few questions about how the editing process was going. I told him not bad. When he spoke it was in a quiet manner, as if somehow he was practicing restraint before speaking.

"OK." He breathed out. "I'm ready."

The tape ended with a scene of a middle-aged man carrying a handbag and running full speed toward a burned-out train. He was running for his life. He ran in perfect beat to "Numb,": *"Don't check/ just balance on the fence/ don't answer/ don't ask/ don't try and make sense."*

"That is the best use of a U2 song I have ever seen," he said when the tape ended.

He asked me what my plan was.

"To make a full-length documentary," I said.

"Good."

Then I said I had been told to leave town in two days.

"By whom?" he asked.

"Well, I think by U2," I said as if asking a question.

He nodded and scratched his chin as if this made sense.

"We need to get Bono to look at this."

Later, as the party was winding down, Bono and I spoke about having dinner together. He suggested his home, the following evening. There was no agenda, just a social get-together. I didn't mention the tape. The following day the phone rang around one in the afternoon at the hotel. It was Bono.

"When you come over for dinner, bring that tape you showed Edge."

I called Stephen and told him I was coming down to the studio. I told him to put whatever he was editing on to a new tape. I also told him about the dinner date.

"He asked you to bring the tape?"

"Yes."

"This is it."

74

The taxi drove me through a myriad of small streets to the outskirts of town. It was overcast and, well, very Irish weather—always threatening to rain. Near the gates to Bono's home sat a drove of fans, who, when the taxi waited for the gates to open, ran up to the window. Their faces were open and expectant, but when they saw the cab driver and me they frowned and walked back across the road, disappointed. Later, Ali, who was cutting carrots for a home-cooked meal, said, "I don't know what they are possibly waiting for." She said it not as a person tired of something, but more with a deep curiosity. I wondered myself, but there they stood in the dark waiting for something.

Present were Bono, Ali, their two children, and Ali's parents. We ate chicken and vegetables and talked of everything from sport to politics to music. They asked me my plans for the future, a reasonable question but quite honestly one I hadn't thought of for what seemed many years. As far as I knew, my future plans included going back to the hotel later that night. Perhaps if I rode the lift long enough that woman in the sari would show up again. Beyond that I had no idea.

"So tell me the truth. There must have been a woman," said

Bono with a boyish grin as he used his fork to clear his plate into the sink.

"Why do you say that?" I asked.

"To stay that long in there it had to be a woman." Now he was wiping his hands on a towel.

"I guess that makes sense."

"So come on then," he said, chuckling.

The rest of the dinner party was waiting as well. I felt caught, wanting to prove my storytelling abilities in an Irish home and at the same time wanting not to open an emotional can of worms to people I didn't know that well. Still, I felt it was time to come clean with my motivations. Bono had stepped forward and taken a huge chance on my behalf and now I was a guest in his home. It seemed like the time to put all the cards on the table.

"There was a woman but she didn't live in Bosnia. It was before the war. We were in love and she died."

There was a brief pause, but it wasn't awkward, more the silence of giving respect to the dead.

"Was she Bosnian?" asked the father-in-law.

"No. No, she was American," I said, feeling the sweat beads forming on my forehead.

For the first time I felt vulnerable, as if by exposing my personal story I could now be attacked for everything I had been doing. Still, I could hear myself thinking, I had to stay open to those who had been open to me. It is the agreement of the living. The fuel to take the next step.

Someone poured some wine and soon the conversation shifted direction. Then Bono motioned for me to follow him. He leaped up the stairs, two steps at a time, urging me on so we could watch his new music video. His energy and sudden movements made me feel like we were teenagers escaping from the parents to somewhere we could blow our cigarette smoke out the window.

He waited until everyone at dinner had followed before putting on the video. He seemed nervous; not insecure, just excited. The video was of a song called "Lemon" and the images were of the band wandering around in what could best be described as an abstract visualization of a mathematical equation. They were dressed in modern suits and walking in front of a digital world of clocks, ladders, and transparent ledges that led nowhere. After it ended we put my tape in. Even though it was slightly altered from the day before, it ended the same way it had when Edge had watched it, with a man running across Snipers' Alley, carrying a handbag, toward a burned-out train.

Quietly stern, Ali's father said, "Paul"—Bono's real name—"you have to help this young man."

"So where are we?" asked Bono, his legs dangling over the arm of the chair.

I told him I was supposed to leave town in two days. Someone in the room sighed and it hung there for a few moments, like thick dust floating through the air.

"I have to tell you I don't understand what is going on," I said with some frustration. "Ned is telling me to leave town and yet in Verona we talked about me editing this film. I quite honestly don't know who to listen to. I don't know who this thing called U2 is."

Bono sat up and looked me in the eye. "U2 is five people. Larry, Edge, Adam, Paul, and myself. Everyone else works for us. I pay people a lot of money to make decisions for me. And Ned is one of them. He said he reviewed the tape and didn't see a film."

"Ned?" I said. "Well, I can assure you he didn't watch thirty hours of film, and besides, he doesn't know what to look for in this footage. I do."

Bono didn't hesitate. "OK, you work like the clappers until next Friday at the studio. I don't care about cost. Use anything you need. Add another five great minutes and shape this up, and Ali and I will come in and watch it. If we like it we will finance it ourselves."

Stunned but happy to be back on track, I agreed and we shook hands. Still holding my hand he said, "But don't jerk me off here. Make something we will be proud of in ten years. In twenty years."

"And what about me leaving?"

"Don't worry about that," he said.

Later that same night, in the hallway, he asked if I had a title for the movie. I told him I had a notebook full of titles but none seemed to be working. They were all too obvious and gloomy.

"Didn't you say there was a Miss Sarajevo beauty contest in the war?" he asked.

I told him there was but I didn't have any footage of it. All I knew was that women in bikinis strode the catwalk with a banner that said "Don't Let Them Kill Us" while outside the artillery barrage continued.

"That's it then," said Bono. "The title. *Miss Sarajevo*."

"I don't want it to be too poppy. I don't want to make people think it's about a beauty contest."

"It's the perfect metaphor. Miss. It can be a woman. It can be a city. You call it *Miss Sarajevo* and I will write you a song."

"Deal," I said.

Over the next week, as Stephen and I sat in front of the monitors for sixteen hours a day, we worked under a few guidelines, which I stuck up on yellow Post-its. The main one was that the editing must reflect an element of insanity and surrealism.

The most notable difference was a sudden influx of people to look over what I was doing. Although kind and respectful, everyone had suggestions. Perhaps subtitles would be an interesting idea; start it with radio broadcasts to help the viewer; use a narrator. I told them these were all good ideas and when they left I told Stephen to ignore everything they said. I had already learned in Sarajevo that one key to success was never to listen to the suits, even if they were the ones giving you the money. Especially if they were the ones giving you the money.

They eventually hired a "supervisor," a pleasant film-maker named Gerry Hoban who stopped in from time to time to check on our progress. I liked him, mostly because he told me he felt uncomfortable interfering with another person's work. Instead we met in the nearby pub at the end of the evening and drank Guinness and talked about how the film was going.

That Friday, as promised, Bono and his wife came by in the early evening. I had changed the order of the film and added pieces and dropped a few storylines. Stephen had dubbed in some new music. Overall it was a stronger piece and we knew it.

When it ended Bono edged to the front of his seat. "OK, we are in," he said. "Let's make a budget and decide what it will take to make it great."

Although I was excited to get the green light on the project, there was still no promise that it would ever be seen. But something felt right about the work. The act of work. The fifteen-hour days of putting images together in a way that made sense out of senselessness. The voices of friends in Sarajevo who were once just voices in a room were now becoming authorities on something. What? I wasn't sure yet. I wanted to make a great film, a document that captured the essence of a time, in a place. But in truth it was the promise of more work that felt so good; the hour-by-hour effort of creating something that would last.

75

As it turned out, Ned's production company, Dreamchaser, which handled almost all U2's video work, ended up co-financing the postproduction of the documentary. My co-producer was Liam Cabot, a young Dubliner who arranged for me to move into an flat near downtown, a few minutes from a pub that had Guinness on tap. It was all in the budget. It had been only two weeks since I had left the war zone. This fact weighed on my mind like a bag of bricks as I walked the streets of Dublin. Still, I found great relief in imagining Beckett bumbling around the side streets actually talking like he wrote. It was mysterious and yet, like most places on earth, there were reasons to be wary of the one thing the place was well known for. In India and Nepal, known for spiritual insight, there are plenty of men dressed as yogis who prey on the naive and ignorant American or European looking for a path to God. A few rupees will get you further down the path of enlightenment. In America it's the entire consumer-driven economy. To be happy you must buy. In Italy a woman must be on guard against the Italian man who considers himself God's gift to women. In Ireland, as I was finding out, it was subtler. It was their speech. It was their command over the English language and their ability to use it as a storytelling device and at the same time to weave a web of confusion as their last line of defense. One man, Gavin Friday, whom I found to be refreshingly candid about all things Irish, told me, "The reason the English hate us is because we speak their language better than they do. It is our greatest weapon."

One night, while talking with Stephen about all this, I realized I had forgotten Ned's promise regarding the camera I had lost in Sarajevo. I hadn't shot anything new since losing the camera, which was fine; I had the footage, which mostly consisted of interviews with people I knew in the city, street scenes and shots of Graeme and me running around looking scared and slightly ridiculous.

Still, I had plans to use the camera again, maybe even for this documentary. I called Ned and immediately he talked about how I had most likely misunderstood him at the time when he had said, "I really don't think that should be a problem."

In war there is clarity. Not good or bad, just clear intent. There you knew the guy on the hill wanted to kill you. No punches pulled. If he got the shot he took you out. And the old man who invited you in for coffee? He really wanted to share his time, his coffee with you. But here in Dublin I was getting confused between language and intent.

After viewing all the footage, it became clear to everyone involved in the project that I was missing key interviews with some of the major characters. And my footage was not as clean, in either video imagery or sound quality, as it would have to be for broadcasting. Also I needed stock footage of the war and the Miss Sarajevo contest to round out the film.

The only way to get everything was to return to Sarajevo.

I borrowed Bono's camera, which was exactly like the one I'd lost except that it was formatted for recording in PAL, the European format. This would make it easier to use the footage in Dublin.

From the budget I took $3,000 in cash, a few cigarette cartons, and a duffel bag of booze and gifts and flew to Aviano, Italy. There I sat in my hotel room, in the dark, poring over the last six months. None of it made sense. It felt like a dream I was just wandering around in, waiting to be woken up.

Also, to be honest, I was terrified of returning to Sarajevo. I had a feeling I had already taken too many risks and that death was in my future. At the same time I wanted to see my friends, tell some stories and try to get some footage that would make this documentary stand out as different from so many others that had been made about the city.

Actually I ached to be in the southwest, where the canyons run red and deep and the sky is like blue silk stretched taut across the earth's skin. Back when I'd ridden across that desert I would build a fire just to watch the fire ants. Have you ever watched this phenomenon? The flying ants circle the fire for some time and then suddenly they alter course and nosedive straight into the fire, evaporating in the heat. I wondered, are we like that? Do we circle our own lives like ants hovering around a fire, and then in one violent but decisive moment face the inevitable truth and fly purposely into an act of personal evaporation?

I caught the first morning flight to Sarajevo on a French C130 military cargo jet. I caught a ride downtown in a French Foreign Legion APC. First I delivered new Levi's to the sisters and a new set of guitar strings and some whiskey to Vlado. I told them I was here for one week and would visit soon, but first I had to see Ciba.

At Ciba's, Amra cooked the chicken I had brought, along with the vegetables. We opened a bottle of wine and put out a plate of bread with cut cheese slices.

"So you are fat now?" said Amra. "You have eaten very well."

Survival guilt flows highest when a person's very presence is a reminder of what others can't have.

Over dinner they told me something that had happened while I was gone. One day the phone had rung in their house. That in itself was unusual enough for a story. But, they explained, the person on the phone had been a man named Dinko, a Serbian, who had been on Ciba's soccer team before the war. They'd been the best of friends. At the beginning of the war he had left to join his family abroad. Ciba and Amra had wished him luck. This flat was his and they were taking care of it in the hope that they would see him again.

Telling the story, Ciba explained that he was very happy when he realized it was Dinko. He asked where he was calling from.

"He said he was calling from the mountain," said Ciba.

"With the Chetniks?"

"Yes. He is captain of an artillery gun."

"Jesus. Why did he call?"

"To find out who was living in his flat. He said he was going to bomb it if Muslims were in it."

"We are Muslims," said Amra.

"I have never been to a mosque. Ever," said Ciba.

"Can you imagine this?" asked Amra. "But he said he would not bomb it as long as we were living here. I tell you we are all crazy here in the Balkans."

"Enough of this stupid place. Tell us about Ireland," said Ciba.

Before I answered I gave Ciba a new set of blank canvases I had bought in Italy. He shook his head and smiled.

"Thank you. I will do a new show with these."

"And Ireland? Is it wonderful?" asked Amra.

I told them about the food, the hotels, the concerts, and the editing of the film. I also told them about the woman who said she had fallen in love with me while watching the satellite link-ups. They smiled, glad, it seemed, I'd used the word love. Then I told them how I had fallen asleep while she was giving me a mas-sage. They giggled. And then how I'd run downstairs half-naked looking for a woman with a slit in her dress. They laughed. Fi-nally I told them that when I'd seen her the next evening she'd re-fused to talk to me. They laughed so hard they could barely eat.

Come to think of it, we never spoke again about the man on the hill with the cannon pointed at the living room.

76

I have never believed in the idea of coincidence: something that happens by chance in a surprising or remarkable way. It is the word chance that bothers me and I wonder sometimes if it is a word invented for those who just don't want to see the intricate magic that happens in our lives, every day.

Likewise, one can never predict the moment when the past will intersect with the future and find us standing in the precarious balance of the place we call the present.

Like that afternoon, when I turned the corner and walked into the alley with my camera rolling. I never imagined that the thirteen-year-old girl sitting on top of the Volkswagen would suddenly, almost as if time had never existed, pull together my past, present, and future life.

I went straight for her. The first thing was her laugh. It had a sweetness to it that harbored no cynicism or malice. It almost drifted, like an echo. This young girl had dark brown wavy hair that fell down past her shoulders. Her eyebrows were a slight shade darker than her hair and her voice was scratchy and strong. Her face was that of purity in bloom, an angel in waiting. Her round brown eyes didn't betray the slightest hint of wanting, even in a place so full of need. And when she laughed her joy was like a ray of light, spreading to all those in sight. It has been said that there are some people who, by their very existence, walk through this life creating a slipstream, a draft that makes you want to follow wherever it may lead. If so, I was already beginning to drift.

"Are you the guy who did all that U2 shit?"

"Yes," I told her. "Are you the ones who throw rocks at me all the time and call me asshole and motherfucker?"

"Yes," she said, which made her friends laugh. For months these teenagers had thrown rocks at me and called me names whenever I passed by the entrance to their flat building.

"Why?"

"Because."

Suddenly, for what seemed like the first time in my life, that answer made perfect sense.

"And why are you talking to me now?"

"I don't like U2 music. I like techno and black music, but what you did was good."

They invited me into their Volkswagen. I accepted. It had no engine and the guts had been scavenged long ago. Four of us squeezed into the car while the rest of the gang stood outside the windows, which had no glass.

"Do you want to go somewhere?" she asked.

"Sure," I answered. They made car noises and changed gears and stared at the scorched building in front of us. They sang songs and told me it was the radio playing.

"What song is that?" I asked once, while rolling camera.

" 'Pump Up the Jam'," the girl said.

Another girl made chocolate cake from the seat cushion and offered me a slice. In one five-minute stretch we went to Italy and back.

The camera was still running and I finally asked about the war.

"I have lost many friends," said the thirteen-year-old, her slipstream becoming stronger as each minute passed. "In the beginning we were all in shelters . . . ah, forget about all this war shit. Let's go to the beach," she said. And again she drove, making engine noises and swerving to avoid the people in the way of her mind's journey. Then I saw the waves breaking on the shore. It was a sunny day with large pelicans diving for surface fish. I was jolted into remembering that day at the beach with Corrina. Corrina was there and she, this young girl, was there playing in the water between us. If it wasn't for the constant gunfire I would have stayed at the beach. Instead I was caught staring out the window.

"Hey!" she yelled. "Are you coming or not?"

"What's your name?" I asked her.

"Alma."

"What does it mean in your language?"

"Soul."

I kept on filming, trying desperately to make sure the camera didn't betray my inner thoughts. I scanned her friends from time to time, but only as a decoy. I was in love with a thirteen-year-old girl. How could that be? I wanted it not to be true. No, that's a lie, I wanted it to be true but in another time, another dimension. Even now, years later, as I write this, I want to lie and say it wasn't so. That instead of love it was just a wonderful and poignant moment of seeing a lively little girl in a place of death and destruction. How sad, how wonderfully pitiful. Still, there it was. I was in love, not with her, but with her essence or spirit. Is there a difference? I do not know this either.

An older teenage boy passed and said something to Alma. He made a suggestive gesture with his hip.

"Stupid boy. He always wants to know what we are doing," she said and then she laughed.

I had no idea how long the battery light had been blinking, but the tape had stopped rolling.

Like I said, she was thirteen. And her smile rarely left her face.

I filmed Vlado speaking about losing his friends. His mental health was still fragile and he was still on a leave of absence from the army. Johnny joined us as we sat smoking a hash joint. Then at one point Vlado, laughing, shook his head and said, "You know what the problem is?"

"No."

"How many people I have killed. So many people. I sometimes think they are stupid or something. They just keep going to the same spot and I keep throwing mortars at them. It's too simple."

On a lighter note, he was now sleeping with Brigitte. I never asked how that came about. Whatever the reason, it didn't matter. It seemed to be helping. For now.

Graeme was also there. He had taken a leave of absence from the Road Trip and was working with Karine, a Belgian girl from Equilibre, to get a circus school up and running in Sarajevo.

A few days before I left, we shared a vodka and lemonade on our way to the disco.

"A circus school here would be wicked," he said, excited as ever.

Then, sounding like a gambler who just lost his last dollar at

the table, he added, "I am so tired of all the bullshit." He was talking of the politics in Geneva, the politics of the Road Trip, the
UN, the waste, the lies, the war, the death, the stink, the drunks,
the guilt of feeling like you are doing something but how much?

"Are you thinking of leaving?" I asked.

"Nah. Take a break and then back at it."

Gambling, throwing the dice at life. Sometimes it's the only
way to make a difference. Win, lose, or draw, at least you know
you took a chance.

I got the footage of the Miss Sarajevo beauty contest from
Mimo, a local newsman who edited for the Sarajevo press
pool. He also gave me several minutes of stock footage to use
in the film. Mostly raw war shots. When I could I played football, visited friends and drove around town with Ciba in the
VW Golf, feeling strangely happy to be here, but even happier
to know I was leaving soon.

And secretly, in every spare moment, I ran down the alley to
see Alma and her friends. I spent hours with her, listening to
her tell stories and answering all her questions about music,
pop culture, and America. She was eager to learn more of a
world she only hoped to see one day. Yet, whenever I asked if
she wanted to leave the city, her answer was immediate and
clear: "Never. This is my city. I will never leave here."

And then, with the camera rolling, I told Alma and her
friends that the world believed their country was in a war over
religion.

"I am Muslim," said Alma. "I am a Muslim but sometimes I
go to church, you know, and I go to the mosque. I believe in
one God."

"God is God," said Darko, a fourteen-year-old boy.

"It's not three Gods or four Gods," said Alma. "God is God."

More and more she reminded me of what I'd lost. That
spirit, that laughter, those dark brown eyes. At the time I remember thinking, this thing called life . . . it was looking up.

77

I told Ciba and Amra I was leaving but would be back soon.

"Why? Do you need more filming?" asked Amra.

"No. I think I have it all."

"Then you must not come back," she said.

I was shocked even though she said it with her usual caring tone. Ciba smiled and nodded, agreeing with his wife.

"She is correct. You must now leave here. I would."

I set down my cup of tea. The motion felt oddly monumental, like my hand resting on a rudder in the water, helping to steer me to open water. After a few moments I asked them why I should not come back.

"You have a big job to make this movie. After that, who knows what is next. Don't take chances you don't have to with your life," said Amra.

"Everything is a chance," I said, not knowing what else to say.

"Bill, you are our friend. You are now part of our family. But you can leave, we cannot," said Amra. "You can survive. If we die you will remember us. If you die here then the movie does not get made and all the friends you know here will disappear."

Memories. That was what I was doing here. Crystalizing hope through the act of bearing witness. Documenting these people and their day-to-day effort to live gave hope that all people, no matter where they lived, were capable of surviving all manner of horrors.

I left on a hot sunny day in late September. It was almost hot enough to forget that another harsh winter was only a month away. I drove with Ciba, Shibe, Vlado and Johnny. In the second car rode Branko, Amra and Alma. I had become fast friends with Alma and, although I hadn't realized it, she had suddenly become the center of why I had come here in the first place. To bathe in her glow was a reminder that innocence can live in the worst of times.

We drove to the gate, as far as Bosnians were allowed to drive. There were two guards. One was a Bosnian and the other looked like a Bangladeshi. He had a UN blue patch on his shoulder and was armed with a machine gun. They stood on either side of a thin chain dangling from two rusted poles over a dirt road. Down the road, 500 feet beyond, was the UNPROFOR headquarters and the way out. Beyond that, the Serb positions. Beyond that, free Bosnia, Croatia. Further beyond, Hungary in one direction, Italy in another.

And what about that winter? What would happen to all these people in the freezing days of December? How would they eat, keep warm? How many sofas were left to burn? The old man downstairs from Ciba was two feet deep in the ground, in a ditch, chopping the roots of a tree long since sliced up for wood.

One by one we hugged, each of us smiling, holding back the tears.

I had come with one duffel bag but was now carrying the equivalent of three duffel bags. Ciba had given me a series of paintings. Others gave me sketches, notes, or music tapes. Seo, a jeweler and a friend of Ciba's, gave me earrings for my mother. Lejla and Selma gave me a note and a kiss.

Alma, the newest of this band of friends, shifted her weight, left foot to right. She smiled, I died a little and we hugged. She said, "Be cool."

A shell flew overhead and landed far away on a hillside behind us. No one flinched.

Ciba handed me his still camera and told me to hold on to it. I told him he would want it for something and regret giving it to me. He said, "No film. Besides, you have to keep telling stories."

"I'll see you soon," I said, looking at Amra, stunned by Ciba's offer and his words.

She smiled and mouthed the words "I know."

"We'll be here . . . maybe," said Vlado as he puffed a cigarette. "And tell Bono if he doesn't play here he will have to answer to me." That made us all laugh.

Once on the other side of the pathetic gate, it occurred to me how thin the separation is between life and death. In this case it was as thin as the blue pass dangling around my neck. I could leave and they could not. In a couple of hours I would be eating pasta and drinking wine with my toes in the sea, while the friends standing before me would be finishing their daily odyssey of getting water from a leaky pipe in a basement somewhere on the other side of town.

The thin line between sanity and insanity. Between grief and love. The line is so close you can smell the grass on the other side. But as I stood on the other side I also realized the separation between here and there had nothing to do with the physical frailty of this gate and everything to do with how one chooses to live one's life. All the people in front of me were not exceptional in the sense that their country would ever remember them in a history book. They were exceptional at the art of living boldly and truthfully until, and not before, death puts the black bag over their heads.

I waved goodbye and with each step I felt no better than a coward who, in fear of his own life, had abandoned his loved ones in their darkest hours. I was the nameless neighbor of Anne Frank leaving my friends in the attic to save my own skin. I remembered Amra's notion of preserving memories. Walking away, I turned back to see my friends. They were still waving. Alma stood off to the side, not waving. I could still see her eyes. They were round. So round. So big and so round. So chocolate brown, so round, so full of hope.

Walking, I found it difficult to balance the weight of my cargo. And my heart felt like it would crack in two. It was as if Corrina had split her essence into a series of souls and they were all standing on the other side of that gate staring back at me. And I was walking away from that. Again.

Halfway down the road I lost my grip on the bags and they fell to the ground. Just then an older man on a bicycle came to a stop next to me. A Bosnian, he must have been a custodian or day laborer in the UNPROFOR building. He said a few words in his language and I nodded as if to say yes to anything he asked. He could have my money, the camera, the gifts, the blue card, whatever he wanted.

He reached out and placed my duffel bag on the rusty rack behind his seat. He motioned for me to put my other belongings on his seat. I suddenly had to see my friends, just one more time. But when I looked, the cars were pulling away. All that was left was a chain fence and a puff of dust from the tires, as they drove back toward downtown. I turned to the old man, who smiled, his skin like the bark of a weathered oak tree.

Together we walked, side by side, down the road.

Part Three

78

Miss Sarajevo would eventually win several awards, play in several countries and raise money for charity. How much? I have no idea. I traveled with the film to college lecture halls and town hall meetings, and in each place the reaction was always the same: a stunned look that said, "Did that really happen?" And wherever it played Alma mesmerized the audience.

The first question when the lights came up was always the same. "Who was that girl?"

I told them her name was Alma Čatal and that she liked to dance. That she had lost several friends in the war and that she carried five gallons of water up fourteen flights of stairs every day. And that when the snipers fired an incendiary bullet into her bedroom and burned down the flat, all she worried about was her dead parrot. One day walking through the ashes she said to me, "My father told me Cuckoo didn't die of fire. He died softly by smoke."

It's true, the real pulse of the film is captured in Alma's moments on tape. I edited those first two hours I spent with Alma into small segments that became the beginning, middle, and end of the film. The person I spent the least amount of time with had become the thread holding the story together. When people said, as they often did, "the spirit of Sarajevo," it was her they meant. Armed only with a laugh that bellied up pure soul, a thirteen-year-old had stampeded over the technocrats and politicians so intent on talking shit until people like her were dead and buried.

Here's the thing though. I have sat in the back of so many

rooms, playing the film for others to watch, and each time I am accosted by the same fearful thought: that some day her laugh may vanish.

After the airing of *Miss Sarajevo* on MTV Europe, some people took an interest in me and some even offered me work. There were offers to go to another war and do the same thing all over again. Some suggested I go to Rwanda, where the brutal massacres were just finishing. Others pushed the Congo and still others hinted I might travel, with my camera, to the far western regions of Pakistan.

I thanked them for their offers and advice but explained that I hadn't gone to Sarajevo either to make this film or to become a war journalist. And I didn't want to work for a humanitarian organization because, although I respected their work, I knew too much about how they operated, top heavy with bureaucracy. At the same time, by the sheer feat of surviving it, I had become an instant expert on the Bosnian war. To those who asked, and even to those who didn't, I usually expressed my opinion of how the war started and how it should end. My answer was always the same. To bomb the hell out of the Serbian artillery positions in the hills surrounding Sarajevo.

So what now? That was the question. After leaving Dublin and paying a short visit to Chico, where my mother and stepfather lived, I ended up in New York. There I went from party to party, usually introduced as "the guy who just came back from Bosnia." After six months I was broke, again. Unable to find a way of making a living, I flew to Los Angeles, where I decided I would parlay *Miss Sarajevo*'s success into my budding career as a film-maker. I would take the story of all the people I had met in Sarajevo to the big screen. How? I wasn't sure.

I arrived in Hollywood with a few phone numbers in my pocket. To be honest, besides wanting to bring the story of the Bosnian war to the masses, I was also seeking the flicker of eternal fame and had aspirations to use the medium to alter perceptions, to ignite passionate discussion. OK, sure, I wasn't thinking straight. I broke into dry sweats at the slightest burst of fireworks, car backfires or even when someone dropped a plate in a café. But that wasn't all. There was a growing sense of ambition, a rising ego that told me—and at this time I was often talking to myself—that what I had done was important. That somehow this would be enough to help me to "succeed." I should have known. This kind of thinking was the tripwire, the mechanism that would send me round the bend.

For months I worked on a screenplay about Sarajevo. Like a monkey chained to the whirling music box, I told anyone who would listen stories about the war, but when you boiled it right down to the nut, I was just retelling a series of bad events. Maybe that's what war is, not a story, just a series of bad events. And you can't write about that. To write you must have something to say or else the events are like raw nerves getting whacked in a root canal when the novocaine is just not enough to cover the pain.

I moved into an flat in Silver Lake. The money was tight. I had a sleeping bag for bedding and a card table to write on. I stayed indoors a lot, mostly because I couldn't imagine myself talking with people about the things people liked to talk about. I was too raw for idle chat about sporting events, gossip or almost anything that didn't cut to the core of the matter. What money I did have I saved for the bars. On most nights I rode home drunk on my motorcycle, sometimes cradling a sixteen-ounce Budweiser between my legs. Occasionally a woman came round and slept with me. But that never lasted very long.

Here's the truth. War and death are really not good for the soul, but they are good for soul-watching. Like when grief has you by the balls, life and death situations bring a distinct clarity to your life. Sarajevo had given me an ability to see whether a person was happy or not by a quick glance in their eyes. The eyes told everything. Not the surface details but a person's depth of happiness, their capacity for compassion, or to feel death, pain, hunger, and mercy. It made me want to wear sunglasses or, more accurately, carry bags around with me and hand them out so I couldn't see the eyes. Lonely lost eyes, all hopelessly dejected that the dream hadn't panned out.

79

I kept writing. Everyone would have a part in the movie. Vlado, Graeme, Amra, Ciba, the sisters, and Shibe were the main characters and Alma was the spiritual centerpiece. I found that the very act of writing allowed me to keep my friends in Sarajevo alive and healthy. There was no way to communicate with them and most of the time I accepted that one or more of them would die before I found a way back. And in the script they all lived—even though, at the suggestion of one producer, I did eventually kill Vlado in the story. He said it would increase the "dramatic arc" of the movie.

But as I worked on the script there was another award ceremony to attend for *Miss Sarajevo*. The film had already won the International Monitor award and the Golden Hugo but I hadn't attended those ceremonies. I decided if I won again I would go, to see what would happen. So when a film festival invited me to collect their Maverick Director award, all expenses paid, I told them I'd be there. Strangely enough, my experiences at this ceremony would illuminate why the war wasn't over yet.

The night of the screening, a dramatic film called *Vukovar* was to play before *Miss Sarajevo*. I knew a little about Vukovar. It was a town destroyed in the war between the Serbs and the Croats, a year before the Bosnian war began. Depending on who you talked to, either the Serbs destroyed it and killed the Croats or the Croats destroyed it and killed the Serbs. Either way the place was decimated.

I had seen the movie on videotape the week before. Its realism was good; it was filmed in warlike conditions. The problem, which was subtle, was the same one that plagued the international community in relation to Bosnia, and I suspect many other wars and humanitarian disasters around the world. The movie didn't blame either the Serbs or the Croats; instead it inferred that this war was a terrible tragedy of history catching up with the place. I have come to realize that this argument works when talking in a social setting to people who are generally ignorant of geography or history. They end up agreeing with the person spouting this argument, especially if that person has any roots in the area or, worse, has relatives living there. Instead of asking questions and standing firm on the pillars of right and wrong, not political or social but moral, they become victims of not wanting to seem stupid and in the end agree with the speaker. Because, after all, they tell themselves, "I'm not from there. What do I know?"

To those people I say this. If a Navajo Indian walked into an Arizona hotel lobby and killed a dozen white men in suits, but while he did so screamed for the revenge of his forefathers, what would we do as a society? Try him for murder and put him in prison. Done. The Navajo's historical plight is not in question; the act of vengeance is. A Serb sniper in Sarajevo shooting children has no defenders except those who put history before people.

There was to be a charity event after the screenings. The proceeds were earmarked for all the children of Bosnia, regardless of their ethnic backgrounds. Who could argue with that?

I spoke first. I said something about having been fortunate to witness such grace under pressure. That the Bosnian ability to maintain their sense of humor, their pride and their dignity was a true testimony to the depth of the human spirit.

Then the director of *Vukovar* spoke. I glanced over at his table. Sitting there was a famous basketball player in the NBA, America's pro basketball league. A Serb expatriate living the high life in America. Surrounding him were several other men, whom I assumed also to be Serbian. The director spent the next five minutes telling the audience that *Miss Sarajevo* was a propaganda tool. That I was telling lies and that there are no such people as Chetniks—a word commonly used by those in the film to distinguish between the Serbs on the hills and the Serbs living in town, who, like everyone in Sarajevo, were being killed by those Serbs on the hills. In conclusion he said he was appalled and would never have attended if he had known that *Miss Sarajevo* would be shown.

No one in the audience moved. I had come alone and was sitting toward the back, drinking wine. I had been attacked like this before so it didn't rattle me much, but the director of the festival leaned over and told me that I had every right to go to the microphone and respond to the attack.

I walked to the podium. The audience, here to spend money for children, did double-takes, from the Serbian table and then back to me.

"For the record," I began, "I didn't make up the war in Bosnia. The people you saw in my film are real. It's a documentary, not a fictional film. I also did not make up the word Chetnik. It is an old word which was used by soldiers in the Bosnian Serb army to describe themselves."

The audience looked like they were ready to flee the building in case there was a fight.

"But I do have a question for this man who just attacked me," I continued, looking at him sitting behind the NBA star. "I am guessing by the way you are talking that you were never in Bosnia during the war. Is this correct?"

There was no response. I had guessed correctly.

I walked away from the podium and, badly in need of some nerve medication, headed straight for the bar. There, one of the older Serbian men from the director's table introduced himself. He smiled and flashed me a charming wink.

"A good film, really," he said.

"Thanks," I replied.

"That is why I am sorry to tell you we will be suing you for slander."

"We?"

"Yes. The American Serb community."

"What?" I was still not sure what he was talking about.

"We are going to have to sue you."

I laughed. I was certain I was caught up in some good old

Balkan sarcasm, which I have learned the Serbs are great masters of.

"Great. Take everything I don't have."

"Your depiction of Serbs in your film is slanderous." He was serious, which meant I knew immediately he was an expatriate. Expats of any country are quick to lose their sense of humor, beaten down by a lifetime of defending the land they no longer live in.

"Half the people in my film were Serbs."

"Why didn't they say so?"

"Well, that is the point, isn't it? They live as Bosnians, not ethnically divided groups, like Karadzic and Milosevic would prefer."

"I don't think you understand," he said. "You can't."

"OK . . . Let me ask you . . . how long have you lived in America?"

"Almost twenty years."

"Did you visit Serbia during the war?"

"No."

"Well, that explains it."

"Explains what?" he asked.

"Your country fucked up pretty bad. So you get defensive. I know. I'm American. Most places I travel America has already raped the place in the name of money. But that doesn't mean all Americans are bad. There are plenty of screwed-up Bosnians. Some are war criminals. And the Serbs too. Not all of them are bad, but come on, admit it . . . someone over there has been kicking people in the teeth using your name."

"I suggest you be careful this evening." He smiled.

I looked over at his table. Five sets of eyes were watching me.

Two young men standing nearby walked up and began speaking with the older Serb man. One of the young boys had dark shades on, blacking out his eyes. He turned to the old man, speaking steadily but sternly in Bosnian at him. He pointed a finger at his forehead. I understood nothing. The old man talked back, putting up his hands from time to time in a casual way as if to say "oh, you young boys," but the boy just continued. As he did the older man's face began to turn white. Finally, the boy stopped talking and the older man paused, and then, looking defeated, he turned to leave.

The two young men walked up and shook my hand.

"I am from Sarajevo," he said. "And my friend is from Srebrenica."

"How's America treating you?" I asked.

"Good."

"I shouldn't have come to this event," I said.

"Mr. Carter, don't say that. Your film is the most important document of our city. I first saw it on MTV."

"Thanks. Has your friend seen it?"

"No," said the man with the glasses, "I am blind. But I have heard it and I know it is a great thing."

"I don't think that man will bother you again," he continued, resting his hand lightly upon my forearm. He stared just beyond my right ear. I asked him why. He said he had told the older man how he had been blinded.

It seems that when the Serbs came to Srebrenica they took him prisoner. As history has documented, eventually those troops would massacre upward of 7,000 men. But they spared this young man. Instead of death they took a spoon and pulled out his eyes. And that was what he had told that older man, who I imagine had been living in some Chicago suburb, in a three-bedroom house, with a Yugoslavian flag over his fireplace, wondering why his people were always getting blamed.

"Want to know the good news of losing my eyes?" the blind man asked, smiling.

"I'd love to."

"Now that I've lost my sight my hearing is so much better."

80

Toward the middle of August 1995 my life took another turn. A television company asked me to make a documentary on war journalists in Sarajevo. The siege had now been going on for more than three years. Going back to Sarajevo conjured up a debate in my mind. I had no desire to be a war junkie or observer. Or worse, a tourist. Still, I wanted to see my friends. Thus I had to have a purpose when I returned, and the cloak of being a journalist at least gave me some excuse.

So I agreed to make the documentary, but only as long as I was able to pick the subject. My subject was to be the bureau chief of one of the largest news services in the world. The chief—we will call him Brock—was a man who had spent nineteen straight years in war.

August in Sarajevo is hot. The war was dragging on, as if it had been put on remote control some time ago and no one knew how to stop it. Supplies were scarce. Water was scarce. Snipers were busy and the shells were still falling. My friends were all alive but much skinnier and their smiles were for the most part long gone. What they didn't know was that the war was about to take a radical turn. What I didn't know was that I would be there when it happened.

The bureau chief had a tricked-out stereo in his Land Rover that played only Bob Dylan. His favourite was "Lay Lady Lay." On the third day of filming, we drove downtown after word that a few shells had hit the marketplace. I knew there was something wrong when I started running toward the market and met all the Bosnians running, not jogging, trotting, or shuffling, but running for their lives, in the opposite direction. In two years of this war I had never seen Bosnians run like they did that day. Whatever was behind them was more than even they could endure.

When I turned the corner there were body parts stuck to the walls of the buildings. Pieces of arms, asses, and heads were splayed on the cement. In all around 90 dead and 180 injured, maimed, or dismembered. A sea of body parts floated in a stream of blood. I felt like praying, crying, and screaming at the same time. Most of the injured and dead had already been taken away—in the war the Sarajevans wasted no time in clearing the carnage from their streets.

I walked silently through the marketplace, as if I was looking for something. I don't know, perhaps I was looking for a clue, a physical piece of evidence of why this had happened. In the middle of the street a man kneeled down with a bucket of water and calmly began washing the red-stained pavement with a sponge. At the time it seemed a more implausible task than putting a man on the moons of Jupiter.

I took a cab to the hospital. My friends, if injured, would be there. I knew Alma was in her parents' flat. I had seen her that morning. Ciba and Amra were no longer in the city; they had escaped in the spring to a village in northern Croatia—finally a Spanish officer sitting for his portrait had come through with the necessary blue cards. Johnny had escaped to Paris. Vlado could have been downtown. So could the sisters or Shibe. Or Alan or Senad. Or so many others.

"Be careful," the cab driver said and pointed to the back seat, where I was sitting. I hadn't even noticed—there was blood on the seat, on the headboard, on the window. There were streaks of blood on the window lever, on the back of the front seat, the seatbelts, the ashtray.

"Three men, two with no arms. I took them to the hospital five minutes ago. Two died before I arrived."

Outside the hospital people were being dragged from the backs of cars. A Polish photographer, whom I had met a few times in town, walked up to me. He looked up at the shockingly blue sky, his camera dangling from his neck. He rubbed his forearm back and forth, like he was trying to peel off his own skin.

"It is now over," he said.

"Why now?" I asked, even though I had the same sense.

"There." He pointed to three foreign cameramen sitting on the grass with their heads in their hands and blood on their clothes. I recognized two of them. Hardened, jaded professional journalists. "Once those people can't take it then I don't think the world will be able to take it."

He was right. A few days later, some time in the middle of the night, sixty NATO jets screamed over the Croatian coastline and over the mountains of Bosnia. On the slopes of Mount Igman, a fiercely fought-over piece of land, a French artillery division pounded the Bosnian Serb army positions. In the end, the whole horizon turned into an Alaskan summer night. Burned orange.

During the bombing, I shuttled back and forth between downtown and the television station with the chief. Once, high on wine and weed, he opened the back door of his armored car in Snipers' Alley and yelled, "Fuck you, you Serbian fucks."

The Spanish driver slammed on the brakes and told me to turn off the camera. "Have you seen the bodies? This isn't a joke." He was fairly new to this war.

"Don't worry. I've seen the bodies," I said in a quiet voice.

"*Relax. He's seen the bodies*. Turn up the goddamn music!" yelled the chief. "And drive the fucking car." Dylan's "Lay Lady Lay" reverberated through our bending minds.

We drove on, him singing out the back door and me filming him as images of the broken city went roaring past in the background.

81

On my last night of filming, with the US jets dropping one-ton bombs in the hills, I was with the chief and one of his cameramen, a punchy South African who was a likeable but jaded war veteran. There we sat in the office, in a far-off corner of the television station, with no lights except for the glow of the stereo. Bob Dylan's "A Hard Rain Gonna Fall" was playing. Loudly. The NATO bombs shook the floor. Brock's eyes were relaxed but closed and he was singing along with Dylan. The wine bottle went round and round like a peace pipe.

There was a tiredness in us, or at least I saw it in them and felt it in me, like suddenly we had barely enough energy to stay alive. The adrenaline of years in war was wearing off, sending us into a crash dive. Dylan was on repeat and half a dozen television monitors showed frozen images of the market massacre, which the South African had filmed. I stared at the two veteran journalists in front of me and made a note to myself: I do not want to live my life chasing war. I do not want to be paid to make consumable soundbites. I do not want to make war digestible.

Breaking the silence, the South African cameraman lifted the wine bottle to his mouth and said, "I've gotta get out of here." And then he wiped a few tears from his eyes.

The next day Brock stopped the filming. He said I had seen enough of his world. Actually he said I had seen too much. He quickly sobered up and demanded back any tapes that showed him drinking or talking harshly about the business. I told him he was sounding like the people he despised, the ones who ran corporate news. I argued, using his own words, that it was important to tell the news from the street, from people's points of view, not from politicians' points of view. Not from the lawyers' or shareholders' points of view. Not from a soundbite perspective. In the end I gave him copies of the tapes he wanted and when I tried to arrange a meeting to discuss his decision, he stopped answering my calls, and in the next few days he made it clear I was not allowed to visit his office, with or without a camera.

Now, something for the record.

The US and European press had argued for years that fighting the Serbs would be like fighting a pack of rabid badgers in a den that had tunnels as long as rivers. They pointed out that the Serbs over the centuries had turned back Napoleon's and Hitler's armies. Funny, the only Serbs I had met on the Bosnian Serb front lines in the mountains outside the city were either high, drunk or scared, and they were sometimes threatened by their own commanders to kill or be killed.

Everyone would say the word Vietnam. Please . . . Vietnam is Vietnam. Does it have to be the yardstick for how every foreign policy decision is made until all the Vietnam memories are dead? No one argued for foreign troops in Bosnia, not even the Bosnians. Not once. What they wanted was to get the tanks and artillery off their backs so that they had enough time to take a breath.

Once the NATO bombing started, the Serb soldiers ran like hairless rats back to the villages they came from.

The whole thing, which had gone on for nearly four years, was over in a week. The final tally in the pursuit of a Serbian Empire (excluding what was to come in Kosovo)? The numbers fluctuate to this day, but they seem to hover around 250,000 dead in all of Bosnia, not including injured, maimed, or driven mad; 1.5 million displaced or refugees; 30,000 women raped. In Sarajevo? Statistics put out by the Bosnian government estimate 10,000 dead by snipers and/or artillery, 1,600 of whom were children; 50,000 injured; 500,000 pieces of artillery landed in the city. Although most of the fighting ended in September 1995, officially the siege would end on 26 February 1996, after 1,395 days. This makes the siege of Sarajevo the longest known siege in modern history.

Should it have ended sooner? Who knows? Not me. And some will ask: what about Rwanda, Angola, El Salvador, Cambodia? And on and on. I don't know about that either.

And the tapes? The chief had been right. He'd told me they would never get on the air. In truth the footage, when reviewed, made little if any sense, which I attribute to Brock's and my states of mind. It is hard to capture chaos on camera. As far as I know the tapes are in a basement somewhere in Hollywood. After I delivered them via express mail from Croatia, the only comment I remember from the production company was along the lines of "We just don't feel this footage is suitable for our current programing."

82

So the war ended. And it was just another day. The rain fell like the day before and when the sun broke through the afternoon clouds it was still sinking. Not that I want to admit it, but I had always thought the end of the war might change *my* life. Well, there was a small consolation. I didn't worry any more that my friends would be shot in the head. But they were still over there and I was back in my home country surrounded by strangers.

Meanwhile Bono had written that song to my documentary and called it "Miss Sarajevo." It was a stunning piece of writing, which captured the surreal essence of war. He also decided to write an operatic piece in the song, and later collaborated with Luciano Pavarotti, who sang that part. Stephen re-edited the ending of the documentary using the song, and the results were almost immediate. The U2 "Miss Sarajevo" song was a hit single in Europe and the music video, made by Maurice Linnane, from Dreamchaser in Dublin, created a renewed interest in the documentary. There were no work offers but plenty of phone calls from interviewers looking for the story behind the documentary. Usually the television and radio interviewers wanted to know more about the music, the satellite link-ups, the war, the film. No one seemed to care when I pointed out that the war was over. Better late than never, they say. But is this actually true? What about hurricanes, wars, bad news, death, love turned to hatred, uncooked meat, debt collectors, cancer, . . . and so on? Why not just "better never?"

Then U2's record company set up a radio tour that flew me from city to city, talking to radio stations about the film and the war and raising some money for charity on the side. One morning, when the radio rodeo ended and the planes stopped flying, I found myself back in Los Angeles, sitting in the director's suite on the top floor of a hotel near the Beverly Center. I hadn't lived in LA for six months, since I had accepted the documentary job with the bureau chief in Sarajevo. My flat had been abandoned long ago. There was no one I wanted to call in this town.

The hotel room was actually a suite with two sofas and

a loaded minibar. The hotel management kept sending me baskets of fruit and telling me to ring them if I needed anything, anything at all. I thought of calling and asking if they could get rid of the body parts on the wall or, worse, my Bosnian friends with the laughing eyes who were in the next room. And while they were at it could they please, please, please send someone to find Corrina's hair.

The sun blazed hot white light into the room. I sat on the edge of a king-sized bed staring at the window but unable to see out. And then the phone rang.

"Thank you, Bill, it was a pleasure working with you," said the woman on the phone. She was the person from the record company who had organized the radio tour.

"Thanks for the room and board," I said.

"Yes, well, good luck in LA."

"I don't live in LA."

"Oh, I'm sorry. I was under the impression you lived here."

"No."

"No problem, we'll arrange a flight home. Where do you live?"

I looked at the full-length mirror and saw myself sitting on the edge of the bed with a white phone in my hand. My hair was wet and my facial twitches were acting up every twenty seconds or so. The worst part was that my dad had a twitch in the exact same place. It tended to flare up right before he gave a lecture about God or the communist threat or when he was getting ready to lay the board on me.

I guess I was homesick, but after the many years I'd traveled I had no home to return to. I had begun so long ago, wanting to see the world. But seeing was never enough. I wanted to feel the world. And so I did. Then I wanted to change the world, and in the end it seemed the only thing that had changed was my clothes. In truth I was tired of not living my own life. I was living by other people's notions of life. And who was that man in a suit at the airport holding a sign with my name on it? And the women? I was beginning to think women found the idea of surviving war very attractive. It was enough to make me wonder sometimes if this wasn't why men started them in the first place: to prove beyond a doubt that they could survive one more day and were therefore worthy of getting the women.

But really I needed a job.

"Mr. Carter, where do you live?" said the voice on the other end of the phone.

It was my moment to break free. I was tired of the news and politics. I needed space, wide open space where the landscape was large enough to swallow a person whole, a big wide space to remind me on a daily basis that I was only a small step from heaven and an even smaller step from oblivion. I needed the world to shrink back to being a blue map hung on the wall with tape, where my toes could be in the Pacific Ocean and my fingers in the Indian Ocean.

It was as if I was again sitting in that blue Skylark, Mom was driving, and we were cruising next to the river. The peach trees were in bloom and the only sound was of the tires humming along the road under our seats.

"Mr. Carter, where would you like me to make the flight for? Your home?" the woman asked again.

Then I remembered a friend once telling me that in Tucson, Arizona, on a good day from the top of the mountains you can see for seventy-five miles. All the way to Mexico. He said it was like being in a sea of nothing.

"Tucson will be fine. Thank you."

83

In Tucson I rented a hundred-year-old adobe flat in the downtown barrio. The walls were three feet thick and crumbling but it provided for nature's finest air conditioning against the 100-degree-plus summer heat. Outside my back door I had a small desert garden of bougainvillea and Mexican primrose. In the spring I planted lettuces and spring onions and some Serrano peppers. The desert suited me. The wildness of the place suited me. John Steinbeck was right. "There are true secrets in the desert. In the war of sun and dryness against living things, life has its secrets of survival." In the evenings, after the heat receded, at least until dawn, I went for long hikes in deep canyons or up pine-covered mountain slopes. I looked, in vain, for the mountain lion that was surely tracking me. Or the elusive Mexican jaguar that has been known to wander across the border. At sunset, if I walked the ridge tops of the Mule Mountains, near Bisbee, where I sometimes lived, I would come across the javalina, a wild collared peccary. Occasionally I'd spot a coyote lying on its side in the riparian grass, unbothered by my presence. Thank God for that. And there was the coatimundi, a strange creature that looked something like a raccoon with a mongoose's tail. And if not the hills, then I walked the dry washes at the feet of the saguaros, the rare cactuses that grow only in the Sonoran desert and stand up to forty feet tall with branches like mutant multi-limbed human beings.

There is something I learned quickly here and it is what has kept me here. This desert is lush compared to most of the earth's deserts but, like all deserts, the moment you take it for granted—don't bring enough water on a day hike, lose your sense of direction or journey out too far with no way back—it will kill you. As Steinbeck continued, "The desert, being an unwanted place, might well be the last stand of life against unlife."

I got a job building adobe houses for $10 an hour. Every day I woke up and mixed mud, water, and lime and stacked fifty-pound bricks next to one another. It was back-breaking work, but it cleared the mind. Besides, when the job was done there was something there, a physical signature of something I had been a part of.

One afternoon I came home for a tuna-fish sandwich lunch. I had to be back on the job in less than an hour. We were framing a house in a new adobe village. It was one of those fancy developments for rich people moving here for the air, which was quickly becoming polluted from too many rich people moving here for the air.

I was sucking down an iced tea when the phone rang.

"Bill. Is this Bill Carter?" asked the voice. It was female and foreign, definitely Balkan. Immediately I felt the present slip away and Sarajevo came rushing before my eyes.

"Amra?"

"Yes, it is Amra. I am calling you from Toronto."

Amra and Ciba had fled to Canada several months before and we had exchanged letters and phone numbers but we hadn't spoken on the phone.

"And Ciba?" I asked.

"He is painting, of course. He has an exhibition soon."

"If I can I will visit."

"Yes. Of course. And how is Graeme?"

"I think he's OK, but I haven't spoken to him in a very long time."

"Have you found a woman yet?" she asked.

"Not yet."

"You cannot be alone. That is not good for a man."

"Yeah, yeah, I know. What else is new?"

"Anja is in school and speaks perfect English."

"Do you like it there?"

"To tell you the truth, no. Ciba does and Anja seems happy, but actually I don't like the ways of people here. There is no family, no culture. There is no center for the people. Do you understand me?"

"Yes. It's a bit trickier here than in Sarajevo, but it is there. You just have to look for it in a different way. At least that is what I tell myself."

So we talked and filled in some of the blanks in our lives since the war, and then we hung up. The thing is, we have not spoken since. I used to wonder why. But I suspect it is because with our voices comes the memory of a time that part of us wants to forget. Not the time shared, but the circumstances through which we found each other. I dream of that family often and imagine they are just the way they always were, laughing and loving and accepting. The only difference is that they have food on the table and blankets in the closet for the cold nights. And I imagine they occasionally cook chicken dinners for all their friends.

Still, to move forward in one's life one has to find a proper hiding place in the mind for the past and allow the future to envelop us.

After hanging up I stood perfectly still in my crumbling adobe flat for some time. Then I walked over and put my ear up to my dirt wall. It was cold against my face. It felt refreshing, as if I was buried inside an earth tomb. The guy next door was listening to Mozart. The sound was slightly muffled and somehow this was just right.

84

After a year in Tucson, I still hadn't fully found a way back into this time, this life. I needed to find some ground to stand on. I had become part of a community of artists, vagabonds and desert rats. I had also met Patti Keating and Rainer Ptacek. Married, they lived in a small two-room house on a plot of desert in the middle of Tucson. They had two sons and a new-born daughter. Born in Berlin of Czech descent, Rainer had moved to the US as an infant. He grew up to become a master blues musician and a friend to many in the community. She was a desert rat with Irish-Mexican ancestry who liked to tell people that Tucson had a vortex to it. "Once you have been here in the wide open desert you just can't help but keep coming back."

I had something in common with them. Death. You see, Rainer was dying slowly from brain cancer. And it was his dying that was so familiar to me. Of course, thanks to his calm sense of life and spirit, his laughter was the deepest of everyone around him and his ability to be present was never clouded with what-ifs or regrets. He was on his way out and, like so many I had met in Sarajevo—and in other places where death is like the stranger who hangs out on the front porch so long he actually becomes welcome—he wanted to look it straight in the eye when death came.

After his death, some who knew of my past thought I could

help. Offer words of condolence, that sort of thing. In truth I was done grieving for the dead. I was only interested in the living. It was the only option. Otherwise this world would smother us in tears. Here was the interesting part. A few months after Rainer's death, Patti made plans to build an extension to their house. That was what it was called. An extension.

I told her I would build it.

We dug two feet into the earth to sink the room. I got a pile of sand delivered and bought twenty bags of cement. I hired an assistant and for the next three months I stacked bricks on top of bricks and in between I threw in the mud. It was dusty, hard work, but other than a little bit of tightness in my ankle from gout, I had no complaints.

As I worked she took care of her kids and peeled off layers of paint and tile from all the floors in her house. Sometimes through the walls I'd hear her sobbing, and other times I'd hear her laughing. It was the glorious wave of life, up and down, living and dying. I wasn't surprized that it gave me great joy to feel it, if only through another. After all, to laugh deeply or to feel pain deeply must be directly related to how much a person is able to feel love. For it is the very act of being.

One afternoon Patti and I were sitting on the porch. Clouds streaked across the sky. The weather was pleasant, cool.

"Do you ever feel Corrina watching you from inside your own head?" she asked.

"Sometimes, but I can't handle it as easily any more. I think the two worlds can interact for a short time, but not for long. We tend to freak out. It's like the war in Sarajevo. I can't think of it all the time or I can't live here. I can't calm down that way."

"Sometimes I think Rainer and Corrina are watching this," she said.

"What?"

"Us building this room."

"I wouldn't doubt it."

"Bastards are probably eating chips and salsa and drinking Tecates," she said.

It was around this time that I realized something. It seemed so simple I almost didn't give it much thought. Patti was building the adobe room to create a new life *inside* her old life. She said she needed another room to walk around in. She wasn't tearing down her old house, her old life, just adding on. If the heart of love has many chambers then she was creating a new one, which by definition wouldn't exclude the old one. In fact that would only make the new chamber stronger and wider. I said in the beginning of this story that I needed a new ending. I see now I don't. I need to build a new chamber inside my old self. One that doesn't replace the old love, but allows room for a new one. A simple idea, and probably obvious to most, but some of us take a while to grind through the mud to make our own way.

She and I spent many afternoons waiting for the mud to dry, drinking beers in the mesquite grove. I was envious of her loss. Not the pain of the loss, but that they'd had twenty years together. Three children and all the trimmings of a life lived. I knew her pain would be deep, a twenty-year hole, but I also knew that in the years to come she would find solace in knowing the answers to the questions I could never answer. What would have happened? What could have happened? What would we have done when we reached that point when two people lose the initial amour and have to rely on pure guts to get through the night? That has to be worth something.

85

In the following weeks I poured the bonding beam and put on the roof. After that we put in brick pavers for a floor and then a ceiling fan. The adobe work had served me well, in that my memory was no longer dominating my present life so much.

But still I tried to keep track of what had happened to everyone I'd met in Sarajevo. Good or bad, each one had left a mark on me.

In the end The Serious Road Trip delivered over 1,200 tons of food to Bosnia and tens of tons of building materials for reconstruction. As for the original members, most of the Road Trip people I knew were long gone, scattered around the world telling their own versions of how it all went down. Not long after the war ended, Graeme went to Africa to run safaris on game reserves. He would eventually move back to England and become an ambulance paramedic. At the time of writing he had upped and moved to Australia, where he was working in a dive shop, taking people out to the Great Barrier Reef. I only heard second hand about the others. Josh moved to Sarajevo, where he worked for a large, well-funded aid organization. He got himself a steady girlfriend and wore a suit and tie. Tony Gafney and I saw each other once more, in a London pub, down the street from the Road Trip office. I was there on a layover from Dublin and wanted to set the record straight. In the passing years the Road Trip had seen fit to use *Miss Sarajevo* footage and photos I had given them from the war, for Road Trip purposes, which didn't bother me, but at the same time they took it upon themselves to trash my name. Everyone said it was Tony who had done the trashing. At the pub I had asked him about it. He lifted his drunken head from the bar and said, "Sorry about that, mate. Guess I've been dragging your name through the mud for a few years now." I asked him why and his answer was, "I really don't know."

English Roger had gone to the Rolls-Royce school of driving and was now a chauffeur. I don't know what happened to the Kiwis. Christophe, the Frenchman, went back and served his time in the French army. Wally, from Equilibre downstairs, would eventually jump ship and run Road Trip offices in other countries.

Jason and Ivana got married, went back to graduate school in Massachusetts and were both promoted. Jason became country director for Croatia for OTI, the Office of Transition Initiatives, a group funded mostly by USAID. Ivana, also in Croatia, was working for the NDI, the National Democratic Institute. Now they both travel the world, working at executive levels for various aid organizations.

Brigitte eventually married Dutzo, the keyboard player in Vlado's band. They moved back to Paris, where Brigitte became the manager of an emerging Bosnian band called Sikter. Ironically, its lead singer was Enis (a.k.a. Burre), the young fireman who'd done the U2 satellite link-up to Stockholm. Johnny had also escaped, through the tunnel under the airport, and was also in Paris. He left with nothing but the clothes he was wearing and not long after arriving in France he woke up in a psychiatric hospital. It happened after he learned that his mother had died in Sarajevo. But eventually Johnny and Dutzo started a band called O'djila, which married Balkan gypsy and modern musical rhythms. Alan, the bass player in Vlado's band, moved to Minnesota, where he is happily married.

Vlado, of course, was still in town. He was teaching English again and still playing music. The sisters were still there. Lejla had a new boyfriend and Selma the same one as before. She was talking of getting married. Shibe got married to his girlfriend and moved to Switzerland, but was often in Sarajevo for holidays. Mustafa, the café proprietor, moved to Prague. Branko's café was finally bombed and he escaped somewhere.

My brother Cliff was a successful lawyer and had three children, all happy and glad to have such a great father.

My mother would eventually retire, after thirty-three years of teaching secondary school. She lives in Chico with my stepfather, who is still working as a principal.

And Alma?

In all my storytelling and lectures I never revealed the truth, that I felt a tenderness toward her. That I knew, wherever my life journey now took me, I would know her for the rest of my life. But I wouldn't try to own her or even marry her. I just wanted to keep track of her, to be there for her. I wanted to squeeze all my urges to save everyone I knew in Sarajevo down to one person. I already knew I would do anything she ever asked of me, even though she has never asked me for one thing.

86

One night, near the end of building the extension, after a shower to wash away the mud I stepped out onto the porch. It was another beautiful night in the sea of Arizona. Something felt slightly different, as if I was feeling the ground beneath my feet for the first time in years.

And so who does die? And where do they go? That was the fundamental question that had been plaguing me ever since Corrina's death. Do we ever die? Or are we just sketches left over in others' memories? And if so, when we are alive and creating memories with others, is there a rhyme or reason to our actions? Or should we just chuck it all and party until we don't wake up? And what about this one: is death from a sniper round in the chest somehow more tragic than a person dying because they fell asleep at the wheel? Is it? I say no.

That room, square and cold to the touch. Corrina's last days were spent in a state of silent beeps from machines keeping her alive. When I was a kid on the ranch I would often lie down in the orchard and daydream my greatest death, which, by definition, was always linked to my greatest love. I was in a bed. A girl was holding my hand. Maybe she was my attending nurse. It was her that I would gasp my last breath to. Strange. My life's most dramatic moment, my own death, would be shared with the one I most wanted to breathe with.

Yes. I sometimes wonder how to wake up and open the door. Out there the sun is always rising and the moon sure to follow, but do I have to? Yes, in fact, I do. I have to carry on, at least for another three or four weeks. I carry her with me not because I want to relive the past but because she made me a better person. It was she who released me on her last breath and sent me screaming naked into the world. Because of that I cannot live a life of regret, of doubt. I cannot ever look back. Never. Only forward with no guilt or regret. For this I swear on her death. And for this I can finally say I am thankful.

An elderly Mexican man selling tamales strolled by, ringing the bell on the handlebar of his pushbike. I stepped barefoot onto the dirt sidewalk. The earth crinkled between my toes. It was cold, like wet clay. Maybe the art of life is simply always being ready for what may come next. Take Kundera's words at the beginning of this story. "Living: carrying one's painful self through the world." I was done living. But being, that's different. "Being: becoming a fountain, a fountain on which the universe falls like warm rain."

The setting sun was blazing bloody red straight out on the horizon, but a monsoon was blowing through town blocking out all the stars above. I stood with my head back, tongue out and eyes closed. A soft gentle rain fell on my face one drop at a time. It felt like liquid love.

EPILOGUE

It wasn't until 23 September 1997, nearly two years after the signing of the Dayton Peace Agreement marking the end of the war in Bosnia, that U2 finally played a concert in Sarajevo. Up until a week before the concert I didn't think I would be attending the show. I was broke again and too proud to beg. Almost. But after a few phone calls to Ireland, and U2 having bought me a ticket, I landed in Zagreb. From there I took an eight-hour bus trip to Sarajevo.

That day the weather was perfectly mild, not hot or cold. The cafés were full and the streets busy with people hurrying to work and getting on and off the trams. The flagpoles on top of the ski run, which used to fly the Serbian flag, now flew NATO and UN flags. The only killing in town these days was the run-of-the-mill city stuff. The buildings still had their shell-pocked scars, but now people entered using the front door. A small thing, but somehow it seems worth noting. The country was crawling with war criminals but, without their armies and with no war to fight, I imagined most of them spent their time drinking in bunkers and wondering if they would one night be duct-taped by British special forces and dropped on the tarmac of the Hague airport.

I walked past the UNIS towers under the sunshine. I felt light. I felt like a kite, floating up and away. But then there was that feeling of weight around my knees. It had started when I visited the sisters, Lejla and Selma, earlier in the day. They were both healthy and filled their jeans nicely once again. During lunch the parents wouldn't stop feeding me. Lejla said they were trying to make up for all the times Graeme and I had brought them food. I told them they would have done the same for me.

"Not me," said Lejla and winked.

At first they were excited about the concert, but then they both became angry when they talked about it. They told me that last night they had watched the news.

"A Bosnian politician was talking about how he had arranged all the satellite connections when he met the band in London, and that the concert was his idea," said Lejla.

"How can they do that? It's history. I mean, it is documented history," I said.

"Our history books are being rewritten while we are in class. It's all lies," said Lejla.

"Every politician is using this concert as a way to feel big, like they are important. Most of them weren't even here in the war. They came here to look cool," said Selma.

"This place is shit. Really," said Lejla.

I would have to say this is where the heavy feeling inside my chest started.

I arrived at the stadium a few hours early and climbed to the top, where I did a slow 360-degree turn.

Everywhere I looked was like staring at a living X-ray of the twentieth century. Or, to be more specific, a cross-section of Europe's wars, which have a way of dragging the whole world into a downward spiral. Out of sight, down by the river, was the Bridge of Friendship. It was on that bridge on the morning of 28 June 1914 that Gavrilo Princip, a Serb nationalist, shot dead the Archduke Ferdinand and his wife. When the Austro-Hungarian Empire retaliated against the Serbs, the Russians stepped up for their Slav brothers. In came the Italians, the British and the French. And so on. History proclaims it as "the shot heard around the world," the beginning of World War One. For all intents and purposes that day, that shot, was also the beginning of the bloodthirsty twentieth century. A century highlighted by two world wars, dozens of regional ones, and a few genocides.

Between the stadium and the bridge was a series of grave-yards. Some of the graves, old and engraved in stone, dated from World War One. Closer to the stadium were more graves, some dating from World War Two. Butting up against the Olympic arena were new graves. And directly in front of me I saw a large yellow arch, a stage prop for tonight's concert, not unlike a single McDonald arch rising out of the top of the stadium.

So, I thought to myself, why not declare today the end of the twentieth century? Why not? The bridge where it began was in a perfect line with the stadium and in between lay the dead bones of the last hundred years. And what about that big yellow plastic arch rising up into the sky like a McDonald shrine? It made the X-ray complete. After all, it was the perfect symbol for the end of the century: when the worship of pop culture and celebrities had long ago become the religion of the masses.

Back down on the stadium field I noticed a man walking toward me, surrounded by security. It was a Bosnian politician I had suggested Bono get in touch with months before, regarding the concert. Although I knew of this politician, I had only met him once, several months before in LA, at the U2 concert. Back then, when I had introduced myself he had stood up and shaken my hand. Still holding my hand he'd turned to his Bosnian assistants and said, "This man's name is spoken on the street corners of our city. *Miss Sarajevo* is known to every Bosnian. He is a hero to us. It is an honor to finally meet you."

As he passed I said hello. He said, "Oh, what are you doing here?" He looked startled, even a bit shocked.

I thought nothing of it. After all, today was a day of celebration. A VJ day for all of Bosnia. It was their party, I was just glad to be here. Besides, I was quickly distracted when I passed the bar. Celo, the warlord, was standing there. I walked away. I didn't have the energy right then to ask how he got back.

Before the concert, I found myself leaning against a railing just when the U2 band members emerged from backstage. They walked toward four black Mercedes with drivers anxiously waiting to take them somewhere. With them was Brian Eno, who had produced the song "Miss Sarajevo."

I stood there in plain sight with my new backpack and brand new boots. I was proud of the upgrade. The band members moved slowly and purposely to the cars. One of their security guards, the same one who'd said, "Balls," in Ireland the first time I met him, saw me and shrugged his shoulders as if to say, "You coming?" I felt this was a moment to act, but I was unsure what the action should be. So I stood still.

After they had driven away I turned round and there stood one of the many U2 assistants.

"So where are they going?" I asked.

"To meet with the President. They are receiving honorary passports and keys to the city," she said, scribbling something on a notepad.

I felt slightly dizzy. I said nothing, but felt lost, as if I didn't belong here. Then, as my mental balance began to slip further, I heard a voice. It was far away but I tuned to it like a beacon.

"Bill," the voice said. "Over here."

I turned and it was Alma. She was dressed in jeans, a windbreaker and a wool cap that said Snoop Doggy Dogg on it. "Where have you been?"

We walked to the top of the stadium and looked out over the city. God. She still had those round brown eyes.

"I wonder if how all this happened is going to be erased?" I asked her.

"It's Bosnia."

"Meaning what?"

"Yes, it probably will be."

We watched as tens of thousands of people began filling the stadium.

"What matters is that it happened," she said.

"How old are you now?"

"I turn eighteen in April."

The night came suddenly and soon 50,000 people were crammed into the stadium. The idea that music crosses all boundaries was literally being proven this night. It was truly an awesome and thrilling sight. It wasn't so much the anticipation of the show that was thrilling but the sheer size of the gathering.

Stationed on the roads were NATO tanks and NATO soldiers weighed down with weapons, 4,000 NATO troops in all. This was to be the largest gathering since before the war. To bring people together, U2 and NATO and the local governments and municipalities had spent great political effort to get the trains running again outside the city for the first time. Serbs and Croats were coming into Sarajevo by train, many for the first time since the end of the war, to see the show. On my bus ride from Croatia all the teenagers had gawked out the window as they saw with their own eyes the destruction that had happened in the country right next door. More than fifty eighteen-wheelers loaded with stage gear had made the cross-country trip from Austria over temporary bridges and through military checkpoints.

It was truly a staggering undertaking.

The politician I had passed earlier in the day approached the microphone. He took a moment to thank some people. I inched forward in my chair.

He thanked security, NATO, the UN, the U2 management, the other politicians, the military brass, the press, and the opening band—Sikter. The politician went on to thank the crowd. He thanked the train and bus drivers for getting people there. He thanked Pavarotti and Brian Eno. He thanked almost everyone who had power or the promise of power. And then he screamed for everyone to have a great time.

Alma looked over. "Why didn't he say your name?" she asked with a sense of utter bewilderment.

"Should we get closer?" That was all I could muster at that moment.

"Sure," she said, without a care in the world.

The show was a hit. The crowd sang every word to every song. They even played "Miss Sarajevo" and showed footage from the film on the massive screens behind them. Everyone sweated and laughed, and some even cried. People brushed up against each other. Serb to Croat to Muslim to Roma to Jew. Standing next to me, on a VIP section of raised platform so we could see the show better, were Jason and Ivana, who in turn were next to Johnny, Vlado, Selma, and Alma. Lejla was somewhere in the crowd with her boyfriend.

At one point during a song, Vlado leaned in and said, "Do you know that you actually changed the course of this war?"

"Oh, relax," I said.

"It's true. Whatever happens in your life, know that."

The show was fantastic. And then it was over. After the show I stood on the grass watching the big yellow arch being torn down. So here it was, the full circle of something started on a whim. Or was it? Of course not. And so what exactly was I waiting for? For someone to tell me it was over?

In truth, my journey to this night was over long before I had even arrived. I had made a deal with the universe, with God, when I came to this city. To feel everything I did here. To find something in the outside world that would allow me some equilibrium inside my own soul. To give until either I was dead or I learned to live again. Looking back, it's probably accurate to say I came here as a traveler and ended up being a catalyst. I wasn't alone. There were others who played the same role, but I can't speak for them. And now, for me, there was nothing left to wait for. The two sides, the city and the outside world, had connected and the catalyst, by its very nature, had long ago faded into both. I had survived Sarajevo and when I had to I had used the cameras, the press and the thank-yous all to my advantage. But now it was over. Being in the spotlight was never part of my deal. Being here was.

Further, I wasn't sure when it had happened along the way, but the moment I had begun to want something from my work, whether it was money, fame, or recognition, everything had stopped working. Like dominoes tumbling in my mind, my work had faltered, my conviction had begun to lose its impact. I suspect it was because it no longer came from the hollow of my chest but from the empty chambers of my being, thick with doubts and weeds. So there's a lesson. Do it from the gut or don't do it at all.

I was suddenly anxious to get back to the desert, to walk into the great wildness. To get swallowed up by the horizon that stretches so far we are inclined to believe there is more. I wanted to hike the barren ground only to find the odd purple flower sticking out from the top of a prickly pear cactus, as if announcing, "*Ha!* Life is everywhere."

After the crowd had left the stadium, an American NATO officer walked up and pointed at the stage.

"Can you believe it?" he said. He had a kind smile and was excited, like a schoolboy.

"What's that?" I asked.

"Five billion dollars has been spent by the international community to get these folks to speak to one another. *Five billion* dollars, and we can barely get two old men to agree to play a game of chess. This music group spends their own money, rolls into town and 50,000 people come from all over the Balkans. People who hate each other are dancing together."

"I guess music does cross all borders," I said.

"We are in the wrong business."

"I have always thought so," I said.

"You are probably too young to know what war is, but trust me, you don't want any part of it. And I'm sure these people didn't either."

"Well . . ." I started, then stopped myself.

"War is an ugly thing," he said. He was not lecturing me, just sharing his own story. He was both excited at the evening and frustrated at the system he lived in. "Your generation has too many romantic notions about war. Just ask the young people here tonight, they know. It isn't pretty."

Vlado, Johnny, Alma, and Selma were standing near the tunnel waiting for me to join them to go to the green room.

"Think we can get some champagne," yelled Vlado.

"I'm sure of it." I waved.

The officer looked over at the Bosnians.

"Friends of yours?"

"Yes. Friends of mine."

"So," he said, and then, sizing me up, he took a hard look at me from head to toe. "What's your connection to any of this? A journalist?"

"No." I took a breath. "I'm just traveling through."

And just like that I felt a strange yet freeing sensation. It was as if I suddenly remembered something I had learned as a child: that I was just a dot in the middle of the map. A dot surrounded by so many other dots. It felt like nothingness, and in that space, surrounded by the bones of the ones less fortunate, I wondered if the ultimate reward of life was simply realizing you were still in it. At that moment the weight sitting on my shoulders—you know the one—slipped away. The lightness lifted like a balloon racing toward the sun and the heaviness passed down my legs and out through my feet. It felt like your life being saved when you thought you were a goner. Yes. That's the best I can describe it. Like one life leaving and another one coming in.

ACKNOWLEDGMENTS

I owe my thanks to many, not just for their literary advice but for their friendship and sense of community, which have played a large part in being able to finish this book.

I want to thank Graeme Bint for his excellent company during our time in Bosnia, and for his humor and friendship ever since. And to the individual members of The Serious Road Trip, who made it undeniably surreal.

Many thanks to Jason Aplon and Ivana Sirovic—their hand in all this can't be overstated; to Bob Phillips and Tracy Child, whose friendship and generosity over the years have gone a long way in enabling me to keep writing.

Thanks to Jann Wenner at *Rolling Stone* and Wenner Books, who along with editor-in-chief Bob Wallace believed in the book without hesitation. And thanks to Kate Rockland at Wenner Books for handling the details.

In London, thanks to Transworld Books, especially my editor, Michele Hutchison, and to Deborah Adams, Emma Dawson, and Helen Edwards.

To Bono, for his friendship and support throughout the years, but even more for his tireless ability to create art and at the same time go toe-to-toe with the politicians of the world. And to the rest of U2: Adam Clayton, Larry Mullen Jr. and Edge for taking a chance that fateful day back in 1993. And to Paul McGuinness and the staff at Principle Management for all their kind assistance over the years.

To Elliott Lewitt and Julie Kirkham for taking my late-night calls; to Jim Harrison, Charles Bowden, Mitch Cullin, Bob

Datilla, Sid Evans and Tom Foster for getting the word out; to Mike Fagen and Michael Cannon, who each carried the weight with laughter; to Robert and Linda on the Vineyard, to Bob Guccione Jr., to Theresa Reuter and to Jennie Meador, whose support has been unwavering.

I owe a special debt of gratitude to those who gave me shelter while writing the book: Peter Barnes and the Mesa Refuge at Point Reyes, for the months of solitude I needed to begin the writing; to the Blue Mountain Center, where I was able to continue; and finally to Debbie and Bill Lloyd for the use of their cabin in Mendocino.

In Tucson, I want to thank Howe Gelb, Sofie and the kids; Patti Keating, the oasis in the Sonora, and Niki Freegard, for bringing me in; and John Convertino, Joey Burns, Steve Valdez, and Amy Harrington. In Bisbee, thanks to Pauli and Michelle Heaukulani, Juliette Beaumont and Linsey Blake. At Café Roka, thanks to Sally Holcomb and Rod Kass. Each has contributed in some way to this process, whether by sharing meals, reading drafts or maybe just hosting poker nights.

And a very special thanks to Leigh Schubert, for everything.

I want to thank many people I met in Sarajevo, but there isn't space, and it is my hope the book serves as a more meaningful expression of appreciation. But to Vlado, Alma, Lejla, Selma, Ciba, Amra, Djani, Doutso, Alan, and Shibe: Hvala Lipa. I am indebted.

And a warm thanks to my family: my parents, Susan and John Lalaguna, brother Cliff and his wife, Peggy, and the kids; and to my cousin Wendy Carter, for all their help, maintenance, and continued support.

Finally, I would like to thank Joanie Barton for having brought such a bright light into this world.

Bill Carter was born in 1966. He has spent the last fifteen years traveling the globe, visiting and living in over forty countries; his jobs have ranged from English teacher to commercial fisherman, bartender to adobe mason to assistant film director to photo-journalist. He has also produced and directed several documentaries, including the award-winning *Miss Sarajevo*. Bill currently lives in southern Arizona. *Fools Rush In* is his first book.

For more information on *Miss Sarajevo* or to see some of Bill Carter's photographs please visit his website: ***www.billcarter.cc***